D1120494

French Literature

Cultural History of Literature

Christopher Cannon, *Middle English Literature*
Sandra Clark, *Renaissance Drama*
Glenda Dicker/sun, *African American Theater*
Alison Finch, *French Literature*
Ann Hallamore Caesar and Michael Caesar, *Modern Italian Literature*
Roger Luckhurst, *Science Fiction*
Michael Minden, *Modern German Literature*
Katie Normington, *Medieval English Drama*
Lynne Pearce, *Romance Writing*
Charles J. Rzepka, *Detective Fiction*
Jason Scott-Warren, *Early Modern English Literature*
Charlotte Sussman, *Eighteenth-Century English Literature*
Mary Trotter, *Modern Irish Theatre*
Andrew Baruch Wachtel and Ilya Vinitsky, *Russian Literature*
Andrew J. Webber, *The European Avant-Garde*
Tim Whitmarsh, *Ancient Greek Literature*

French Literature

A Cultural History

ALISON FINCH

polity

First published in 2010 by Polity Press

Polity Press
65 Bridge Street
Cambridge CB2 1UR, UK

Polity Press
350 Main Street
Malden, MA 02148, USA

ISBN-13: 978-0-7456-2839-4 (hardback)
ISBN-13: 978-0-7456-2840-0 (paperback)

A catalogue record for this book is available from the British Library.

Typeset in 11.25 on 13 pt Dante
by Toppan Best-set Premedia Limited
Printed and bound in Great Britain by MPG Books Group Limited, Bodmin, Cornwall

The publisher has used its best endeavours to ensure that the URLs for external websites referred to in this book are correct and active at the time of going to press. However, the publisher has no responsibility for the websites and can make no guarantee that a site will remain live or that the content is or will remain appropriate.

Every effort has been made to trace all copyright holders, but if any have been inadvertently overlooked the publisher will be pleased to include any necessary credits in any subsequent reprint or edition.

For further information on Polity, visit our website: www.politybooks.com

In loving memory of my husband Malcolm Bowie, 1943–2007

Contents

Acknowledgements   *ix*

Note on References, Bibliography and Translations   *x*

Introduction   *1*

1   From the Beginnings to the Renaissance   *6*

2   From Sun King to Enlightenment (1630–1789)   *26*

3   Between Revolutions (1789–1830)   *53*

4   Balzac and the Birth of Cultural Studies (1830–1870)   *74*

5   Republic, Reaction and the Murder of Taste (1870–1913)   *99*

6   Despair and Optimism (1913–1944)   *119*

7   Commitment and Playfulness (1944–1968)   *138*

8   After May 1968   *159*

9   'Foreignness' Early and Modern   *177*

10 Francophone Literature: Recent Developments   *199*

Conclusion   *220*

Bibliography   *222*

Index   *233*

Acknowledgements

My first debt of gratitude is to Andrea Drugan, my editor at Polity, who has been unfailingly encouraging and patient, and a fount of shrewd advice. My warm thanks go to her, and also to the readers enlisted by Polity to comment on the draft of this book, Laurence M. Porter and Timothy Unwin. Their suggestions were enormously helpful; any faults remaining are entirely mine. Finally, I want to thank my family, in particular my son and daughter Sam and Jess Bowie, for all their support during the writing of the book.

Note on References, Bibliography and Translations

Since this book is aimed at a wide audience, I avoid footnotes and give page references only for major quotations, but I have drawn on the work of many specialists and provide as full a bibliography of secondary works as possible. (Page references always refer to the editions cited in the bibliography.) Life-dates are given for most authors discussed, except very minor ones or those mentioned only in passing; some dates are repeated where this might be helpful. Italics, ellipses and translations are mine unless otherwise stated. Published translations are sometimes slightly adjusted.

Introduction

The body of writing that we call 'French literature' has had a striking impact on the rest of the Western world. Courtly romance spread all across Europe from the mid-twelfth century on, as did French models of chivalric behaviour and love, originating in these romances and the troubadour tradition whose golden age was between about 1160 and 1230. These still shape our ways of thinking, even of feeling. Montaigne's essays (1572–92), translated into English in 1603 and rapidly into other European languages, influenced Shakespeare and have left an indelible impression on European culture. The ideas and even the phrases current in France during the eighteenth century spurred on the American Revolution and contributed to the wording of the American Declaration of Independence (1776); theories of democracy and tolerance either conceived or publicized by the French Enlightenment continue to govern Western liberal political thought. Plays written by French authors have become the libretti of some of Europe's greatest operas: Beaumarchais gave us *The Marriage of Figaro* (the play was first performed in 1784, Mozart's opera in 1786); Hugo gave us the plot of *Rigoletto* (play, *Le Roi s'amuse*, 1832; Verdi's opera, 1851). In the early twentieth century, the Bloomsbury circle turned to French poetry to embolden it in its experimentation; the mid-twentieth-century New York School poets were francophiles (Kenneth Koch sometimes wrote in French and John Ashbery was a Columbia doctoral student in French). Samuel Beckett preferred to write in French rather than English. Post-Second World War French thinkers such as Lévi-Strauss, Foucault and Derrida have taken the humanities by storm in the universities of anglophone and other nations; while Simone de Beauvoir's *Second Sex* (1949), translated into English only a few years after publication (1953), led the growth of late twentieth-century feminism in anglophone countries.

Indeed, for centuries the French language itself had unparalleled prestige in Europe. Many English works owed their diffusion in other European countries to the fact that they were translated into French and then from French into another language such as German. All over Europe, French succeeded Latin as the international language: famously, the Academy of Berlin offered a prize in 1782 for the best essay (in French) on this subject: 'What has made French the universal language of Europe?' ('Qu'est-ce qui a fait de la langue française la langue universelle de l'Europe?') Although the revolutionary and Napoleonic wars would reduce this vogue for French, it remained the language of choice in many parts of Europe: as readers of Tolstoy will know, the Russian aristocracy was still speaking it in the last decades of the nineteenth century.

In other areas, too, French culture has shaped our representation of the world. Monet was the begetter of Impressionism; Paris played a spectacular role in nineteenth- and twentieth-century painting, drawing into its ambit many artists of other nationalities such as Picasso. France has bequeathed to the world its cuisine (a French word), its fairy-tales (such stories as those of Sleeping Beauty and Puss-in-Boots were first collected and written down by Perrault in the seventeenth century), and its films. For despite the current commercial domination of Hollywood, it was in France that cinema was invented, and it continues to influence world cinema in more ways than are widely realized. Such key concepts as film noir, cinéaste and 'auteur' cinema are French; Jean Renoir's *La Règle du jeu* (*The Rules of the Game*, 1939) is still rated among the top ten films ever made, one of the only two non-American films to have had that accolade in every decade for the last fifty years. (The other is Eisenstein's *Battleship Potemkin*, almost always, however, lower on the list than the Renoir. *Sight and Sound*, the magazine of the British Film Institute, conducts polls of leading film critics every decade to establish the ranking.) The major international film festival is held in Cannes. And Anglo-American cinema owes some unexpected debts to France: for instance, the plot of Hitchcock's best film *Vertigo* (1958) is based on the French novel *Sueurs froides: d'entre les morts* (1954, by Pierre Boileau and Thomas Narcejac).

This is not to deny that other nations have formed Western culture too, among them Arabic and Eastern ones. From the Renaissance on, primary movers have been Italy in art and music; Britain in literature and philosophy; Germany and Austria in music again and in modern theories of politics and the mind. Artists and thinkers from minority European cultures have made a trans-European contribution, those of Jewish origin being particularly prominent. Nor is it to deny that France has turned to and absorbed what these others have offered: during the Renaissance, it eagerly embraced Italian art, the Petrarchan sonnet, and aspects of the Italian language; in the eighteenth century, it declared its debt to British political structures and thought. Cervantes's *Don Quixote* (1605, 1615) and Sterne's *Tristram Shandy* (1759–69) suggested the form and scenarios of numerous French novels; France's major nineteenth-century authors looked to Germany and other 'Northern' lands for inspiration – for the new movement of Romanticism, to take only one example. And in a sense, it is somewhat absurd (and outdated) to break down the history of Western culture, which has thrived on interchange as much as it has been damaged by strife, into the history of separate countries. Yet France has 'exported' far more than it has 'imported', and has played a multifaceted role in the world far beyond what might be expected from a relatively small nation. That role has been made possible in part by means of aggressive conquests both in Europe and elsewhere. (While France today has a population of about 64 million, French is spoken as a native language by 90–100 million world-wide and is a second language for some 200 million more in countries that include Vietnam, Senegal and Tunisia.) France's acquisition of overseas territory helped create the wealth that enabled it to foster and subsidize many forms of culture. And such works as Jared Diamond's *Guns, Germs, and Steel* (1997) remind us, if we needed reminding, that the modern supremacy of the West arose not from innate genius but from geographical luck and ruthlessness. But within that broad picture, it is revealing to examine the cultural contribution of one nation-state – a nation-state that both regards itself as exceptional and has been so regarded by many outside its borders, even at times when France's military domination has been weak or non-existent.

How has this impact been achieved in the sphere of literature? From very early on in the country that came to be called 'France', good writing and debate were regarded as contributing to social prestige. They became part of the consciousness of a national elite. French culture is much more thoroughly permeated than anglophone by a common literary and intellectual history, one that is viewed with pride. Not only do French journalists frequently allude to the classics, but literature as a distillation of human experience also functions as a valid source of exempla: not so much a 'guide to life' (as for some anglophone critics who suggest: 'Read X [*Middlemarch*, or *Anna Karenina*, or Toni Morrison's *Beloved*] and you will become a better person'), but rather as a shared frame of reference. In the work of the post-war paediatrician Laurence Pernoud, for example, one finds an eloquent, sensitive statement as to how it feels to be pregnant. One expects to see the name of a living woman as the source. No; it is Balzac. But this shared frame of reference, if a cause of pride, does not create complacency. On the contrary, it has led to constant self-questioning and to a politicization of the relationship between elite and 'low' culture.

In short, France perceives itself as both a 'literary' and a 'political' nation, and this has endowed it, over the course of a millennium, with hundreds of plays, poems, narratives and discursive texts that are especially linguistically aware; especially engaged with social issues; and especially inclined to weave that awareness and that engagement together. My book traces the history of this interweaving, going further back than most 'cultural histories of literature' do. Cultural studies are often confined to the mass-media era, but a longer time-span can open up revealing perspectives. So, although I devote more space to the post-1789 period than to previous ones, I bring out continuities that have their origins in the earliest French literature. There are ruptures and discontinuities too; but overarching preoccupations still emerge, sometimes in surprising places.

As an example of the approach the 'cultural critic' can take, let us look at Van Gogh's *Parisian Novels* of 1887–8, shown on the cover of this book. Van Gogh's painting has international dimensions. Its title, telling us that the provenance of the novels is Paris, announces therefore that it is by a non-French national drawn to Parisian culture. (Indeed, Van Gogh painted it during his two-year stay in Paris.) The 'yellow novels' were the popular fiction produced for a newly literate readership in nineteenth-century France; regarded as scandalous outside France, they would be taken up by anglophone writers who wanted to trail-blaze on both social and literary fronts. (Oscar Wilde's circle founded a magazine called *The Yellow Book*, illustrated by Aubrey Beardsley, and the British 1890s would be referred to as 'the yellow nineties'.) Thus the painting may remind the viewer 'in the know' that France had been, and would continue to be, a beacon for experimental work abroad.

There are more internal meanings too. Literacy was spreading only because of post-Revolutionary political reforms; the large-scale marketing of novels occurred only because inventors and businessmen realized it was in their commercial interests to make and use the cheap paper that could bring prices down. This knowledge is in the hinterland of the painting, which is saying a number of different and perhaps incompatible things about art. Far from disdaining popular culture, the artist makes it an aesthetic subject, as if to say that any artefact can be beautiful and that 'elite' and 'popular' can enrich each other. Yet at the same time the artist needs to preserve his social distinctiveness: after all, he has to make a living from being 'different' – he has to suggest that the (eventual) sale of this painting is *not* the same as the sale of novels, not essentially a matter of mass-pro-duced commodities. So the artist challenges the spectator to set the cheap novels both with and against the work of art that makes them lovely. In other words, there is a double self-positioning here that we shall encounter again. The artist expresses solidarity with the novels and at the same time lays claim to cultural prestige by appealing to a viewer more sophisticated than their average reader.

1

From the Beginnings to the Renaissance

The medieval period originated in the break-up of the Roman Empire, shifting the global cultural struggle from 'Europe' (Greece, and later Rome) versus 'Asia' (Persia) to Christian Europe versus Islam; a recognizable 'French' monarchy started in 987 with the election of Hugues Capet as king of France. The Capetians survived in a direct line until 1328, and branches of the family continued to rule thereafter. This continuity, with relatively few dynastic struggles, already gave France an advantage; but, as yet, the early French monarchy was centred in the tiny territory of the Ile-de-France, and the king ruled precariously over unreliable vassals. Nevertheless, capable of rebellion though they might be, they recognized the king as a figure to whom loyalty was owed, and it was less through violent annexations, more through diplomacy and the building of ties by marriage, that the Capetian kings slowly strengthened and extended the royal sphere until the French crown became the foremost one in Europe, and the one with which the Popes had the closest alliances. (This is one reason why the Papacy moved temporarily to Avignon from 1309 to 1377.) But 'Gallicanism' was also developing in the French Church, limiting the Pope's authority, tilting the balance of influence to the bishops or the monarch, and ensuring a degree of Church autonomy that would continue right through to Napoleon.

From early on, therefore, there existed an independent land called 'France', one whose nationhood was still weak and whose powerful princes and local lords had to be won round to any sense of 'the centre', yet one in which the monarchy's gradual consolidation normally proceeded without all-out collisions like those which in England led to the assassination of the Archbishop of Canterbury Thomas Becket in 1170, or to the signing of Magna Carta forced on King John in 1215.

Fault-lines, naturally, existed. In *The Identity of France* (1986), the historian Fernand Braudel has declared: 'Yes, France is certainly diverse, and that diversity is visible, lasting, and *structural*' (his italics: II 669); and he suggests that France is 'too good' at internecine strife, wars of religion, even civil war. 'Every nation is divided, and thrives on division. But France illustrates the rule rather too well: Protestants and Catholics, Jansenists and Jesuits, blues and reds, republicans and royalists, right and left, Dreyfusards and anti-Dreyfusards, collaborators and resisters – division is within the house and unity is no more than a façade, a superstructure, a shout in the wind' (I 119). Here then are some of these divisions, already declaring themselves in the Middle Ages: between centre and regions; between the two great medieval civilizations of North and South (with their different languages, *langue d'oïl* and *langue d'oc*); between the assertion of authority and the rejection of it; between different belief-systems and ideologies. But if there was 'division within the house', there was still a 'house', providing room for the arts to develop locally and centrally, particularly during what has been described as 'the twelfth-century Renaissance' – and room for Paris to become established as a European focus for intellectuals. For the Middle Ages gave us universities, and in the twelfth century that of Paris became pre-eminent, attracting students from all over Europe to learn from its great thinkers, the most renowned being Pierre Abélard (1079– 1142/4). By the time the famous Louis IX was reigning (1226–70), it was taken for granted that national and international prestige could be demonstrated through centres of learning and through religious architecture and art. Through other means too: Louis IX, like his predecessors, led a Crusade, albeit one during which he was captured and had to be ransomed; and he sanctioned the Papal Inquisition in Languedoc. But along with these acts of violence (for which he would be canonized), he encouraged artistic production, for example building the exquisite Sainte-Chapelle in Paris.

Partly, then, because the initially weak Capetian kings kept power internally through negotiation not battle, 'France' was able to develop art and writing, the latter at first in the monasteries but soon spreading to secular communities. While the commissioning of music and expensive artefacts fulfilled a social function as affirmations of luxury, hence status, regional seigneurs often favoured writing as a means of enhancing their position. Thus ducal patrons might commission chronicles designed to highlight their achievements or genealogy – to demonstrate, say, their descent from Charlemagne, which affirmed their legitimacy vis-à-vis the present king; these histories could shade off into fictional narrative. But it was not only commissioned chronicles that contributed to prestige. It is often supposed that in 'undeveloped' societies antagonism was and is settled purely by might and main; the anthropologist Michael Herzfeld has however noted that fine verbal performance can sometimes more successfully contain an opponent than physical violence. If, in an angry dialogue, one interlocutor makes a clever riposte, 'to respond with knife or fist would demean the assailant by suggesting that he was incapable of responding with some witty line of his own' (*The Poetics of Manhood*, 1985, 143). Herzfeld's comments indicate that in certain contexts skilful language is a particularly effectual non-physical demonstration of status. It can hold conflict in equipoise. France's elite would appear to have learned this lesson early on – to have placed high valuation on a linguistic dexterity that can both express tension and be used to deflect its bodily enactment.

Of course the application of the lesson would be uneven; nor should we suppose that all medieval French literature expresses tension: the saints' lives (hagiographies), among the earliest of chronicles, voice duty to God in pure form and thus generally lack the mental *agon*, the contest, of self against self to be found in almost all the literature the West now values, going back to Homer. But much of this early literature does depict both outer and inner strife. For instance, in the medieval French epic, loyalty was owed first to the Lord God, then to one's liege, and, later, to one's Lady: these loyalties could however clash. The first masterpiece of French literature, *La Chanson de Roland*, shows how works can both describe struggles and paradoxically be 'used' to consolidate political aims. Composed in Northern France in the late eleventh century, the *Roland* narrates the end of the Frankish Emperor Charlemagne's campaign against the Saracens of Spain. The Christians accept the Saracens' deceitful offer of peace, an offer opposed only by Charlemagne's nephew Roland. Roland's treacherous stepfather Ganelon conspires with the Saracens, who ambush Charlemagne's army; Roland, commanding the rearguard, at first refuses the advice of his friend Olivier to blow his oliphant (ivory horn) and summon help from the rest of Charlemagne's retreating army. Roland dies, Charlemagne takes vengeance on the Saracens, and the traitor Ganelon is executed.

This epic enjoyed great popularity in the Middle Ages and was translated and adapted into Latin, Norse, Middle High German, Dutch, Welsh and Middle English. Arguably, at the time of its dissemination it reflected, and even contributed to, some sense of quasi-national community: it refers to 'dulce France', 'sweet France' (line 109 and elsewhere), and to the bitter tears, the swooning in dismay, of '100,000 French' ('Cent milie Franc en unt si grant dulur, / N'en i ad cel ki durement ne plurt'; 'Cent milie Francs s'en pasment cuntre tere', lines 2907–08, 2932). It illustrates, too, the literary representation of history for purposes of propaganda: the original battle, in 778, was against the Basques not the Saracens. But the Crusades were now on the horizon: the *Roland* was composed soon after 1086, and the Pope's first call to the Crusades was in 1095. These Crusades have been described as Western Europe's first colonial venture, and differences between 'Moor' and 'Christian', with concomitant distortions of Islam, mark many works of medieval French literature. Thus this early masterpiece serves a directly political end. Nor does the story end there. As the most widely known of the hundred or so medieval French epics that have come down to us, the *Roland* shows how culture can be commandeered by posterity as well as by contemporaries for purposes of national solidarity. For it is uncertain whether the origins of the tale are Germanic or 'French', and, as we have seen, at the time it was written there was no undiluted French national feeling in the modern sense. Nevertheless, in later centuries the *Roland* was held to be a prime example of 'Frenchness', never more so than in the late nineteenth century, in the wake of France's defeat in the Franco-Prussian War (1870–1).

But the *Roland* is significant in other ways. It has been described as a 'liturgy of genocide': in haunting verse it details multiple dismemberings and disembowelments of both French and pagans with no visible compassion for the pagans. Yet it is a tale of moral as well as of physical conflicts. These moral conflicts arise when Charlemagne wishes to cease fighting and accept a truce; in Ganelon's treason itself; and when Roland puts his pride above his duty to preserve his men. Psychological and political complexity fuse when the *Roland* shows the different reactions of individuals to the same communal crisis, and when it suggests that though this may be a tale of ultimate 'triumph' for the French, theirs is a Pyrrhic victory. For the work depicts the horror of the French losses at least. 'When Count Roland sees his fellow-nobles dead, / including Olivier whom he loved, oh so much!, / he feels tender and begins to weep. / His face lost all its colour; / so great was his suffering that he could not stand upright' (lines 2215–19). The verse structure itself can recreate the shock of the violence. 'When the emperor goes to search for his nephew, / in the grass of the meadow he finds so many flowers / that are crimson with the blood of our barons' (lines 2870–2): the third line, with deliberate suddenness, contrasts the natural beauty of the flowers with the slaughter that stains them. Charlemagne is often said to be weary, not to know what to do; and when, at the very end, the angel Gabriel summons him to further warfare against the pagans, he weeps and says, 'God! how hard is this life that I lead' (line 4000). In short, as much imaginative energy goes into the temporary defeat of the French as into their ultimate victory, as much into tragedy as triumphalism. The *Roland* serves as a model of a certain kind of literary engagement with history, an engagement that shapes a multiperspectival awareness of national events, and heightens sensitivity to the relationship between the personal and the political.

This model was followed by other medieval authors. The *Roland* is a *chanson de geste*, that is, a 'song about history, about deeds'. The genre flourished until the early fourteenth century; these long and often rough-hewn epic narratives recreate the trauma of violence. The late twelfth-century poem *Raoul de Cambrai* even explores the point at which a lord's ill-treatment of his man justifies the man's disloyalty, and asks whether, after a formal renunciation of fealty, the slaying of lord by man should be regarded as treason or not. Somewhat later narrative forms like the first-person *dits*, and historical accounts like Froissart's *Chronicles* (1360–1400), evoke the sufferings of terrified victims; whether directly or ironically, they can query the necessity for violence, and can stage not all-powerful monarchs but uncertain or weak kings. Thus many of these works – including those commissioned as propaganda exercises on behalf of nobles – described a political system in which, in theory, abuses could be challenged, authority-figures held in check. Arguably they helped to maintain such a system, or the idea of it: an idea that, for much of France's history, guarded against the worst excesses of absolutism.

And this varied governance allowed for the spread of culturally rich regional courts whose seigneurs not only enjoyed works about their own ancestors but also, as I have suggested, created communities that vied with each other in elegance and refinement. For as well as an intense engagement with 'history', French literature was developing another typical characteristic. From the late eleventh century on, the troubadours – poet-musicians – performed at, and were financially supported by, all the major courts of France; they were also in demand at those of Spain, Portugal, northern Italy and England. The troubadours' depiction of love sometimes resembles a game with defined rules; their exquisite verse deploys intricate, virtuoso rhyme-schemes. Later in the Middle Ages, lyric poetry became still more intricate, almost mathematical in its structures. This delight in the 'rules' of love, and in linguistic patterning and ingenious play, is perhaps more consistently self-conscious in French than in other national literatures. Sophistication must not only exist but can be advertised as such: it creates importance.

That sophistication depends too on a foregrounding of the female figure. Here we encounter one of the major contradictions of French literary culture, a culture that has almost from the start both demoted and promoted women. For eight centuries France has argued about the role and 'nature' of women – arguments doubtless affecting mainly the well-born, but nevertheless a live part of social and literary interchange. The earliest examples of these 'querelles des femmes', 'women-debates', are to be found around 1200. Feminist critics have focused on the demotions of womanhood; there is another side. The model of courtly love, *fin'amor*, that France transmitted to the rest of Europe is, to be sure, reliant on an idealized and sometimes condescending gallantry, but it also recognizes that women have desires, and gives their feelings prominence in however stylized a form. Numerous hagiographies laud female martyrs and saints, endowing them with the role of representing 'ordinary' Christians. And while much medieval literature is scurrilously misogynistic, comparing women to animals and lumping them all together for negative generalizations, many of the finest writers of the period like Chrétien de Troyes do create nuanced female characters who act with intelligence and initiative.

How did this contradiction arise? We may suppose a basic assumption that the female sex is the inferior one, since this exists in most societies. The early nineteenth-century writer Germaine de Staël was the first commentator to argue that belief in the Virgin Mary began to change men's attitudes to women (in *De la littérature*, 1800). Since then, others have discussed the 'Mariolatry' that swept France in particular in the Middle Ages, pointing out how many churches and cathedrals are dedicated to Mary (the greatest being Chartres) – not only dedicated to her, but sometimes exclusively depicting scenes drawn from her life. This cult of Mary may have arisen from an early questioning of authority. The Trinity was feared, whether God the Father, the Holy Ghost, or Christ himself. All male, they could be expected to apply laws rigorously (and the king shared in their divine power); whereas Mary might bend the rules, was on the side of the sinner – she could intercede for the thief or mischief-maker in the most unlikely, the quirkiest, of circumstances. The age was not ready for atheism, much less for revolution, but Mary offered a way of 'thinking round' the prevailing ideology; and some of the grateful devotion she thus earned spilled over onto real women.

Certainly, France has an ambivalence towards women still more visible than in other European countries, and this has affected both its politics and its literary culture. On the one hand, that culture can be unremittingly sexist. On the other, intellectual women can be lauded, given 'space' in which to be creative individuals and to engage with issues of the day. Here are a few examples of the ambivalence. Reigning supreme among the antifeminist works that proliferated in the Middle Ages was the *Roman de la rose*, highly popular not only in France but throughout Europe (composed *c*.1225–78; it was begun by Guillaume de Lorris and continued by Jean de Meun, whose part is much longer and more significant). This verse dream-narrative of a young man's initiation into love looks misogynistic. It stages coarse advisors and ends as explicitly as may be with a sexual congress that implies painful deflowering for the woman, even hinting at rape: 'there was a barrier within, which I could feel but not see . . . Therefore I forced my way into it . . . in order duly to pluck the rose-bud . . . I can tell you that at last, when I had shaken the bud, I scattered a little seed there. This was when I had touched the inside of the rose-bud and explored all its little leaves' (*The Romance of the Rose*, 333–4; translation by Frances Horgan). Even this work, however, plays so learnedly with literary conventions, and with allegorical figures of Love and Friendship, that it can be interpreted (and has been) as predominantly a 'debate' about love and sex; in other words – so its modern supporters argue – the ambiguous structure of the *Rose* should not be understood as tending in one direction only.

And there were some women writers in the Middle Ages, for instance female troubadours (the *trobairitz*) and the twelfth-century Anglo-Norman writer Marie de France, who composed a series of witty and dexterous verse tales, the *Lais* (*Lays*) and adapted into French fables from Aesop and other sources (including Arabic ones). Marie de France was writing at about the mid-point of the two-century period when, for the elite, 'English' and 'French' language and culture overlapped to the point of being often indistinguishable. She lived at a court (that of the Plantagenet king Henry II) in France's first large overseas colony – England. (That colonization meant that the French language fused with 'English' and for centuries would shape English ideas not only of cuisine, but also of war, diplomacy, couture, ballet, equestrianism . . .). Marie's tales evoke a world of magic and marvels in which, almost by sleight of hand, adulterous relationships are taken for granted if the marriage is a loveless one; her passionate heroes and heroines see love as an ultimate value. Still more radical are the fables, which describe power-struggles among different 'ranks' of animals – in the manner of all fables, but given a sometimes startlingly contestatory twist by Marie.

The most renowned female author of the medieval period is Christine de Pizan (*c*.1364–*c*.1431). Extraordinarily, she was a professional writer. Male writers could count on making a living from Church attachments at varying levels of formality, which left them free to compose (thus the medieval Church, paradoxically, helped to support secular literature). But no such flexible structure was available to women. It was precisely this that led Pizan to make a living from her pen. Her output was large and diverse, including political and moral works, but her best-known work now is *Le Livre de la cité des dames* (*The Book of the City of Ladies*, 1405), and she is held to have been the first woman in the Middle Ages to tackle literary misogyny or anti-feminism openly. The aim of *The City of Ladies* was two-fold: to refute the equation of women with sinfulness, and to instil a sense of their own worth into female readers. Pizan is not a modern feminist: she does not advocate that women perform striking deeds or seek 'equal opportunities'; rather, she promotes their moral qualities, and on the face of it her title alludes not to activism but to St Augustine's conception of the 'city of God'. Yet the 'city' of this political writer does become something secular. It is a community that stretches back in historical time, an entity that denotes mutual protection and 'civilization'. Furthermore, the work proceeds in a way that we are beginning to discern as another recognizable strand of French culture, in that it self-confessedly focuses on representations. It is just as much about literary, biblical and mythical portrayals of females as about men's treatment of women, and one of its key targets is not a legal system, but another book – the *Roman de la rose*, about whose misogyny Pizan at least was in no doubt. Pizan's own book *is* the protective 'city'. The social unit and the written artefact stand for each other.

One specially arresting case of a work deliberately blurring gender, racial, political and genre boundaries all at once is that of the anonymous part-prose, part-verse *Aucassin et Nicolette*. (It survived into the early modern and modern periods and was revived as an operetta as recently as 1979–80: *La Belle Sarrasine, The Beautiful Saracen*.) Written in the late twelfth or early thirteenth century, *Aucassin et Nicolette* draws attention to its mixed form by calling itself a *chante-fable* (song-story). Full of gentle parody and deflation, it tells the tale of two young lovers separated by the wishes of a tyrannical father. Nicolette has Saracen origins; Aucassin, although the son of a Christian count, has a Moorish name. Naively besotted with his Nicolette, Aucassin is an 'anti-knight' who, placing love above all other considerations, refuses to fight. This was potentially scandalous in noble feudal society as well as in the world of 'courtoisie', chivalric courtesy, where love is the source of prowess, not a reason for running off into a private world. As for Nicolette, far from being a lady on a pedestal, she is resourceful, amusing – this is part of what Aucassin likes about her. 'Nicolette, . . . so beautiful when you joke and tease' ('biax borders et biax jouers', VII line 15). The work may well have been unpopular at the time: all copies of it but one disappeared, and no mention is made of it in contemporary texts. But what is important is that it could be written. And certainly popular in the same period was the subtler Chrétien de Troyes (he flourished between 1160 and 1185). Chrétien is the author of five Arthurian verse narratives that put questions about status and rank enigmatically, elegantly, even whimsically. Out of love for Guinevere, Lancelot abases himself so far as to ride in a cart (in *Le Chevalier de la charrette*). Is this ignominy, or should true love steel the knight even to abjure his social standing?

Drama and other public performances of the period contributed to the crossing of borderlines between 'noble' and lowly, dignified and undignified. The *chansons de geste* were often recited by travelling performers, *jongleurs*, who would also compose and perform satirical and parodic *fabliaux* – short comic verse works that could be peopled by pimps and beggars, take the clergy as butts of ribald humour, and be graphically scatological. (Even Marie de France talks about faeces, indeed diarrhoea, in her fables.) Church drama itself evolved from the enactment of the Mass liturgy to racier content. At first didactic and comfortably familiar, these liturgical plays over time acquired more and more props, stage-directions and secondary characters; fervour might be relieved with musical interludes; serious religious themes combined with often humorous scenes of low life. The ass that bore Jesus might be revered but also mocked; dramatized conflicts between Church and Synagogue could end with the discomfited 'Synagogue' being bodily pushed off the stage. The Roman soldiers present at the Crucifixion could become comically stupid figures. And the lives of the saints lent themselves to a variety of eye-catching props and off-beat minor adjutants. These developments correspond roughly to the transition from 'mystery plays' to 'miracle plays': the dividing line is not always clear, but miracles, being full of surprise and suspense, were inherently more theatrical. The Church itself was in a cleft stick, realizing that lessons had to be enlivened if they were to hold the attention of the faithful – and these dramas were aimed primarily at 'le menu peuple de Dieu', 'God's humble folk' – but anxious lest the entertainment itself become too alluring and all-encompassing. This danger presented itself soon. The earliest French comedy – still religious but with an admixture of farce and vulgarity – was Jehan Bodel's miracle play *Le Jeu de Saint Nicolas*, of about 1200; also early in the thirteenth century, *Courtois d'Arras*, a short and lively dramatization of the parable of the prodigal son, is set in contemporary Artois: the country-bumpkin son, ironically named 'Courtois' ('Courteous'), is robbed by two prostitutes in a tavern. And another area in which the sheer pleasure of the medium could take over was in the writing itself: the outstanding thirteenth-century author Rutebeuf wrote, inter alia, a play in complexly patterned, sometimes punning, verse (*Le Miracle de Théophile*, 1264).

Eventually, purely secular dramas were performed. The first French play that is serious yet non-religious is the *Estoire de Griseldis* (*Story of Griseldis*) of 1395, based on a tale made famous by Boccaccio and Petrarch; numerous others followed in the fifteenth century, as well as comedies of varied types: farces, 'soties' (satirical farces), humorous monologues. Guilds of actors ('confréries') already existed in Paris; now societies sprang up devoted to the writing and performance of comic pieces, including lampoons of specific public events. Medieval drama was, in short, becoming risky. Ever more stringently policed, it eventually died away, but not before it had produced outstanding works and bequeathed fertile possibilities to successors, not least to Molière. One means of self-policing, increasingly in evidence as the period went on, was for playwrights to hover on a borderline between harsh and gentle ridicule of social 'types'; another was to combine coarse with sophisticated topics. Dramatists could thereby appeal to different levels of society, both protecting themselves and increasing takings. One play in particular demonstrates this: the anonymous masterpiece *Farce de Maître Pierre Pathelin*, thought to have been first performed between 1456 and 1469. This play remains popular, and one of its phrases has passed into the language: 'revenons à nos moutons', literally 'let's return to our sheep' – 'let's get back to the point'. Its neat plot draws to some extent on familiar elements of farce and comedy of situation, revolving round a ruse that backfires, so that in the end the 'biter' is 'bit' to amusement all round. But what is significant is the transmission of this stock-in-trade through a more ostentatious comedy of language than had yet appeared in French drama. The Pathelin of the title, an impecunious lawyer, is a conman who tricks a stupid draper out of some cloth, in part by dazzling him with a display of verbal fireworks. At one point, pretending to be delirious, he speaks no fewer than nine languages in succession. But Pathelin is in his turn tricked by a shepherd who has to appear in a lawcourt and whom he has advised to answer all questions with 'baa'. When Pathelin finally asks the shepherd for payment, he naturally replies – 'baa'. The feigned inarticulateness of a peasant can outwit the clever lawyer. The play could thus speak both to the 'common man' and to a relatively educated audience. We shall see this same double-sidedness in Molière. As well as a survival mechanism and a means of ensuring one's livelihood, political flexibility in the hands of the great French comic writers pulled together the viewing public.

Some critics have proposed that the author of *Pathelin* was the celebrated late medieval poet Villon (*c*.1431–after 1463). Whether he was or
not, Villon demonstrates another major change that took place by the end
of the Middle Ages. Almost all texts in the early medieval period are anonymous, and even somewhat later books were very often 'compilation'
works in which the identity of the authors scarcely mattered if it mattered
at all. Even so, many writers, including anonymous ones, do refer to their
own act of writing with a frequency that may surprise modern readers
brought up on the notion that this first happened in the twentieth century.
But by the end of the medieval period the concept of individual authorship
has truly taken hold. *Le Voir Dit* (*True Story*), by the brilliant poet and composer Guillaume de Machaut (*c*.1300–77), both narrates its own day-by-day
composition and is a 'confessional' love-story. Christine de Pizan may be
writing on behalf of women, but she is also writing as herself. This change
has been located in the fourteenth century, when it became possible to
make a living by writing: anonymity became rarer since authors wanted
to claim works as their own. Nowhere is this promotion of personal
authorship clearer than in Villon. That does not mean he has no sense of
the community in which he is embedded, nor of its past and future: far
from it. The two perspectives – the distinctiveness of this particular writer,
and his sardonic relationship with his society – combine to produce one of
the most influential works of the medieval period. Writers from the sixteenth century to the nineteenth and twentieth – Marot, Baudelaire,
Rimbaud, Brecht – have admired Villon; one of his phrases has passed not
just into the French language but into other European ones: 'Mais où sont
les neiges d'antan?', 'But where are the snows of yesteryear?' His best-
known work (from which this phrase comes) is the *Testament* (1461–2).
What could be more solemnly expressive of a unique individual's wishes
than his or her will? And Villon often (unsolemnly) draws attention to this
individuality by rhyming with his own name – for example, in French 'bell-
peal' and 'testicles' rhyme with 'Villon' ('carillon', 'couillon'): 'Ici se clôt le
testament / Et finit du pauvre Villon. / Venez à son enterrement, / Quand
vous orrez le carillon, / Vêtus rouge com vermillon, / Car en amour
mourut martyr: / Ce jura-il sur son couillon / Quand de ce monde vout
partir' ('Here closes and ends the will of poor Villon. / Come to his burial, /
when you hear the carillon, / dressed in vermillion, / for he died a marytr
to love: / that's what he swore on his balls / when he wanted to depart
this world': *Testament*, lines 1996–2003). Individuality, yes. But that plan-
gent refrain 'Mais où sont les neiges d'antan?' is part of a social lament: it
appears in a section called 'Ballad of the ladies of olden times' and is

echoed in the immediately following 'Ballad of the lords of olden times', which now explicitly reminds us that worldly power is transient: 'Mais où est le preux Charlemagne?', 'But where is the valiant Charlemagne?' As a literary 'will', this work is then also political, a statement bequeathed to the society that will come after the man. And not only is it a mock testament, it is also a public testimony, since in it the poet bears witness to everything he has suffered at the hands of the authorities. He pokes fun at them, uses rhyme and other poetic games to draw attention to torture and capital punishment, deflates powerful personages and tells them the rich are damned while the poor are saved. The verse of Villon, on the cusp of the French Renaissance, enacts an intensive, deftly realized, authorial specificity *and* an engagement with a particular community.

This French Renaissance occupies what is often called the 'long sixteenth century', 1470–1630. It was during these 160 years that the vernacular took on a politically prominent role – that the use of French started to be perceived as an instrument of state. Important characteristics of sixteenth-century French literature follow on from this politicization of the French language, which has indelibly marked succeeding centuries too. But in a sense, from the very beginning of written French recognition of the vernacular had been political. The earliest text we possess in the vernacular of Gaul is that of the Strasbourg Oaths of 842, a pact between two of Charlemagne's grandsons, forming an alliance against their brother and swearing in each other's language as a sign of trustworthiness: one of those languages is the precursor of French. From the late ninth century on, hagiographies were also in the vernacular – mostly translated from Latin, and aiming to edify the non-Latin-speaking laity. This was a challenge to the language of 'authority', Latin, for it meant that, as Sarah Kay puts it, 'the saints speak French' (*A Short History of French Literature*, 2003, 31–4): the challenge was as yet low-key. The vernacular gradually supplemented Latin as an official language; finally, in the late thirteenth century, the authorized history of the realm, the *Grandes Chroniques de France*, was translated from Latin into French. From this point on, 'literary' and 'political' uses of the vernacular fed into each other. By the late fourteenth and early fifteenth centuries, history-writing in French reached a peak of prestige with Froissart and Pizan, and by the end of the fifteenth century the vernacular was not only supplementing Latin in formal and legal documents but had almost completely displaced it. And, as is plain by now, it was not only in hagiographies, histories and official texts that the vernacular was set down in writing. Over the course of the four centuries before modern printing (that is, from the late eleventh century to the late

fifteenth), the oral body of French fiction and verse had come to be comple-
mented by a huge number of written works. Many were still read out to
listeners, but the moment a work was committed to manuscript, and
however often it was subsequently performed, it ceased to be oral and
entered the realm of writing. Medieval writers were well aware of the
implications of this: the transition from oral to written vernacular often
led them not only to refer to their own act of composition, as we have
seen, but further to play ironically with their texts' literary status. Along
with these developments, and even though the status of verse still superseded that of prose, prose was nevertheless taking over in many areas of
writing, particularly in the vernacular fictions that, from the twelfth century
on, were translated into all neighbouring vernaculars and would play a
leading role in subsequent European literature. The spread of written
prose was also propelled by pragmatic considerations. It, along with the
vernacular, became a prime medium for the history: prose was perceived
as a way to ensure an impression of 'truth', to avoid association with the
'entertainment value' of verse, and was thus a useful strategic tool.

The printing press gave this sanctioning of the vernacular a mighty push
forward. Movable type came to France in 1470 (over twenty years after
Gutenberg's invention). Books could now reach a far wider audience than
was conceivable in the age of manuscripts; although the reading public was
still very small, the demand for literacy grew as reading matter became
more readily available. From 1516 on, this development was in part bound
up with the growth of Protestantism, hence did not lack opponents. The
diffusion of printed material in the vernacular made the Catholic Church
anxious. For example, one of the most widely read books of the sixteenth
century was the translation of the Psalms into French verse, begun by the
Protestant court poet Marot (1496–1544: his *Trente Psaumes de David* was
published in 1541). Such dissemination of Biblical texts among the laity – a
central aim of religious reformers, and inconceivable a hundred years
earlier – also displeased the Sorbonne (by now an arm of the Church); it
went so far as to attempt to suppress printing in the 1520s. Both authors
and printers could be in real danger: the publisher and evangelically minded
scholar Estienne Dolet was burned at the stake for heresy in 1546. But
despite this brutality, printing irrevocably consolidated the use of French
as opposed to Latin, and by the mid-sixteenth century the nation was ready
for a formal and public appropriation of its own written language.

The term 'French' itself needs further definition. 'Early Old French'
(mid-ninth century to end of eleventh) was divided into *langue d'oïl* (northern France), *langue d'oc* (southern) and *franco-provençal*. Variations contin-

ued to exist in 'Old French', but by the end of the twelfth century 'francien', the dialect spoken in Paris and the surrounding regions (including the Loire valley – in other words, the areas favoured by the royal court) was taking over, being regarded as the most prestigious spoken and written form. From the fourteenth century on, 'French' came in effect to equate to 'francien'. So, while the great Renaissance poet Ronsard (1524–85) urged that one way of enriching French was to draw on all manner of dialects, he also had to concede that since France was now ruled by one monarch, 'we are forced, if we want to obtain some honour, to speak his court language; otherwise our work, however learned, would be judged relatively worthless, or (perhaps) totally scorned' (John Lough, *Writer and Public in France*, 1978, 33). But despite Ronsard's reluctance, for him too the endorsement of this 'court language' was bound up not just with personal fame but also with France's unity and standing. Under his leadership, a group of seven poets known as the 'Pléiade', active for most of the second half of the sixteenth century, focused on the renewal of a national poetic language. Thus the vernacular came to be presented overtly as a means of forging a sense of nationhood; while the adaptation and dynamic 'incorporation' of classical literature ('innutrition' was the word used) was a way of raising the status of French to that of Latin and Greek. Advice on this assimilation was proffered in both poems and theoretical statements, the first and best-known of these latter being Du Bellay's essay *Défense et illustration de la langue française* (1549; that is, roughly translated, 'Defending the French language and rendering it illustrious'). This work, contrary to what one might suppose, is not without its snobbery: Du Bellay (*c.*1522–60) dismisses previous French literature in order to promote a renewal based on the most celebrated ancient (and Italian) models, arguing that French, thus 'glorified', would become the language of works fit to enter the Pantheon. So begins the linguistic elitism that would reach its peak in the following century.

The Pléiade group was active in the period just after the reign of François I (1515–47) and could not have existed without his encouragement and subsidizing of the arts. Under François I, the drive for national unity and prestige did not translate into rampantly imperialist ambitions vis-à-vis the rest of Europe. France could and did continue to press key territorial claims, and François I had aspired to the title of Holy Roman Emperor; but when this failed, he focused France's self-assertion as it were inwards. The wise king Grandgousier in Rabelais's *Gargantua* (1534–5) advises that 'the time is past for conquering kingdoms . . . at the expense of our Christian neighbour and brother' (322). The idea of a European empire was in decline, not to be revived until Napoleon, and these words from Rabelais's royal character may, claims Terence Cave, be interpreted as propaganda in favour of another kind of French sovereignty (*A Short History of French Literature*, 2003, 100–1). François I laid the foundations for France's double evolution into the most powerful nation-state in Europe and into a beacon of European culture, now with a clearly wordly aim. Indeed, the French Renaissance, which derived immediately from Italy, and more distantly from Constantinople (Istanbul) via Islamic expansion, can be most neatly summarized as a comprehensive secularization of high culture. More than ever before, wealthy French nobles and monarchs wanted splendid palaces and rich decoration, after the manner of the northern Italian city-states. The construction of cathedrals faded into the background. Painting – instead of displaying religious figures against gold backgrounds signifying paradise (with at times a tiny image of the donor appearing to the side) – now glorified material wealth in portraits of rich and powerful contemporary secular figures.

During and soon after the reign of François I, France produced two of the major European literary works of the sixteenth century, both of which had an incalculable impact on Western writing and thought: Rabelais's narrative sequence about a family of giants and Montaigne's essays. In this period, they are rivalled only by the plays of Shakespeare (1564–1616) and the early seventeenth-century *Don Quixote* of Cervantes (1547–1616). We should be wary of simplistically seeing the 'radiance' of François I as a direct causal factor in the appearance of these two astonishing writers: we are not yet looking at a fully unified or centralized France. Although Rabelais (1483?–1553) came from Chinon in the Loire valley, he lived for much of his life outside this region (in Montpellier, Lyon and Rome), and was first published in Lyon (1532–4), while Montaigne (1533–92) lived, and was first published, in Bordeaux (1580). Furthermore, ironically, one catalyst of Montaigne's humane and tolerant world view was the civil conflicts, atrocities and economic collapse brought about by the struggles for ascendancy between Catholics and Protestants (in the Wars of Religion, 1562–94). Yet by the time Rabelais had begun to publish, the nation France, in its regions as well as in its royal court, could lay claim to an exceptional valuing of all the arts and of philosophy. And the acknowledgment of Paris as a centre of learning is integral to the book's structure. Rabelais sends his young giant Gargantua to Paris for his education, even if he satirizes the dry scholasticism of the Sorbonne – the Sorbonne which, for all its reactionariness, still ranked as a leading European university with a three-hundred-year-old tradition of intricate theological debate – or ranked, at least, as an institution that had to be contended with because of its powers of censorship. Rabelais, then, was read throughout Europe from the six-teenth century on; two early translations into German and English, loose but vigorous, ensured his fame (respectively, Johann Fischart's and, some decades later, Sir Thomas Urquhart's: he gave English the adjective 'Rabe-laisian'). Rabelais's central characters are the giant Pantagruel, Pantagruel's human companion Panurge, and Pantagruel's father Gargantua, whom we see growing up and, for example, releasing a flood of urine from the top of Notre-Dame that nearly washes away the Parisians, drowning 260,418 of them – 'not counting the women and children' (155); the narrative is written with incomparable exuberance, issuing long and joking lists of activities or objects, creating mock-puzzles, punning, celebrating food and drink on a scale that is not merely copious but hyperbolic.

Rabelais did not spring from nowhere. The bawdiness and the delight in verbal texture are there in many of his medieval predecessors; his con-man and debater Panurge is the 'son' of Maître Pierre Pathelin (Panurge, like Pathelin, is a polyglot); and the 'Grands Rhétoriqueurs', a group of poets active in the immediately preceding decades (1470–1530), had written works clotted with elaborate rhyme-schemes, alliteration, puns and verbal puzzles. But the confidence with which Rabelais weaves all these together is both unique to him and belongs to the French Renais-sance. He creates what Cave calls a 'cornucopian text' that glories in the riches of ancient and present culture. New to the century's literature too is Rabelais's humanism. He was not, as we have seen, the first to challenge the Church and other authorities. But complementing the enjoyment of the body is a sophisticated emphasis on education of the 'whole person'. Rabelais's work promotes the radical values that were changing Reforma-tion Europe; and, albeit the protagonists are male, when eventually Gar-gantua creates his ideal community, the Abbey of Thélème, men and women live together in a harmony and companionship that go beyond 'courtoisie' and gallantry. Sophisticated, too, is the interweaving of body, book and narration in metaphors or quasi-allegories. The body can be a kind of text to be worked on, played with; the text or book is, as Rabelais often reminds us, a physical object -- and, comically, the word itself can become almost physical (in one episode in the Fourth Book, the characters on their travels encounter 'frozen words'); finally, Rabelais's tongue-in-cheek narrator is particularly knowing: 'I, who am telling you these oh-so-true tales' ('je, qui vous fais ces tant véritables contes', *Pantagruel*, 417). Rabelais makes us relish the relationship between authorial, linguistic and bodily self-awareness.

The motto of the Abbey of Thélème is 'Do as you will' ('Fais ce que voudras'); Montaigne's motto was also a flexible one: 'What do I know?' ('Que sais-je?'). This is not nihilistic – not: 'I believe nothing'; rather, it betokens a need to question both the outside world and the self perceiving it. These two mottoes could be taken as the key ideas of Renaissance France. This is by no means to suggest that they had universal currency: as we have seen, attempts at suppression could be ferocious. But their open-mindedness reinforced revolutionary new agendas that would come to characterize radical thinking among Europe's cultural elites over the following two centuries. Montaigne's mode of writing is different from Rabelais's: while Rabelais's is joyously dynamic and explicitly celebrates the body, the physicality of Montaigne's is conveyed often in quiet, submerged imagery. But, like Rabelais, Montaigne is a master of eloquence. His tone is teasing as well as grave; his very syntax suggests a relativistic outlook, supple enough to embrace differing viewpoints and to move easily between 'noble' and 'everyday' (for example, between so-called 'great' human accomplishments on the one hand and, on the other, the spider's web as an illustration of the unrivalled craft to be found in Nature). He even smooths away the potential political clash between Latin and the vernacular by quoting extensively from classical Latin texts in such a way as to blend these almost seamlessly with his own prose.

Montaigne's most renowned essay is 'Des cannibales' ('On the Cannibals': it influenced Shakespeare's *The Tempest*). Here, 150 years before the Enlightenment, Montaigne queries European assumptions of superiority over 'savages', and claims that we are too inclined to take our own country as the pinnacle of success: 'There' – he slyly remarks – 'we always find the perfect religion, the perfect polity, the most developed and perfect way of doing anything!' (203; translation by M. A. Screech). Sometimes cautiously, sometimes firmly, he points out that our own customs are as 'savage' as those of the natives of the newly 'discovered' country we now call Brazil. Like Rabelais, too, Montaigne deflates imperialist pretentions, now by way of a far-reaching allegory that brings together political, private and physical experience. In only the second paragraph of 'Des cannibales', he revives the myth of Atlantis. According to this, in ancient times the major land masses of the world were disposed quite differently, and somewhere beyond Greece lay a large island called Atlantis. The Kings of Atlantis had enlarged their territory to take in Northern Africa and Europe as far as Tuscany; they subjugated all Mediterranean countries and carried on into Asia. But some time later these kings and their island were swallowed up by a flood. 'It is most likely,' says Montaigne, 'that that vast inundation should have produced strange changes to the inhabitable areas of the world; it is maintained that it was then that the sea cut off Sicily from Italy', and that 'elsewhere lands once separated were joined together by the filling-in of the trenches between them with mud and sand' (201). It is unlikely that Montaigne believed in a real Atlantis: by the beginning of the Renaissance few did. But through it he creates a fable, part fantastical but part founded in observable geography, that depicts the sea bringing mighty, hitherto unimaginable, alterations. The sea can symbolize uncertainty of all kinds, physical and mental (the 'liquid' can make 'solid' certainties dissolve or at least re-form); it is also an image of mortality, life being a 'river' that finally disperses into the ocean. And the sea can utterly destroy temporal power. Typically, Montaigne constructs these pictures laterally and tactfully. The allegory is not trumpeted as such; and Montaigne says not 'It must have been the case that . . .' but 'It is most likely [bien vraysemblable] that . . .'. But for all his understatement, he has exploited the myth of Atlantis to invalidate, almost immediately the essay opens, regal and colonialist ambition.

At the end of this same essay (212–13), Montaigne relates that 'someone' (apparently Montaigne himself) asked three of these 'cannibals', on a visit to France, what they thought of their experiences there – these included a visit to Rouen and a conversation with the late King Charles IX, then aged only twelve. They replied that first, they found it most 'strange' that so many full-grown men 'should consent to obey a boy rather than choosing one of themselves as a Commander'. Second, 'they had noticed that there were among us men fully bloated with all sorts of comforts' ('gorgez de toutes sortes de commoditez'), while at the doors of these well-endowed ones their fellow-men were begging, racked with hunger and poverty; and they found it 'strange' that those destitute ones 'should put up with such injustice and did not take the others by the throat or set fire to their houses'. (The French words for 'strange' and 'foreign' are close: 'étrange / étranger'; which behaviour is the more 'foreign' in this situation?) The leader of the trio of 'cannibals', a commander, is questioned as to whether his authority at home lapses when war is over; 'he replied that he retained the privilege of having paths cut for him through the thickets in their forests, so that he could easily walk through them when he visited villages under his sway.' Montaigne concludes with the now-famous comment: 'Not at all bad, that. – Ah! But they wear no breeches . . .' ('Tout cela ne va pas trop mal: mais quoy, ils ne portent point de haut de chausses!') Perhaps we should not be too eager to impose our own post-Revolutionary perspective on this episode, and Montaigne is still expressing himself moderately, casually, drolly – and with safeguards (saying he had a bad interpreter: this is presumably a precaution should the interpreted views be challenged). But there is no mistaking the sense of incongruity highlighted by the 'savage's' remarks about the poor, nor the strength of 'racked with hunger and poverty' ('décharnez'), nor the violence of the picture of the poor rising up from their passivity. Indeed, arguably the low-key presentation makes the throttling of the rich, the arson, emerge all the more fiercely. Just before that scenario, Montaigne had claimed he was told three things by these foreign visitors but has forgotten one – 'I am very annoyed with myself'; just after, we have the amusing exclamation about breeches – that is, about our prizing of local modes of dress. One could almost mistake the whole passage for a reflec-tion on the parochial, on flummery be it regal or bourgeois. But one also has to understand the more serious meaning: 'we overvalue *all* our own customs, however absurd they may seem to outsiders'. A century-and-a-half before it will become commonplace, Montaigne casts doubt on his own nation's values through the figure of the foreign visitor who wonders 'But how can this be?' Montaigne is a political writer, manipulating style and structure to raise disturbing questions about social organization.

Many other less celebrated sixteenth-century authors also use their rhe-torical skills to connect literature with the politics of the period. For example, the Protestant satirist and polemicist Agrippa d'Aubigné (1552–1630) could almost be deemed the 'war poet' of the century; following on from the *chansons de geste*, his *Les Tragiques* (written 1577–9) is a verse account of the Wars of Religion and a justification of the Protestant cause. But the somewhat earlier Marguerite de Navarre (1492–1549) is a particu-larly apt figure with whom to end this account of French literature up to the early seventeenth century. The sister of the monarch who definitively set France on its course as the cultural standard-bearer of Europe, François I, she was herself a patron of the arts and a prolific writer. Passionately interested in Protestant ideas at the time when France nearly became a Protestant country, she protected leading Reformers. The Reformation's desire to make the Bible accessible to individuals, unmediated by the priest-hood and open to discussion, is reflected in Navarre's own choice of liter-ary genres, in particular of the vernacular prose narrative, governed by an ideal of 'the plain and available text'. Navarre's writing also demon-strates the fluid relationship between French and foreign, 'high' and 'low' cultures in the sixteenth century. First, like many contemporaries, she took inspiration from Italy: the tales in her best-known work the *Heptaméron* (first published in 1558) were based on those of the *Decameron* by the fourteenth-century Boccaccio. Thus she exemplified what was now the acceptable way of 'appropriating' another European country's 'riches'; but she gives them a 'French' stamp, for – unlike in Boccaccio – each story, once told, is discussed at length by the group of listeners, who raise a range of questions in debates that reach no firm conclusion. Second, although the tales are related by high-born ladies and gentlemen, they are often ribald, staging situations that could as easily be found in medieval farces or *fabliaux*. There were other female writers in sixteenth-century France: Louise Labé's sonnets are passionate poems in which women as idealistically sexual beings find a voice. But Navarre is the politically more significant figure, in part because she was more powerful: she shows that in sixteenth-century France as well as in England, a queen could be a protector of and conduit for the arts and could herself write; and she could furthermore promote a new standing for 'lowly' themes and popular literary modes.

2

From Sun King to Enlightenment (1630–1789)

Monarchs, for the time being at least, would remain passionately involved in the artistic production of the nation; nobles continued as patrons, and as authors themselves. But the social origins of writers were changing. Many, from the sixteenth century on, were neither penniless wanderers nor landed seigneurs; they increasingly came from the gentry or bourgeoisie – not always a wealthy bourgeoisie, and, as Lough demonstrates, it could be painfully difficult for writers to make anything approaching a living by their pens (31–67). They were often entirely dependent on patronage, as the (to us) embarrassingly fulsome dedications to patrons in sixteenth- and seventeenth-century works show. Only the lucky ones gained court sinecures; others relied on ecclesiastical benefices to escape penury. Even Ronsard, renowned in his time, had had to make numerous efforts before finally receiving a secure income from the grant of 'custody' of a religious house.

Some of the most famous writers of the seventeenth century were of middle-class origin, such as the dramatists Corneille and Racine. (Corneille, for example, was born into a middle-class family in Rouen: his father was a magistrate, and he himself worked for many years as a lawyer and administrator in Rouen.) These writers, like their predecessors, were regarded merely as 'servants' by a haughty aristocracy, even if statesmen of the highest echelons recognized their utility. Seventeenth-century writers might, then, have an acute sense of social complexity. They needed to please but they saw abuses of power. They knew their own rank was despised, but, well versed in the literature of their nation and of others, they might have a profounder understanding of chivalric ideals, of 'courtoisie', than the aristocrats who condescended to them. This acuity first displays itself in the 1630s, which mark a pivotal change in French literature. It was during this decade that Corneille (1606–84) established himself as the leading playwright of the day. His four great tragedies were all performed during the six years immediately preceding the reign of Louis XIV, the 'Sun King' (ruled 1643–1715): *Le Cid* in 1637, *Horace* in 1640, *Cinna* in 1640/1 and *Polyeucte* in 1641/2. These plays are central to any cultural history of French literature, bringing together many earlier social-psychological concerns and heralding others that would have to wait until the nineteenth or even twentieth centuries to be so explicitly voiced again.

Corneille depicts in his main characters a consciousness divided against itself and with unprecedented clarity links that division to political or communal pressures. He does develop key themes of medieval literature: quarrels between nobles and king; the life of the saint; grief over the harsh situations battle forces on its participants. Thus *Le Cid* stages frictions between a noble elite and a monarch less decisive than could be expected; *Cinna* and *Polyeucte* show group opinion swayed by a powerful moral or religious example. But Corneille brings these into his own period: the rifts in his plays have been seen as reflecting tensions between new and earlier social codes, and between the monarchy of Louis XIII and the old aristocracy – tensions that would come to a head in serious civil disturbances between 1648 and 1653 (the 'Fronde': see below, p. 32). More generally, 'equipoised' contest characterizes the narrative of Corneille's plays. They explore conflicts without explicitly 'taking sides': the effect is almost balletic, with the characters assuming differing stances round an urgent central problem. Also innovative is Corneille's stylistic enactment of the struggle between personal and political. Although a grief-stricken Roland falls to the ground on seeing the dead Olivier, and although '100,000 French' weep and faint over the horrors of battle, it is not until Corneille that this struggle is expressed in the very structure of the verse. His characters' speeches often proceed by antithesis, with the dilemma laid out either in each half of a monologue, or in each line of a couplet, or still more strikingly in each half of a single line. The hero of *Le Cid* must avenge his father, who has been slapped by another man – but that man is his fiancée Chimène's own father: 'Contre mon propre honneur mon amour s'intéresse; / Il faut venger un père, et perdre une maîtresse' ('Against my own honour my love pits its interests; / I must avenge a father and lose a beloved', I.vi). But these antitheses are complex ones. Along with such apparently opposed choices, Corneille's plays often also suggest that family loyalty, patriotism, direct action to assert one's religion against an oppressive state, are not 'antagonistic' to sexual love but are another kind of love (of parent, of country, of God). In the relationship between personal and political, stark dilemmas do exist, but there can also be a sliding scale of attachments, a variety of balances to be struck. Thus, in *Horace*, which tells the tale of the clash between an expansionist Rome and the neighbouring city of Alba, three Roman brothers

– the Horaces – are chosen to fight three Alban brothers. But these families are linked by marriage and friendship. Horace, heroically hard-hearted, tells his Alban brother-in-law Curiace that as Rome has nominated him to fight, he no longer 'knows' Curiace; Curiace replies that he does still know Horace, and that is what is killing him. The rhyme presses the point home:

> *Horace* Albe vous a nommé, je ne vous connais plus.
> *Curiace* Je vous connais encore, et c'est ce qui me tue. (IIiii)

Equally powerful is the elegiac tone Corneille brings to the expression of an unresolvable dichotomy. The characters talk about this insolubility ('Notre choix impossible', 'Our impossible choice', *Horace*, IIIiv), and, as we have just seen, can speak with anguish: it is as if they are being torn apart. Even Horace's father, still stonier than his son, admits, when talking to Curiace, that he cannot find words, that his heart cannot form firm enough thoughts, that tears are in his eyes (IIvii). And some of the most poignant laments are those of women who, albeit pushed to the background of political action, nevertheless have a voice with which to utter agony. In *Le Cid*, Chimène, helpless before the twin demands of love for her fiancé and justice for her slain father, exclaims: 'Pleurez, pleurez, mes yeux, et fondez-vous en eau! / La moitié de ma vie a mis l'autre au tombeau' ('Weep, weep, my eyes, and melt into water! / One half of my life has sent the other to the grave': IIIiii). Women may even weaken the men's resolve. When Sabine, Horace's Alban wife, comes to him in grief before the fight, he tells her she is attacking his 'virtue'; she gives him ironic permission to stop 'fearing' her, since reinforcements are arriving in the shape of his father; and Horace begs his father to keep the women away lest their cries and sobs 'disturb' the combat (IIvi–viii). Female characters make plaint in classical literature too, for example Andromache in the *Iliad*; these are sources for Corneille, but he allows women's distress potentially to infiltrate the action and gives their responses a sustained presence.

It has been said of Corneille that he is 'optimistic', and certainly some of his plays end with generous action, uplifting change, reconciliation; furthermore, he takes the medieval code of 'knightly service' and translates it into a still recognizable but more modern ethic that seeks to combine support for the community with personal self-definition. We might without undue anachronism compare this to the construction of identity still sought by many, especially in times of national or ideological crisis. In the twenty-first century no less than in the seventeenth, the sense of self may be irrevocably bound up with the desire to fight for one's nation or beliefs;

this sense of self may also rely on an image of how one appears to others, how one is perceived 'in public'. A similar view of the self can be found in recent thinkers like Sartre, for example. Whether this really means Corneille is 'optimistic' is another matter. What we may say is that despite the divisions his characters enact and themselves describe, Corneille stages stronger self-directedness than would writers later in his century; that is not because these latter had a truer view of human beings but because they were responding to different cultural exigencies. The essayist La Bruyère would famously comment that Corneille paints men as they ought to be whereas Racine paints them as they are (*Les Caractères*, 1688–94; in 'Works of the mind', no. 54). But this judgement of La Bruyère's is itself conditioned by his period, coming near the end of the seventeenth century and in the wake of many depictions of humankind as governed by passions, as wretched – merely a 'thinking reed', in Pascal's words (*Pensées*, 1670, no. 200). Corneille may have appeared old-fashioned to the two succeeding generations; in reality, with his theatrical pictures of contradictions dialectically worked through and (often) lifted to another plane, he is one of France's key political writers.

With *Le Cid*, Corneille found himself in trouble with the newly formed Académie Française. According to this body, he broke the rules that should govern tragedy. These were unity of action, time and place. (Unity of action means there should be no secondary plots; unity of time and place demand that the fictional time of a play should occupy no more than twenty-four hours and that its events should be confined to the same location.) Interest in these supposed rules had recently revived as part of the attempt to appropriate the prestige of the classics. It was claimed that they were Aristotle's. In fact, Aristotle had prescribed only coherence of action, presenting unity of time and place as mere conventions. However, the Italian Torquato Tasso, in his *Discourse on the Heroic Poem* of 1596, changed these latter two conventions to prescriptions, influencing the Académie Française. *Le Cid*, then, presented too much action to be plausible within the permitted twenty-four hours; it had introduced a digressive sub-plot (the Infanta also loves the Cid); and it had, furthermore, offended against the seemly (the 'bienséances'), for it is on stage that the hero's father is slapped. (Rather than being witnessed by the audience, the slap should have taken place off-stage, then to be reported: disunity of tone was also to be avoided.)

These strictures were matters of more than aesthetic concern. For it was now that France was launching an unparalleled attempt to direct culture from the centre. Although academies had been set up with royal patronage from the late sixteenth century on, the Académie Française would be by far the most significant. It had begun to meet in 1634 and was officially ratified in 1637, the year *Le Cid* was performed. The Académie Française was the first of several instituted by Richelieu, Mazarin and Colbert as part of the continuing French policy of harnessing the arts and sciences to the greater prestige of throne and nation. But now the intention was deliberate and far-reaching. At stake was governance of all kinds. The 'cornucopias' of the previous century could no longer be allowed to overflow; the baroque must be brought to heel. (Some commentators have argued that the idea of 'the Baroque' is unhelpful, even meaningless; nevertheless, it is a useful label to attach to those artistic productions which, from the sixteenth century on, create a sense of restlessness, of hyperbolic emotion, of a striving to exceed formal limits, of stylistic as well as structural surprise. But now such effusions and conceits would be slapped down as childish and affected.) It is not difficult to see a connection here with social and political 'decorum', a decorum calculated to please an increasingly absolutist administration. And French Classicism, once fully adopted, would operate stricter literary rules than can be found at any time in French history before or since.

Richelieu, Mazarin and Colbert, then, were the chief statesmen behind this change. Cardinal Richelieu (1585–1642) was the shrewdest and most ruthless French politician of his age; an outstanding consolidator of France's interests in Europe, he also had an active and interventionist interest in the arts, especially in theatre. On his death, he was succeeded as first minister of the Crown by Mazarin, a naturalized Italian who, like Richelieu, was an avid patron of opera and literature; he trained Colbert, who would become Louis XIV's main minister from 1661. Colbert too promoted the arts as a buttress of national status: he fostered libraries and gave pensions to writers of royal propaganda. Thus the Académie Française was from the beginning a political instrument. Its function was, and remains, to establish and maintain linguistic and literary standards for the nation as a whole. Louis XIV himself would fulfil the role of 'protector' of the Académie, exerting pressure from above. During his reign, it was expected to play its part in exalting the monarchy, and the king influenced the choice of new members; he would, for example, delay the election of an out-of-favour La Fontaine. Significantly, the Académie's membership mingled writers and the social elite: 'literature' and political status were thus intertwined despite prevailing snobberies. In spite of all this, and taking the long view, the Académie's success as an instrument of the state, or even as a culturally prestigious body, should not perhaps be overstated. Many of France's greatest and most influential writers have not been members; from the mid-eighteenth century on, the downward pressure of the monarch and his advisors would be alleviated as the Académie was infiltrated by the thinkers of the day; and from the beginning it attracted criticism, even mockery – as it still does. Or it is simply ignored. At the height of Classicism, when authors were willingly pruning their own writing of the excessive and unseemly, Molière would still open his play *Le Malade imaginaire* (*The Hypochondriac*, 1673) with the main character poring painstakingly over his apothecary's bills for different types of enema and purgative.

The Académie also attacked *Le Cid* for its actively desiring heroine, Chimène, who seemed likely to marry her fiancé despite everything: this was judged to be 'implausible', 'invraisemblable'. Here again we encounter a curiously mixed response to women. Was Chimène really 'unlikely' – was it just that the Académie wanted her to be so? While at all levels of society women were in thrall to patriarchal notions and practices, it was still possible for such works as *Equality of Men and Women* (1622) to be published – if with difficulty. (This text was by Marie le Jars Gournay, *c.*1566–1645, Montaigne's adopted daughter and the co-editor of his *Essais*.) Some lesser academies included female members. And in court circles women were not only building on Marguerite de Navarre's precedent, writing fiction and themselves patronizing the arts; they were also starting to exert an extraordinary cultural influence. They famously founded and hosted the salons in which newly composed works changed hands for discussion; some *salonnières* promoted feminist principles. They even set out what was or was not permissible in both linguistic and literary spheres – in effect, shaping 'taste', 'le goût'. This led to strained usages, albeit often witty ones. Famously, the likes of 'teeth' and 'feet' were prohibited: they had to be called 'the furnishing of the mouth' and 'dear suffering ones' ('l'ameublement de la bouche', 'les chers souffrants'). The derogatory term *précieuses* began to be applied to these women. It was at such affectations that Molière was poking fun in *Les Précieuses ridicules* (1659). As a comedian, he would have been dismayed by any move that threatened to close off too comprehensively his own range of humorous effects; and others clearly shared his views, for this play was the first of his great Paris theatrical successes. But even Molière conformed to some extent, most of his erotic jokes, for example, proceeding by innuendo rather than explicit naming. (They are thereby funnier, something not all translators of Molière grasp.) And many intelligent women were not 'précieuses'. Molière himself probably supported a certain level of education and freedom for women, judging from his butts of humour. In *L'Ecole des femmes* (1662), he creates the ludicrous hero Arnolphe, who imagines he can mould his would-be fiancée Agnès to his liking, keeping her – as he thinks – ignorant and chaste. At a comic climax half-way through the play, he trots out to her a standard list of the reasons why the wife must obey her husband just as the soldier must obey his chief, the servant his master, the child its father – any departure from submission leading inevitably to hell-fire (IIIii): this makes him still more laughable. It has been argued that Molière, with both his *précieuses* and Arnolphe, is targeting bourgeois ideas and pretentions, and that his own attitude to women derives from chivalric ideals: another respect in which 'gallantry' could be interwoven with proto-feminism (Paul Bénichou, *Morales du Grand Siècle*, 1948).

Thus it was that not only state backing, but also the contributions of such women as Madeleine de Scudéry (1608–1701) and the famous letter-writer Marie de Sévigné (1626–96), formed the elite literature of what many still deem France's 'Grand Siècle', Great Century. These concerns coincided with a keen civic interest, from the mid-century on, in smoothing over the antagonisms in French society: a 'smoothing' that sanctioned, and was intertwined with, the new stress on refinement. The 'Fronde' of 1648–53 was a civil insurrection during the minority of Louis XIV (who had succeeded to the throne in 1643 at the age of five). The *parlements* (local judicial and administrative bodies) were trying to limit the fiscal powers of the royal government, while a turbulent high nobility wanted to reassert its traditional independence. An outpouring of pamphlet literature known as *mazarinades* attacked Mazarin, the hated prime minister, and at one point the court was even forced to flee as a series of concessions followed by retractions heightened instability. However, through a mix of force and compromise, Louis XIV, by now aged fifteen, was able to regain control of Paris in 1653, and when Mazarin died in 1661 the king, while still dependent on such ministers as Colbert, took the decision to rule without a prime minister. This inaugurated Louis XIV's absolutism. No more was there to be any question of weak monarchs. Yet for all that, a show of civilization was cultivated. So Versailles was built not only as a crude attempt to surpass the château of Vaux-le-Vicomte by making one far bigger and glitzier (sometimes less is more), but also to house three thousand people, allowing Louis XIV to keep an eye on all the important nobles. If one of them asked him for a favour, but had not been dancing attendance, the monarch would dismiss the petition brusquely: 'C'est un homme que je ne vois jamais' ('I never see him'). Indeed, the Classical period under Louis XIV could be encapsulated as a realization of Bentham's and Foucault's mythical Panopticon, the prison in which you could always be seen but never knew if you were. Currents of muted protest can be found in La Fontaine – one reason he was not well liked by the king. His 'Elégie aux nymphes de Vaux' expresses sympathy with Fouquet, the superintendant of finances who had built the château in 1658–61, thereupon to be arrested by the jealous king. And La Fontaine's fables are sometimes bold: in, for example, 'Les deux mulets' he offers a cautious, indirect admonition to the king himself. French kings had long taxed salt to raise money, but Louis XIV increased the tax. Those who sold it on the black market were sent to the galleys or put to death. La Fontaine's salt-tax mule, proudly bearing his sacks of gold, is beaten and robbed by 'l'ennemi' (not mere robbers, but military adversaries), while the other mule, with his humble load, is spared.

Throughout his reign, Louis XIV devoted from six to ten hours a day to the business of government; and the decade after Mazarin's death (1661–71) saw French pre-eminence in Europe asserted by almost every means from the diplomatic to the expansionist, which latter entailed financially ruinous wars. (These, however, stopped short of wide-scale imperialist designs on Europe: see above, pp. 19–20.) Louis XIV would also tighten his grip on the souls of his subjects. From 1660 on, Protestant children were kidnapped and forcibly raised as Catholics in convents; in 1685 Louis XIV revoked an edict which some ninety years earlier had guaranteed Protestants freedom of worship (the Edict of Nantes, 1598). And in this same year he passed the infamous Code Noir, a decree which restricted the activities of free blacks in France's colonies, forbade the exercise there of any religion other than Roman Catholicism, ordered all Jews out of the colonies, and brutally defined the conditions of slavery in the French empire. Thus, for example: a slave who strikes his or her master, his wife, mistress or children, shall be executed (article 33); fugitive slaves absent for a month shall have their ears cut off and be branded, for another month their hamstrings shall be cut and they shall be branded again, and a third time they shall be executed (article 38).

Louis XIV was then a tyrant, and even if the French would periodically thenceforth laud the Sun King's reign as the acme of French civilization, they failed to write a great epic about him: he was intimidating not inspiring. But, if one may phrase it thus, he was a tyrant in a specially 'French' mode. Inseparable from his despotism was his hedonistic adherence to the arts. The expansion of Versailles is only one example; in his youth, Louis XIV was also an enthusiast for plays, music and dancing, appearing regularly himself in court ballets. These ballets too had their political function: while ballet in its early years (the late sixteenth century) reflected the aspirations of courtly society through representations of celestial harmony or the dawn of a new Golden Age, under Louis XIV it helped to create and sustain the myth of the Sun King. But one of the paradoxes of the period is that Louis XIV's fondness for art, as well as long-standing French traditions of anti-authoritarianism, did allow some chinks – more than chinks: veritable openings for free and wild ideas, expressed with consummate skill in this great literature.

The term 'great' applied to cultural artefacts is now held in some suspicion: it is argued that as well as inappropriately indicating an eternally fixed artistic merit, 'great' reinforces clichés of power and reflects a kind of social fetishism. But whatever name the twenty-first century finally opts to give the seventeenth, it is undeniable that under Louis XIV the two decades from 1658 to 1678 saw one of those extraordinary literary flowerings that it is difficult ever to account for fully – extraordinary in its concentrated production of some of the most famous works of European culture. In the twenty years after Molière's return to Paris from the provinces in 1658, the following appeared: Molière's own *L'Ecole des femmes*, 1662, *Le Tartuffe*, 1664/9, *Dom Juan*, 1665, *Le Misanthrope*, 1666, *Le Bourgeois gentilhomme*, 1671, *Le Malade imaginaire*, 1673; La Rochefoucauld's *Maximes*, 1665; Racine's *Andromaque*, 1667, *Britannicus*, 1669, *Bérénice*, 1671 and *Phèdre*, 1677; Pascal's *Pensées* (posthumously published in 1670); La Fontaine's *Fables*, 1668; and Mme de Lafayette's novel *La Princesse de Clèves*, 1678. And a variety of genres flourished, for one cultural benefit of Louis XIV's stifling centralization was the extension of the idea of literature to cover new dimensions of social relatedness: the sermon, the personal letter, the aphorism ('freeze-dried' conversation) and the caricatural moral portrait. All these were public modes: this body of texts, in appearance formal, was also highly social in its original production, embedded in the elite exchanges of the day and rooted in performance. The funeral oration, the verbal character-sketch, the epigrammatic shaft of wit, the fable, fiction, were circulated, 'tried out' or delivered in a court setting. Even the soliloquy in drama is rare: most speeches in seventeenth-century plays are social acts, delivered in the presence of at least a confidant.

This body of literature is characterized too by the attitude of him or her whom the French have come to call the 'moraliste'. This term has no exact equivalent in English. *Moraliste* signifies not 'moralizer' but one who comments – wryly or compassionately, and non-judgementally – on human customs and foibles. The *moraliste* is visible from the beginnings of French literature, but seventeenth-century writing is permeated with his or her approach. It came to the fore in an epoch when a reserved, non-committal sophistication was always desirable, often *de rigueur*. In the hands of the greatest writers this sophistication led to exquisitely worded pity, wonderment, curiosity, amusement, over the human condition: 'this is how we are'.

If one had to pick out the crucial factor in this mid-seventeenth-century flowering of elite literature, it might be the royal support enjoyed by Molière (1622–73). During these two decades, Louis XIV was in his twenties and thirties. He was to become devout when middle-aged – but not yet. His brother's and then his own protection of Molière induced the playwright to return to Paris after thirteen years in the provinces, and enabled his company to move to its own theatre, the Salle du Palais Royal, in 1660–1. Louis granted Molière a royal pension in 1663; the personal favour in which he was held was made public in 1664, when the king became godfather to his son (named Louis); and his company was given the title 'King's Troupe' in 1665. The importance of this protection cannot be overestimated. It is almost certain that Molière was a freethinker; at any rate he moved in freethinking circles. His plays were often daring: *L'Ecole des femmes* provoked such a stormy reaction that Molière wrote two immediately following short plays in its defence (*La Critique de L'Ecole des femmes* and *L'Impromptu de Versailles*). His next play, *Tartuffe*, was still more controversial. Staging a religious hypocrite, it outraged the ecclesiastical party at court, who contrived to ban it; it did not obtain a licence for public performance until 1669, when it became financially the most successful of all Molière's comedies. (It still ranks as the most frequently performed play in the three-hundred-year-old state theatre, the Comédie-Française.) And Molière's other plays too raise thorny issues, ridiculing affected and vain aristocrats, and in *Dom Juan* portraying an atheistic nobleman. There is no very coherent perspective on this latter character. He is sometimes absurd, always shameless, and he joins the arrogance of rank to personal extravagance: his servant (albeit clumsily) attacks his ribbons and luxurious clothes in the same breath as he criticizes his ruthless exploitation of women (Iii). Dom Juan is, naturally, swallowed up by hellfire at the end of the play. However, he also emerges as curiously admirable: his recklessness leads him to generous as well as selfish actions. And he is given the opportunity to lay out his freethinking views to his servant, who tries to re-establish a moral and religious norm – but in vain, for, as contemporaries saw, 'Molière confides the cause of God to a dolt' (Will Moore, *Molière: A New Criticism*, 1949, 95).

Was Molière writing satire? This question is central to any cultural history of French literature, since satire is one of the areas where 'high' and 'low' culture, aesthetic and political concerns, meet in a particularly blatant form. Satire can, in theory at least, be distinguished from comedy. It has been proposed that satire aims to arouse indignation and to change specific institutions, whereas the target of comedy is more general: the oddities of mankind. To that end, comedy may recruit ridiculous traditions or recognizable social 'types' of the time, but that does not mean it is attempting to foment trouble, let alone bring about change. On this definition, Molière is not a satirist but a comedian, even a droll *moraliste* – he who observes us humans, bizarre and full of incongruities as we are, without implying any 'programme' of reform. The difference is clear if, say, we compare the joyously elaborated fatuity of Molière's 'bourgeois gentleman' with the savagery of Swift's *A Modest Proposal* (1729).

Yet the distinction between satire and comedy at times becomes blurred. Was Molière really not 'satirizing' those contemporary doctors who refused to believe in the circulation of the blood when he staged the pompous quack Diafoirus and his idiotic son Thomas in *Le Malade imaginaire*? Perhaps not. There is something sublime in Molière's comedy that defies attempts to corral it into an argument about local issues; and when he says in a famous preface to *Tartuffe* that the duty of comedy is to correct men's faults, we can read this simply as self-defence in the face of the Church's onslaught. But these favoured plays *were* politically adventurous; they aired communal tensions in a way that enabled other respectable thinkers and writers of the time to do likewise, and they laid the ground for the elite-driven satire of the eighteenth century. And Molière achieved this boldness through his wit; for his plays are hugely amusing, funnier if less 'poetic' than Shakespeare's comedies. The French are sometimes proud of, sometimes rueful about, what they see as their own propensity for raillery, 'raillerie'. (Many nineteenth-century women writers, for example, would deplore 'raillerie' as inhibiting their own efforts.) Whatever place raillery has, 'wit' is a distinctive and central part of the culture – so much so that the word for mind, spirit and wit are one and the same in French: 'esprit'; so much so that Louis XIV valued this wit above important political and religious considerations, himself encouraged Molière to parade court bores in his plays, and sanctioned a wide-ranging mockery which, although it could never include royals, risked offending those whose support was integral to Louis's own rule. He was not so 'absolute' in this respect at least.

The culture was thus open enough to allow the *moraliste* La Rochefoucauld to undercut all the constructed faces we like to present to society, which in his disturbing *Maximes* he proposes is made up only of appearances: 'Ainsi on peut dire que le monde n'est composé que de mines' (from maxim 256). 'Le monde' is an umbrella term denoting not just 'society' but 'polite, elite, society'. So La Rochefoucauld's penetrating analysis refers to the court as well as to other groupings. In the *Maximes*, courage, magnanimity and other noble or knightly qualities are inseparable from our love of self; even that most social of feelings, friendship, is shot through with self-centredness: 'In the adversity suffered by our best friends, we always find something that does not displease us' (*Maximes supprimées*, number 18). In *La Princesse de Clèves*, Mme de Lafayette (under a thin historical disguise) talks of the court as self-regarding, inward-turning, a place of constant dissembling and treachery – not excluding royalty itself. La Fontaine gives metaphorical and corporeal shape to depictions of caste: differing bodily status leads naturally to violence as the larger or sharper-toothed animal destroys the weaker one; all still delicately witty in the narration, however. Bossuet, the court preacher, at first alienated from the king, can, from 1669 on, thunder from the pulpit against the vanity of court pomps in magnificent funeral orations (the most famous is that for Queen Henrietta Maria, 1669). Finally, Pascal (not unlike Montaigne) talks about the flummery of majesty, and asserts that power can be maintained only because regal or official get-up speaks to fancy rather than reason (*Pensées*, 44). More than a century before Romanticism, Pascal explores this troubling, powerful faculty that is imagination; he looks at our capacity for delusion – whether to celebrate the mind or deplore its helplessness – and he sometimes does so in a civic context. Pascal was a Jansenist, and Jansenism was one of the few genuinely oppositional ideologies of the seventeenth century. (An austere theological movement, it had attacked Richelieu's identification of religious interests with those of the state; it defended the claims of individual conscience; and it was suspected of republican sympathies by Louis XIV. Indeed, Jansensism did question absolute government and contributed to a growing sense that private conviction had a right to be heard.)

All these writers, then, were daring, and they were interacting with a society that, along with its encouragement of the non-committal, allowed and enjoyed a certain audacity. This interaction is exemplified above all in the immediacy of drama. With Molière, the other seventeenth-century dramatist who is still world-famous was Racine (1639–99), author of beautiful and gripping tragedies about abuses of power and the horrors of quasi-incestuous courts. Was Racine, too, emboldened by the success of Molière's contentious comedies, by their very 'permissibility'? It seems implausible. Racine had himself objected to *Tartuffe*. And it seems still more implausible if we look at Racine's career. Racine's second play, *Alexandre le grand* (1665), had projected a flattering picture of Louis XIV as the conqueror of the world; he was already in receipt of a royal pension; and his subsequent plays do imply an order imposed from above, however tenuously. In some of his tragedies, turmoil reigns only because the 'real' leader is absent; at the end of almost all, warring parties are in some way reconciled – or at the least, as in Shakespeare, the state will now regain some form of stability. (Thus *Andromaque* and *Phèdre* close with the Trojan captive Andromaque becoming queen of her former foes of Epirus, and with King Thésée adopting as a daughter Aricie, his enemy captive and the beloved of his slain son Hippolyte.) Furthermore, in 1677 Racine would become the historiographer royal in order to secure a handsome salary, and from this point on (after *Phèdre*) he would stop writing secular plays, would become pious, and would produce no more drama for twelve years; when he did, the plots of these late plays were drawn from the Bible, not the ancient classics (*Esther* and *Athalie*, 1689, 1691). Is it credible that even as a younger, more intrepid playwright he would consciously undermine images of regal power and of the omnipotent and beneficent deity with whom the monarch was perforce associated?

Yet the least that can be said is that Racine's protagonists, all of exalted rank, differ sharply from the shining vision of royalty that he would paint as an official historian; and the overwhelming impression left by his plays is one of sadistic or unrestrained rulers, of gods who are the cruel children of Shakespeare's simile: 'As flies to wanton boys, are we to the gods. / They kill us for their sport' (*King Lear*, IVi). Not only the pagan gods: although the Jehovah of *Athalie* is praised, and the outcome of the plot is the re-establishment of the line of David, this Biblical deity is hardly a reassuring presence either; furthermore, the child Joas, who triumphs at the end, is destined – as Racine's audience would have known – to become corrupt himself. Racine had been friends with Molière and the irreverent La Fontaine, and we should at least take note that the first of Racine's great plays, *Andromaque*, appeared in 1667, soon after Molière's most controversial trio *L'Ecole des femmes*, *Tartuffe* and *Dom Juan* (1662–5).

Racine is, in fact, the supreme poet of the fears of his time. Most mid-seventeenth-century literature, polished and restrained on the surface, constantly points to the personal and social darkness beneath. It has been proposed that the emergence from the internecine Fronde, as well as contributing to attempts at refinement, left in its wake a strong sense of the brutishness of humans. But, further, many of these writers express an anxiety that does more than mesh with local historical conditions: it probably underlies all communities. It is a specific fear of tyranny and a more general belief that civilization is a thin veneer that may break down at any moment. Again, what is remarkable is that this anxiety could be voiced under an absolute monarch; and Racine reflects it not only in his taut plots but also in his very style. Like Corneille's, Racine's language is a superb instrument for presenting, indeed creating, inner tensions. To say that he turns to his advantage the 'rules' governing language and drama of the period is too weak. The restraint that the court arbiters of taste and the Académie Française urged on French culture forged, in Racine, a stripped-down language in which key words snowball, accumulating complexity until, by the end of each tragedy, they have an almost unbearable force – such as the words 'jour' and 'fond' in *Phèdre*, 'day' and 'depth, bottom', which express Phèdre's yearning for cleansing and the hidden incestuous love she dares not disclose. The seventeenth-century drive against 'cornucopian' writing means that Racine's great tableaux are not the openly physical ones we found in Rabelais, nor shot through with the densely coloured images that will be rediscovered at the beginning of the nineteenth century; they are based on light and dark, but then these themselves take on a ferociously elemental power and symbolism. Similarly, the strictures of the *précieuses* meant that 'love' was often expressed through dead metaphors of captivity and fire (I am your prisoner, I try to hide my flame), but such words are re-animated by Racine when loved ones are actually captives, when flames did actually consume the Troy from which Andromaque has been dragged, and when Phèdre finds herself 'on fire', 'burning' with desire for her stepson Hippolyte. In Racine, the 'bienséances' that banned physical action from the stage, far from reducing the suspense, heighten it as characters enter to relate some dreadful turn of events: the audience's imagination can recreate even worse horrors than a gimcrack monster in front of them, and the focus falls on the other characters' appalled reaction to the narrative all are hearing. And even if characters could not fight on stage, they could and did refer to their own and others' 'body-language', drawing attention to the blushing that discloses the inadmissible, the absent-looking gaze that willy-nilly betokens a painful indifference to the interlocutor.

The hallowed verse form of French drama is the twelve-syllable line (the alexandrine) and the rhyming couplet – arithmetically neater than the stress-timed iambic pentameter of English blank verse; but both the syllable-timed line and the couplet become in Racine's plays the tools of a symmetry that can hover on the verge of asymmetry. For, as the rules demanded, the twelve syllables are always divided evenly into half, with a break after the sixth (the caesura), but within those half-lines the breaks vary so that some words are elongated, some brutally shortened; while the rhymes, however strictly patterned, can convey confused longing or loss of self. Phèdre has just told Hippolyte that, like his father Thésée, he would have slain the Minotaur in the labyrinth of Crete; she would have helped him. Her speech (the famous 'declaration speech') slips constantly between reality and fantasy, between the yearning to tell Hippolyte she loves him and the knowledge that she should not; and it ends:

> Et Phèdre au Labyrinthe avec vous descendue
> Se serait avec vous retrouvée, ou perdue. (IIv)
> (And Phèdre, down in the Labyrinth with you, would with you have found or lost herself.)

That culminating rhyme of 'descendue' and 'perdue' ('gone down' and 'lost') brings together an extraordinarily wide range of suggestions. The 'descendue' evokes: abasement; the depths of being (today we might say 'the unconscious'); female eroticism ('deep in a labyrinth'). The 'perdue' implies: loss of oneself in sexual ecstasy; ruination; a woman's destroyed reputation; death. And this last climactic word recapitulates everything that has been going on throughout the declaration – for Phèdre has been tenuously grasping at, 'finding', self-control and 'losing' it too.

Finally, the courtesy of Racine's characters, their use of the polite 'vous' form and such titles as 'Madame' and 'Seigneur', do not temper the violence of their feeling but enhance it: the polite terms may be spat out with sarcasm, or suddenly abandoned all the more dramatically. Just after Phèdre's speech, when the shocked Hippolyte pretends to believe that she has not really revealed her love for him, she bursts into the intimate 'tu' form, impermissible between a man and woman of high rank: 'Ah! cruel, tu m'as trop entendue. / Je t'en ai dit assez pour te tirer d'erreur': 'Cruel man, *you*'ve understood me too well; / I've told *you* enough to dispel *your* mistake' (italics indicate the French 'tu').

Racine is, then, the paradigm of the dramatic poet who at one level perfectly adheres to the laws of a newly policing culture while using those laws to depict, equally perfectly, misrule and anarchic passions. He may pay lip-service to the might of majesty (after all, it is the pagan gods who lead his characters astray, with the implication that seventeenth-century France is superior because governed by the Catholic religion, according to which the king rules by divine right). But what he actually shows is troubling. To stage socially powerful characters combines the political and personal in an especially provocative way, and this is not only because the nobler the characters, the greater their fall; it is because the whole body politic is implicated in the fall. Phèdre exclaims about half-way through the play: 'Moi régner! Moi ranger un Etat sous ma loi, / Quand ma faible raison ne règne plus sur moi!': 'I, reign! I, regulate a State under my laws, / When my feeble reason no longer reigns over myself!' (IIIi). Let us contrast this collapse with Corneille's Emperor Augustus, who in the *Cinna* of a generation earlier – 1640/1 – had declared: 'I am master of myself as of the universe; / I am, I want to be' as he resolves to forgive those who have conspired against his life (Viii). It would be anachronistic to describe Racine as 'subversive', but it is also impossible to explain the power of his tragedies without some recourse to a view of society as a tenuous human construction and of authority as threatening to break down moment by moment.

The claustrophobic, crisis-laden atmosphere created in Racine's plays also depends on his adherence to the 'three unities'. The concentration these effect chimes curiously with the increasing centralization of the French state, and some writers of the time even exploit this: not only Racine, with his prison-like settings, but also Mme de Lafayette in her *La Princesse de Clèves*. This, rather than eighteenth-century English fiction, can lay claim to being the first true European 'psychological novel': it has perhaps been suppressed from the British view of things because it is by a woman – a French woman at that. Like the vast majority of novels, *La Princesse de Clèves* takes place over more than twenty-four hours, and does not strictly observe the unity of action, with its sub-plots and brief secondary tales. (These do in fact reinforce the thrust of the main narrative: as court stories, they are exempla illustrating either uneasy compromises that prove unviable for the heroine or unresolvably mixed feelings like her own.) However, 'unity of place' is crucial: almost all the action unfolds in the royal court and, as in Racine, this means virtually nothing can be private: gossip, whispering, even spying infiltrate the characters' waking hours. Balls and spectacles are a *sine qua non*: the newly married Princesse, however reluctantly, *must* attend these events, where her reactions to her would-be lover will be seen by all (the Panopticon). In the end, she can escape only by taking refuge in the 'country' (in this case the Pyrenees), a living death which, although it supposedly occupies some years and is studded with 'saintly occupations', in narrative terms leads to her own dispatch within a few pages of her arrival there.

Thus, the content and form of the elite literature of the time see court and capital 'winning' vis-à-vis the provinces. Yet these are not entirely suppressed from view, even if they are a 'désert', a wilderness (as Molière's loner Alceste says when proposing to flee high society in *Le Misanthrope*).

La Bruyère, the last of the great seventeenth-century writers, sums it up succinctly: 'The court does not make one happy; it stops one being happy elsewhere' ('La cour ne rend pas content; elle empêche qu'on ne le soit ailleurs': *Les Caractères*, 'On the court', no. 8).

With La Bruyère (1645–96), who published his *Characters* between 1688 and 1694, we are on the cusp of the eighteenth century in more ways than simply the chronological. His mix of maxims and character-portraits cannot be clearly defined as those of either a *moraliste* or a *moralisateur*. (This latter figure is one who offers censure and advice rather than just observant commentary.) La Bruyère is sometimes one, sometimes the other. As a *moraliste*, he makes such comments as 'A man who has lived in the centre of intrigue for a certain length of time can no longer do without it: any other life is boring for him' ('On the court', no. 91), which is a perception rather than a judgement; it is usually as a *moraliste* too that he describes works of literature and the formation of taste; and he writes a prose elegy on the passing of time that sets ephemeral fashion against 'the immense spaces of eternity' ('On fashion', no. 31) – again the commentator (and poet) rather than the judge. But he ends this latter piece with a thumping moral: 'Only virtue, so unfashionable now, goes beyond time'. And it is not with dispassion but with an intense physicality that he evokes the habits of a sycophantic, trivial upper-class culture he would seem to have hated, from the frenzied rushing upstairs and down of favour-seeking courtiers to a bird-fancier's adoration of the droppings of his caged darlings. These pieces, driven by a novelist's imaginative energy, are also suffused with a caricaturist's venom and with the disgust of the 'moralizer'. Here he is on those courtiers: 'Press them, wring them [Pressez-les, tordez-les], they drip pride, arrogance, presumption . . . their eyes are wild, their minds crazy: their relatives should take care of them and lock them away lest their folly become madness and society suffer' ('On the court', no. 61). This, indeed, goes beyond moralizing: it is satire, arousing a wish to do away with what is described. And it is the satirist's eye that inspires his famous picture of 'beasts' grubbing in the soil, with its shocking twist:

> You can see certain wild animals, male and female, spread out through the countryside, black, livid and completely burned by the sun, attached to the land which they burrow into and turn over with invincible stubbornness; they have as it were an articulate voice, and when they get up on their feet, they show a human face, and in fact they are humans. [. . .] they spare other humans the trouble of sowing, labouring and gathering in order to live, and so they deserve not to lack that bread they have sown. ('On man', no. 128)

Paul Hazard has traced in detail the development of thought that took France into the Enlightenment (in *The Crisis of the European Mind 1680–1715*, 1935); if we are concentrating on 'literature' only, the conservative monarchist La Bruyère is a significant stepping-stone from the seventeenth to the eighteenth century. The more outspoken Fénelon (1651–1715), writing at about the same time, was banished from the court for publishing what looked like a critique of the regime; La Bruyère, however, marked a decisive change to overt criticism without incurring royal displeasure.

This is not to exaggerate the comprehensiveness of that change. In many respects seventeenth-century French culture moved almost seamlessly into the eighteenth century. The closing years of Louis XIV's reign in the early eighteenth century saw a lessening of showiness under the guidance of the devout Mme de Maintenon, his morganatic second wife. But for his successors Louis XV and XVI (reigns 1715–74, 1774–92) the conviction remained that support for the arts was a good advertisement for France. Patronage was still a necessity for most career writers; here the wealthy Mme de Pompadour (1721–64), albeit a royal mistress (of Louis XV) rather than a royal herself, followed female predecessors in her support for artists and authors, including many thinkers. The French court still led the rest of the country, and Europe, in such areas as dress and cookery; as we have seen, however, elite literature was already in the seventeenth century sketching out some opposition to faddishness and waste, and eighteenth-century French writers would continue to be appreciative yet uneasy in front of eye-catching symbols of economic superfluity. (Cuisine and couture themselves would eventually surface as metaphors for art in such writers as Baudelaire and Proust.) The taste for symmetry remained, in for example the patterned gardens that drew attention to their man-made artificiality. Dare we here make a connection not only with aesthetic self-proclamation but also with the brilliant mathematical tradition of seventeenth- and eighteenth-century France, which after Descartes, Pascal and Fermat went on to produce, in the eighteenth century, Maupertuis (1698–1759) and d'Alembert (1717–83), among many others? At any rate, the even-numbered alexandrine still reigned supreme in tragedies that all imitated Racine: these were more or less pale shadows of the master. In fact, the only memorable drama bequeathed to us by the eighteenth century is prose comedy, that of Marivaux and Beaumarchais – but what is important is the grip of the verse model on most writers of the time.

Another imaginative interest that bypassed the 'crisis of the European mind' and that would endure through to the mid-nineteenth century was the fairy-tale. This acquired fresh importance not only to the 'simple' and to children, but also to fashionable audiences. The bourgeois lawyer Charles Perrault (1628–1703) had collected and reshaped the Mother Goose tales at the end of the seventeenth century (*Histoires ou contes du temps passé*, or *Contes de ma mère l'Oye*, 1691–97). Beautifully written, they created a vogue for fairy-tales both in France and abroad. They were soon followed by Galland's translation of *The Thousand and One Nights* (1704–16), and eventually by the monumental *Cabinet des fées* (a forty-one-volume collection that included Oriental stories: 1785–6); by fantastical tales in the early nineteenth century (now deriving from Germany also); and finally by such works as George Sand's *La Mare au diable* (*Devil's Pond*, 1846). The Bibliothèque Bleue, blue-covered books peddled throughout France from the seventeenth century on, also contained old tales, including in due course Perrault's own. Thus a folk tradition, irrationalist and superstitious, complements Enlightenment rationalism.

So continuity and even conservatism ran through the eighteenth century. Yet something momentous was happening too. Sometimes the developments came quietly: the further opening up of the physical world by scientists, and of the geographical world by explorers, meant that scientific treatises and travel writing gradually brought new perspectives for those who could read and had access to texts. But sometimes (in retrospect at least) the changes in ideology are startling. Thus, La Rochefoucauld's devastating description of human motivation as driven by self-love had been structured not as an 'analysis' but as an approach, a series of fragmentary insights; lateral, not frontal, it was shot through with such qualifications as 'often', 'possibly', 'sometimes', 'if'. It did not look revolutionary. Yet it allowed his eighteenth-century successors to promote the concept of enlightened self-interest – that which could benefit others along with oneself – and this had far-reaching effects on political philosophy and economics.

And there were much more sensational developments. Although pan-European, and East–West, transmission of literature and ideas had gone on for centuries, the eighteenth century decisively switched writing from the national to the international stage, with a feverish circulation of new essays and literary works across Europe, some in manuscript form. The drive to examine every belief that had hitherto been taken for granted was becoming urgent, unstoppable. Here was one of the few periods when British thinking shaped French rather than vice-versa: it did so dramatically. Many French thinkers already admired the British model of constitutional monarchy and such long-standing institutions as trial by jury; and in the seventeenth century the political philosopher John Locke (1632–1704) had advocated the separation of powers in a state's governance and had proposed that revolution was a right, even an obligation, in some circumstances. Locke's arguments nourished the eighteenth-century 'Scottish Enlightenment', which included such thinkers as the atheist philosopher David Hume (1711–76) and the economist Adam Smith (1723–90). Locke and the Scottish Enlightenment had a powerful impact on Voltaire and other French writers, and their ideas would in due course contribute to the new American Constitution. Yet even here it is sometimes difficult to separate out the mutual exchanges. Hume himself admired, as well as Locke, the late seventeenth-century French Protestant Pierre Bayle (1647–1706), who had argued for tolerance and whose *Dictionnaire historique et critique* (1697–1702) had embedded social critique in its copious notes. And it is unclear whether the American founding fathers derived such doctrines as the separation of powers from Locke, from the eighteenth-century Montesquieu, or from both. What is obvious is that a strongly humanist and rationalist outlook came to be shared by the Scottish and French Enlightenments and that the thirst for interchange was unquenchable. Indeed, it could manifest itself in unlikely areas. It was not so improbable that Voltaire should spend more than two years in London (1726–8). More surprising were Voltaire's enthusiastic adoption by the Francophile Frederick II of Prussia (1750–3 – it ended disastrously); Diderot's stay (1773–4) with the autocratic Catherine the Great of Russia, who became his patron; and the invitation to Rousseau in 1772 to present recommendations for a new constitution for the Polish-Lithuanian Commonwealth. (Rousseau was read by drafters of other national constitutions also.) I shall shortly look in more detail at the four great *philosophes* Montesquieu (1689–1755), Voltaire (1694–1778), Rousseau (1712–78) and Diderot (1713–84). (*Philosophe*, like *moraliste*, has no exact equivalent in English. *Philosophe* does not mean 'philosopher', but rather a thinker who, as well as inquiring into the natural world and the functioning of the mind, is also prepared to make political statements, to take an active role in shaping public opinion, and to disseminate knowledge. Furthermore, as we shall see, the *philosophe* extends the peculiarly close relationship that imaginative French literature has always had with historical, social and political thought.)

The eighteenth century launched, too, the again international cult of 'sensibility', apparently far from both seventeenth-century restraint and the *philosophes*' demands for evidence-based thinking. But 'sensibility' had its origins in a rejection of authority, especially Christian authority. Institutionally enforced morality was being called into question, and an inward criterion had to replace it. The cult had begun in the closing years of the seventeenth century and reached its peak in the three decades after about 1760, boosted on the way by *Clarissa* (1748), a novel by the English Samuel Richardson which was highly popular in France. 'Sensibility' consists of extreme sensitivity, expressed often in tears, and on the page in exclamation marks and ellipses. This sensitivity would feed into the early nineteenth-century picture of the Romantic, since anyone who was truly 'sensible', sensitive, was made of finer stuff than the common herd. But more immediately, since sensibility also gives rise to, or is caused by, kindness and compassion, it could become a secular equivalent to Christian charity. Among eighteenth-century French works that display, indeed parade, sensibility are Prévost's novel *Manon Lescaut* (1731); most non-classical dramas; Rousseau's *La Nouvelle Héloïse* (1761), which took Europe by storm; and *Paul et Virginie* (1788), Bernardin de Saint-Pierre's sentimental tale of a young couple brought up from childhood in the lush island of Mauritius (they never marry: Virginie is shipwrecked, refuses to take off her clothes in order to be carried to shore, and drowns). 'Sensibility' was on show in German works too, and English ones other than *Clarissa*, but it was in *La Nouvelle Héloïse* that the European cult achieved its peak of expression – and in French painting, for example in Greuze (1725–1805), with his sugary tableaux of girls weeping over dead birds, fathers reading from the Bible to their families. As with some medieval works, this is one of the cultural phenomena of the past that we now find it difficult to espouse imaginatively: Greuze, for example, may simply embarrass us. Even at the time, Voltaire and others mocked it, coining the derogatory term *sensiblerie*, and early in the following century Jane Austen would oppose 'sense' to it in her *Sense and Sensibility* (1811). But 'sensibility' was also a spur for a growing secular benevolence – leading to homes for foundlings and orphans, hospitals for the poor – and for sympathy with the underprivileged, including slaves. Thus not only was 'sensibility' clumsily groping towards a non-Christian morality; it was also part of a wider movement that was attempting to awaken greater social awareness and to reform contemporary abuses.

Another cultural phenomenon that had antecedents yet acquired a remarkable life in the eighteenth century was the literary figure of the *ingénu*. Naive or ignorant characters, staring open-mouthed at their 'new' surroundings and voicing 'innocent' criticisms of these, were, as we know, not an eighteenth-century invention: Rabelais's Gargantua, Montaigne's Brazilian travellers, the Princesse de Clèves, are all proto-*ingénus*. But it is in the eighteenth century that the *ingénu* comes into his or her own, partly by way of the newly popular picaresque novel, taken from Spanish models.

The picaresque protagonist travels from one region, social setting and episode to another, and in the eighteenth century may as often be a parvenu as an *ingénu*, as in the fiction of Marivaux (1688–1763). One of Marivaux's most famous novels is *The Parvenu Peasant* – the title of this latter speaking for itself. Thus the picaro / *ingénu* becomes a means to draw attention to social barriers and the possibility of breaching them. He continues largely male; however, we do now find some female equivalents created by male writers – Marivaux himself writes a *Life of Marianne* and Diderot's novice Suzanne learns about convent scandals in *The Nun* (written 1760, published 1780). And an outstanding novel by a woman, Françoise de Graffigny, places a female *and* foreign *ingénue* at the centre of her *Letters from a Peruvian Woman* (1747). This international dimension marks Montesquieu's *Persian Letters* (1721) and the still braver *Candide* and *L'Ingénu* by Voltaire (1759, 1776). In these narratives the *ingénu* becomes the instrument of wide-ranging, sometimes searing satire. He witnesses, or suffers, abuses perpetrated by both Church and State, for example burnings at the stake and the infamous *lettres de cachet* (individuals could be imprisoned or exiled without hope of appeal simply on the sending of a letter from the king or one of his ministers). Voltaire is often thought of as dry and biting, but here is a moment in *Candide* when satire and sensibility come together. The *ingénu* Candide is just arriving in Suriname, a Dutch-owned Latin American territory. He meets a black who is missing his left leg, cut off because he tried to escape, and his right hand, because a finger was caught in the grinding-machine as he worked in the sugar plantation. 'This,' says the black, 'is the price of the sugar you eat in Europe.' He tells Candide that his own mother sold him into slavery; that dogs, monkeys and parrots are happier than slaves; but that the Dutch 'juju priests' (in French, 'fétiches') who converted him to Christianity tell him every Sunday that we are all – black and white alike – children of Adam. 'I'm no genealogist,' says the black, 'but if these preachers speak true, we're all cousins. Now, you must admit you couldn't treat your relatives more horribly.' Candide exclaims that he must now, at last, abandon the optimism preached by his tutor Pangloss; and when asked what 'optimism' is, he replies: 'Alas! It's a mania for claiming everything is fine when you're doing badly.' The paragraph ends: 'and, looking at his black, he shed tears; and, weeping, he entered Suriname' (183).

The *ingénu* now not only satirizes 'strange' customs and barbaric institutions but also thoroughly relativizes the very concepts of custom, law, religious belief. If these differ from society to society, perhaps they are not God-given but man-made. And this relativism is vigorously and lucidly propounded in more discursive works. Montesquieu, after his pioneering *Persian Letters*, wrote *The Spirit of Laws* (1748), which examines the variety of political and legal structures in past and present societies. He has been called the father of social science. Only four years later, this work was placed on the Index (the Catholic Church's list of banned reading-matter). Voltaire's historical work *Essai sur les mœurs et l'esprit des nations* (*Essay on the Customs and Spirit of Nations*, 1756) is an attempt at a systematic and secular sociology, alive to the interplay between commerce, economics, politics and culture. Rousseau, in his *The Social Contract* (1762), proposes that social distinctions are not the result of an inevitable inequality; they developed because some were greedy and strong. He puts forward instead a doctrine of mutual co-operation and popular sovereignty. The work was immediately condemned by the authorities, but its arguments, and those of the other *philosophes*, were disseminated in numerous forms: pamphlets, songs, hawked-around popular prints (the *littérature de colportage*, pedlars' literature including the Bibliothèque Bleue, which ensured distribution to far-flung and underprivileged communities). Other banned discursive works were printed abroad, particularly in Holland (or in places claiming to be 'Holland'), and found their way back to France.

As we have seen, all four major *philosophes* wrote fiction, still a some-what low-status form: the intention was precisely to reach a wide audience, and while Voltaire did write elevated verse tragedies, Diderot argued that drama too must target a different public – that it must become 'drame bourgeois'. Although this was not entirely successful in the outcome, and although Diderot is talking about a middle-class theatre rather than one 'for the masses', nevertheless it signals the will to inaugurate an important ideological and aesthetic break. The *Encyclopédie* (1751–72) also embodies a popularizing mission: one of its declared aims was to 'change the general way of thinking', and almost by definition its compilers were rejecting any absolute division between 'high' and 'low' publications, between 'culture' and 'knowledge'. And this latter could be practical and artisanal knowledge too: *Encyclopédie* contributors included skilled craftsmen as well as doctors, noblemen, civil servants and businessmen. Diderot co-ordinated the whole operation, and Rousseau, Voltaire and Montesquieu were among the authors of articles – the latter two writing, inter alia, on literary topics. Thus the imparting of professional and cultural information went hand-in-hand with the construction of a social and political ethic: not directly – censorship was still strong, the Church still had the power to mete out dreadful punishments; but indirectly. Side-by-side with innocuous 'factual' entries on trades and manual arts, others poked fun at monastic orders and credulity of various kinds, and either implicitly or explicitly promoted secular concerns over theology. The *Encyclopédie* was a huge success, making a fortune for its publishers; rapidly pirated, it was soon reprinted in cheap editions.

The most shocking of its articles launched attacks on religious belief itself. Not all the *philosophes* were atheists: it is not absolutely clear that Voltaire was (he may have been a deist: such famous statements as 'If God did not exist, it would be necessary to invent him' need not imply disbelief in a deity), and Rousseau allows some room for 'natural' religion (as in, for example, the section of his educational treatise *Emile* (1762) entitled 'Profession of faith of the Savoy vicar'). But Diderot and many others were atheists; and, crucially for our purposes, in one of Diderot's fictional works, *Jacques the Fatalist*, disbelief in an omnipotent, omniscient godhead governs the form of the plot. This novel, or anti-novel, was begun in 1771 and published posthumously in 1796 in France (earlier abroad). It owes something to *Don Quixote* and Sterne's *Tristram Shandy* (published in instalments from 1759 on): Jacques is a servant travelling and talking with his master, and there are constant 'interruptions' from their own and others' stories. But – most important – the problems of free will and fatalism are here explored both openly and by way of the wandering narrative structure. The novel connects its own lack of goal-directedness with the proposition that there *is* no guiding principle for either fiction or humanity. ' "But for God's sake," you, reader, ask me, "where were they going? . . ." "But for God's sake, reader," I'll reply, "does anyone know where they're going? You, for example – where are you going?" ' (52). If the structure is not entirely new, its linking with the 'disappearance' of God is, and in this the work has been seen as an ancestor of much modernist writing. Still more innovative is Diderot's dialogue *Rameau's Nephew*, begun in about 1760 and never published in Diderot's lifetime. It encapsulates the sheer imaginative and conceptual power of this Enlightenment writer, perhaps the most heroic of them all. *Rameau's Nephew* is a conversation between the author/ narrator, 'Me' ('Moi'), and the anarchic virtuoso performer and mimic of the title, 'Him' ('Lui'). The disruption represented by Him, and the mix of mockery, horror and fascination with which the more respectable Me regards this *alter ego*, inspired Goethe, Hegel and psychoanalytic thinkers, who see the work as embodying 'the unruly' in both social and psychological spheres.

So, while it is too sweeping to see a clear break in all respects between the seventeenth and eighteenth centuries, and far too sweeping to say that all elite French literature of the latter century is politically radical, nevertheless barriers were being crossed that hitherto had seemed unbreachable. An important one remained, however. Amid all the changes, the position of women was more static than might be supposed possible. The salons frequented by the *philosophes* were remorselessly oriented towards the display of male brilliance (whereas the blue-stocking gatherings of eighteenth-century London were on the contrary set up to foster women's education and creativity). And the new promotion of merit versus rank, the efforts to shake off received social thinking, did not detain most *philosophes* long in so far as these might apply to the female condition. For example, the education Rousseau recommends for Emile's little companion Sophie is markedly different from that given to Emile himself. While he is to develop his individual potential to the full, she is to be trained for a traditional wifely role. The patron Mme de Pompadour influenced political as well as artistic developments, but this influence had to be unofficial; as such, it created a disquiet about female 'power behind the throne' that would, in the following century, constitute a real political disadvantage for women. Yet Montesquieu's early *Persian Letters* can be interpreted as feminist: the foreign travellers who cast such a quizzical eye on Europe have left behind them in Persia a harem whose discontented occupants finally rebel, not before raising disturbing questions about both the morality and the good sense of 'imprisoning' any pre-defined group of humans; the work ends with a picture of disorder. Women did in increasing numbers publish fiction, albeit often anonymously; these novels were popular, and some rivalled in complexity *La Princesse de Clèves*: not only *Letters from a Peruvian Woman*, but also works by the outstanding francophone Dutch writer Isabelle de Charrière (1740–1805). Laclos (1741–1803), author of the best epistolary novel ever written, *Les Liaisons dangereuses* (1782), believed in the education of women. His female villain, Mme de Merteuil, explains in a key letter (no. 81) why she has become cold and manipulative: she has witnessed the ways in which women are exploited, kept weak, by men, and is determined this shall not happen to her. She is, she tells her fellow-plotter Valmont, 'born to avenge my sex and master yours'. We may interpret the letter in various ways – nothing is simple in this disturbing masterpiece; but the social 'lesson' is not dissimilar to that of Montesquieu: oppress and enslave, and the consequences will not be to your liking.

If it is a 'lesson'; for Laclos, like most of his literary compatriots, suggests rather than states, and the feminism is hinted at through a multivocal structure and pastiches of many kinds, including parody of stereotypically gendered responses. Laclos juxtaposes simple-minded or stilted letters (like those of the naive Cécile or the pious Mme de Tourvel) with the skilfully manipulative ones of Valmont and Merteuil, who rely on the clichéd thinking of those around them for their victories. These two are able to effect psychological control through their literary style: they adapt their register between letters or within the same letter, and they fluently deploy religious diction, legal terminology, the besotted lover's gushing phrases, the military strategist's jargon. In *Les Liaisons* we yet again find ostentatious linguistic virtuosity, and an awareness of the medium itself that becomes almost the prime motor of the plot. This plot could be summed up as 'a pair of aristocratic predators imposing their sexual will on powerless victims' – but what makes it work is our own dismayed delight in the verbal dexterity, which enables these witty, shrewd, vile nobles to seduce us too.

Two paradigmatic figures bring this account of the century-and-a-half to a suitable end: the marquis de Sade (1740–1814) and Beaumarchais (1732–99). Sade, who has given Europe a word for the enjoyment of cruelty, symbolizes – too neatly no doubt – the dark side of tendencies emerging since the beginning of the seventeenth century. The growth of 'free-thinking' was associated, for many, with a casting-off of hypocritical sexual morality: hence the double meaning of 'libertin' – atheist and promiscuous pleasure-seeker. This association is to be found not only in Molière's Dom Juan but also in Diderot, who as part of his questioning of doxa asks why such simple and natural occurrences as ejaculation should attract such a heavy weight of moral judgement. Indeed, the naturalizing of the erotic and the pornographic was an off-shoot of scientific inquiry, or was interpreted as such. This was more 'liberating' for men than for women. Diderot, it is true, does draw attention to the double standards of morality applied to 'sinful' women in such works as *Supplement to Bougainville's Voyage* (begun in 1772, published posthumously); it is part of his emphasis on the relativism of ethical judgements. But in practice the liberation could go in a misogynistic direction: women were (still) objects of gratification, and the works of Sade are an extreme example of this. It is tempting also to make connections between Sade's works and the Terror that was about to send vast numbers to the guillotine in 1793 and 1794. His *120 Days of Sodom*, written in 1784–85, was not published until the twentieth century, but his other works, for example *Justine, The New Justine* and *Aline and Valcour*, grew out of it and were published between 1791 and 1797. Sade depicts a systematized, categorized, 'aestheticized' pleasure in torment; his eroticism depends on mechanisms rather than instinct.

Other nations have initiated and carried through periods of deliberate, widespread, 'mechanical' cruelty: Nazi Germany, Stalinist Russia, Pol Pot's Cambodia. If we are looking for precedents, the Terror must surely be one (just as it has been argued that the French might not so readily have executed Louis XVI in 1793 if the English had not already executed their king in 1649). What is sometimes forgotten, however, is that within the ranks of the Revolutionaries there would always be dissent: hence the disconcerting rapidity with which purges swung in different directions, and hence the (relatively) short duration of the Terror itself. Enlightenment thinkers did not foresee the Revolution, let alone the Terror; many of those guillotined or forced to emigrate would be the very aristocrats who had welcomed the *philosophes* into their salons and eagerly embraced their principles.

And, as Louis XIV had allowed *Tartuffe*, so too Louis XVI himself, albeit reluctantly and for different reasons, finally gave permission for Beaumarchais's *The Marriage of Figaro* to be performed in 1784. This was a work whose author, an insolent entrepreneur, again could not have foreseen the Revolution, but it was a public performance, a spectacle, which was interpreted as a blow against aristocratic abuses of privilege – and which endowed the world with another public performance, now a sublime one: Mozart's *Le Nozze di Figaro*, performed just two years later (also not without controversy). Beaumarchais's *Figaro* did not cause the Revolution, which was precipitated by the economic crises of the late 1780s and the acute food shortages of 1789. But this play – humorous, complicated, designed to stimulate and tease a cultivated, pleasure-seeking audience – was perhaps the best possible instrument to encapsulate and feed into the prevailing radicalism. Its maid and mistress collaborate across the social ranks against a seigneur too happy to exploit his status, and its manservant – much more truculent than Molière's pert and intelligent maids – voices real resistance. *The Marriage of Figaro* must at the least have encouraged the bourgeoisie and the minor aristocrats of the Estates General who finally forced confrontation with the king.

3

Between Revolutions (1789–1830)

From 1789, public events would grip national and personal consciousness as never before. France was on the verge of an economic collapse whose causes can be traced back to Louis XIV's exorbitant wars. In 1789 the Bastille fell and, after Louis XVI voiced doubts about the Declaration of Rights, there was a mass march on Versailles. In 1791 Louis, who had handled the worsening situation in an inflammatory and intimidatory manner, fled to Varennes but was brought back and imprisoned. The next year, the monarchy fell and the Republic was declared. The king was executed in 1793, representing in his person the French monarchy from its beginnings: he had been referred to throughout his trial as 'Louis Capet'. The Terror followed, ending in 1794 with the execution of Robespierre and other faction-leaders. In the interests of stability, two legislative Chambers, an upper and a lower, were now established, executive power being vested in five directors (the Directoire); this system, despite continuing upheavals and reversals, held good for four years (1795–9). Meanwhile the young Napoleon (1769–1821) was emerging as a supremely successful military commander. France abandoned its foreign policy of European 'consolidation' rather than overt conquest: it attacked Austria in 1792, and invaded Italy in 1796–7 and Egypt in 1798. In 1799 a coup d'état brought Napoleon to power. He would rule for the next fifteen years as Consul (1799–1804) then Emperor (1804–14), waging further ruthless campaigns that by 1809 had established an empire which, through annexation and the establishment of vassal states, covered most of Europe, excluding Russia. However, the British successfully organized a series of coalitions against Napoleon, and his Russian campaign of 1812 was a disaster. The allies entered Paris in 1814; Napoleon abdicated and was compelled to retire to the island of Elba, but returned in 1815 for a hundred days, to be defeated at Waterloo by the European allies. After Napoleon's 1814 abdication, the monarchy was restored: Louis XVIII ruled for ten years (1814–24) and Charles X for six (1824–30). In July 1830, another revolution erupted, fuelled by the king's reactionary politics and his disregard for representative government: this revolution was called 'Les Trois Glorieuses', that is, a 'glorious three days' of insurrection and fighting that forced Charles X's abdication and ushered in the so-called July Monarchy of Louis-Philippe, a member of the Orléans dynasty (family rivals to the Bourbon dynasty that had produced French monarchs from the late sixteenth century on).

Thus, by the end of 1830, within living memory two revolutions had taken place; a king had been executed, another made to abdicate and thereby extinguish a royal line that led directly back to the 'Sun King'; arbitrary and quasi-mechanized killing had been publicly practised on a scale hitherto scarcely imaginable (the 'perfection' and universal use of the guillotine in all capital cases was instituted in the early 1790s – it had originally been designed as a humane device that killed so quickly it would be painless). The country had been invaded by foreign powers and defeated on the battlefield; and France had been ruled by a extraordinarily charismatic leader who had risen from the ranks and whose role would continue to be argued about in numerous forums during the whole of the succeeding century. There was no single view of Napoleon, and he himself adopted apparently contradictory ideological stances. For all his ambition and authoritarianism, he had been influenced by Rousseau; he believed that government should be not only strong but also surrounded by popular approval; he supported the establishment of educational institutions such as the *lycées* and *grandes écoles*, that is, secondary and professional schools. These were for an elite but, within the constraints of a still unequal society, a mainly meritocratic one. Finally, for a variety of reasons (some expedient), he favoured legislation that allowed Jews to be assimilated rather than reviled and rejected, not only in France but in other European countries where he forced the removal of anti-Semitic restrictions and abusive customs. (The legal structure he set up in 1804, the Civil Code, granted freedom to all religions – largely retracted after 1815 by the allies.)

These four decades were to mould succeeding French literature up to our day. But as they actually unfurled, France's main mode of self-advertisement was not artistic achievement but military adventurism and the attempted establishment of an 'empire'. The years between 1789 and 1829 were not outstanding for elite culture. Only one short literary work of this entire period has been consistently rated 'canonical' on both sides of the Atlantic in the twentieth century: that is Constant's *Adolphe* (1816). It is perhaps a cliché that political stability is needed for works of genius to be created on any scale, yet the experience of France would seem to lend some support here. No doubt one reason for this apparent dearth is that certain works of the period have been for some time simply unfashionable, such as Chénier's verse (for example *Iambes*, 1794) and Hugo's *Odes*, published in 1822. Another reason is that young writers such as Stendhal (born 1783) and Balzac (born 1799) were still maturing: Stendhal would not publish his first major novel, *Red and Black*, until his mid-forties, in the same year as the 1830 revolution.

But one of the functions of a cultural history is to look at what was going on outside the 'canon'; and these decades are of exceptional interest in their melding of politics with diverse levels of discourse, for example publishing policy, public rhetoric, theatre and sung music. Revolutionary publishing regimes are a good starting-point. Under the Ancien Régime, censorship had often been fierce, as we have seen, resulting in imprisonment in the Bastille or even execution for publishers. However, it had not been particularly consistent or efficient, and this laxity would become as it were institutionalized in the mid-eighteenth century, when the post of director of the book trade (Directeur de la Librairie) was occupied by Malesherbes (between 1750 and 1763). Malesherbes, a member of a powerful legal dynasty, had realized that the system of censorship did not work: royal control was powerless to prevent an outpouring of pirated and illegally imported works; and, equally pragmatically, he also realized that the enforcement of censorship put the French book industry at a serious disadvantage vis-à-vis foreign competitors. Malesherbes encouraged new techniques of circumventing regulations, allowing tacit 'permissions' and 'tolerances' to flourish; these constituted a promise that the government would not prosecute, and in due course helped works like Beaumarchais's to see the light of day. The Revolution itself inaugurated one of the most liberal periods for publication hitherto known in France. In the first years, censorship was abolished outright, and between 1789 and 1799 over two thousand new newspapers appeared in Paris alone, even if many did not survive for more than a few issues. In the same decade the provinces produced over a thousand new journals. This brief opening-up was not to last: it would be trimmed by Revolutionary authorities and drastically modified by Napoleonic and post-Napoleonic regimes. An Act of 1819, for instance, prohibited books that contained any offence to public decency, religion and morality. But in the meantime, an air of freedom and enterprise that would not be forgotten blew through the print culture of France. It would feed into a continuing defiance of government among many writers and journalists both during and after the Napoleonic period: defiance that ranged from sly innuendo and tongue-in-cheek comments to overt throwing down of the gauntlet. This spirit of rebellion was not new; it had informed French

literature since the Middle Ages; but the freedoms introduced by Malesherbes and the Revolution gave much writing of the following century a newly
sardonic bite even when the surface sentiments were apparently respectful
of current orthodoxies.

Also innovatory in the Revolutionary period was political oratory. The
years 1789–94 were remarkable for the speeches of Mirabeau, Danton,
Robespierre, Saint-Just and others, which marked every important event
of the Revolution. We may nowadays find them portentous or artificial,
but what is significant is the clear inseparability in the speakers' minds of
political passion and 'good speech'. This commitment to rhetoric dated
back to medieval education and had been revived in the Renaissance; but
the National Assemblies, clubs and open meetings of the Revolution provided the forum for a massive 'performance' of public speaking that now
seemed capable of changing the fate of the nation. Eighteenth-century
England had been looked to with envy as a place where political eloquence could flourish; now, however, France was practising it on a far
wider scale. Napoleon himself was famously eloquent. (He was, besides,
a well-read man who in his youth had had literary ambitions, penning
short stories; he had studied classical authors, he enjoyed novels, and he
wrote historical memoirs.) In the rest of the century, rhetoric would lose
some but not all prestige; despite the suspicions it had always aroused
(not least in the aftermath of the Revolution), the syllabuses of elite nineteenth-century schools would still include the study of its two 'parts',
poetics and eloquence. With Revolutionary oratory, we have another
stage in that self-conscious manipulation of language characteristic of
French culture.

The theatre, by definition 'popular' during the Revolutionary years, drew
on old fairground traditions (the 'théâtres de la foire'). In the hands of many
practitioners, fairground performances had been cheeky, parodic, even
satirical; now the satire had gone, and politically and morally uplifting plays,
often lauding a Revolutionary fatherland, became the norm. Melodrama
flourished; its plots, after spine-chilling twists and turns, ended by upholding socially acceptable values: virtue rewarded, vice punished. (The best-
known melodrama of the period was *Coelina ou l'Enfant du mystère*, *Coelina
or The Mysterious Child*, 1801, by Pixerécourt, 1773–1844.) Melodrama was
imported from the English Gothic novel, but in addition the events of
the Revolutionary years had developed a public liking for sensational spectacle, and no doubt a wish to see ethical issues in black and white; both
these tastes could be catered for by melodrama. This does not mean
counter-currents were entirely absent; some dramatists were still turning

to antiquity, and parodies would soon return – particularly of melodrama. Thus one of many in 1805 was advertised as:

> *Roderick and Cunégonde, or the Hermit of Montmartre, or the fortress of Mouli-nos, or the Ghost of the West gallery*, a load of burlesco-melo-patho-dramatic rubbish in 4 acts with no intervals . . . embellished with caves and thieves, enlivened by a ghost and warmed up with a fire.

Parodies of this kind are on the whole politically harmless, and can even be self-congratulatory, allowing the spectator the double satisfaction of enjoying the original and feeling clever enough to laugh at it; we have to wait for the sharp wit of a Stendhal for parody to come into its own once more as a probing political weapon. But in the meantime, these theatrical parodies at least kept alive the ability to step back and mock.

Fairground performances had also led into the eighteenth-century development of comic opera: from 1715 on the term 'opéra-comique' had been used for fairground shows, and as from the mid-eighteenth century a new type of national comic opera had grown up in which all the music was original and the libretti, while at times sentimental, could again be satirical. Eventually, in the late eighteenth century, 'opéra-comique' started to move into serious opera, which often had a social or moral message in tune with the Revolutionary period. Thus opera-houses never closed down, even if lines praising monarchs were withdrawn; while revolution-ary songs and hymns offered stirring poetry, of which Rouget de Lille's 'Marseillaise' is only one example. (Rouget de Lille, a cellist, was no fêted composer; by profession he was an engineer, then soldier, and he wrote the song while serving as an army officer.) Revolutionary music was per-formed outdoors so that the public could attend in huge numbers, in deliberate contradistinction to the supposedly effeminate salon settings of the Ancien Régime. Here again we see both the continuation and the apotheosis of a tradition of political music, a tradition that would still be marking French popular song in the twentieth century to a degree unthink-able in most other Western countries. (See below, pp. 173–4, 218.)

Thus politics infiltrated different areas of verbal production. Also remark-able is the number of post-Revolutionary writers who held political posi-tions, a phenomenon hitherto unusual in Europe and even in France, despite the social intermingling in that country of eminent nobles, admin-istrators and writers from the seventeenth century on. Lamartine (1790–1869) is one striking example. His *Méditations poétiques* of 1820 have been hailed as the first French Romantic poetry. (One consequence of the Revo-lution was that France came somewhat later to Romanticism than did other European countries.) The best-known poem of the collection, 'The Lake', laments the loss of love and the passing of time; it does not look 'political'. But Lamartine was also a historian and politician, a liberal humanitarian imbued with the idealism of early socialism, who believed that literature should be a means of furthering the progress of humanity. His immediate poetic success led to diplomatic postings in Italy and, later, to eminence in national politics. Similarly, it is sometimes easy to forget that the nobleman Chateaubriand (1768–1848), nowadays best known for his short, solipsistic and quintessentially Romantic novella *René* (1802), was also a political journalist, a perceptive observer of the period, and an important participant in the historical developments of his time. At a different point on the political spectrum from Lamartine, Chateaubriand fought in a counter-revolutionary army of émigré princes in 1792. He subsequently gained favour with Napoleon by publishing a work lauding Christianity (*Le Génie du christianisme*, 1802) at just the time that Napoleon the pragmatist was establishing a Concordat with the Vatican and trying to restore Catholicism to France; Napoleon accordingly sent him to Rome as secretary of a legation to the Holy See. However, Chateaubriand became increasingly hostile to Napoleon and resigned in 1804; elected to the Académie Française in 1811, he was not allowed to read his anti-Napoleon inaugural speech; and in 1814 he published a virulent attack on Napoleon which Louis XVIII said was 'worth an army'. He then pursued a political career, albeit one marked by numerous vicissitudes, under both Louis XVIII and Charles X, serving for instance as ambassador to Berlin and London and as minister of foreign affairs. And after the revolution that deposed the last Bourbon Charles X, he would even, in 1832, support an effort to foment a civil war and restore the Bourbons. These two cases demonstrate the distinctively public stance that many French writers, even 'introspective' ones, allocate to themselves.

Constant (1767–1830) is another key author-cum-politician, famed among contemporaries not only as a theoretician of liberalism and historian of religion, but also as a remarkably eloquent deputy in the French parliament. He is now judged to be both a great writer and one of the founding fathers of modern liberalism. He was a Swiss Protestant aristocrat and was the lover of the two outstanding francophone writers Isabelle de Charrière and Germaine de Staël. Constant came into conflict with Napoleon for his attacks on the latter's increasing authoritarianism, but supported him during his hundred days' return to France in 1815, believing his views to have undergone a sea-change. This resulted, after Waterloo, in a period of semi-exile in London. But in 1819 Constant was elected to parliament, launching a successful political career in the liberal opposition: he championed such causes as press freedom and the abolition of the slave-trade, and when he died he was given a state funeral.

It was during his stay in London that he published his short masterpiece *Adolphe* (1816). This work, a novella rather than a novel, narrates the tale of a young man, the Adolphe of the title, who has absorbed from his father a careless attitude to women: his father's approach to casual liaisons is: 'It does them [i.e. women] so little harm, and gives us so much pleasure!' Adolphe enters into a relationship with a somewhat older woman, Ellénore; the rest of the work serves to disprove his father's dictum. Ellénore is the mistress of Count P*** and has borne him two children; she has barely gained respectability after a long partnership with him, and now loses all shreds of reputation, and her children, as a result of the liaison with Adolphe. She becomes more and more possessive as he in turn feels increasingly stifled. He longs to break with her but, feeling pity as much as exasperation, cannot find it in himself to do so. Meanwhile his father and another older man are advising him that he must sever this 'unsuitable' relationship, an unmitigated drawback to his career prospects, and start to make his way in the world. Ellénore is aware of the true state of his feelings; finally, she dies and Adolphe is left to wander abroad – the implication of the introductory 'publisher's notice' is that he too will die before long, and the novella's conclusion bears this out. This simple summary gives no sense of the urgency, irony and concision of the narration itself.

Three aspects of this work are especially significant for any cultural history of French literature. First, *Adolphe* is, in some respects at least, a startling demonstration of the time-lags that can occur in the 'development' of literature. We saw this in the conspectus of medieval writing, which forces one to take into account 'mismatches' like *Aucassin et Nicolette* as well as works that fit more conveniently and smoothly with wider trends. The bare, concentrated style and taut structure of *Adolphe* bear far more resemblance to the neo-classical prose of short eighteenth-century fiction than to the image-studded lyrical prose already ushered in by Chateaubriand at the very start of the century, fourteen years earlier (of whose political significance, more shortly). Second, *Adolphe* fits squarely into that major French tradition which – partly with elegiac pain, partly with intellectual pleasure – delineates patterning in love: you withdraw, my devotion intensifies in proportion; I grow bored, you accordingly try all the more anxiously to possess me. (Among writers who deploy this pattern are Racine, Mme de Lafayette, Stendhal and Proust; it is part of the 'sophistication' of French literature.) Third, Constant represents the conflict between private feeling and 'duty' to the peer-group more passionately and persuasively than any male writer since Corneille. (It had been present in many female writers in a somewhat different form, that of the struggle between love and 'honour'; but since it was still men who held the key public roles, this conflict in a male character raises more immediate social questions.)

Now, however, Constant puts the question in a recognizably modern form, and here he is of his time. Adolphe does at last find himself free of Ellénore, thus free to pursue a career. But he does not: he becomes directionless. As in Corneille, there is no final resolution between sexual feeling and society's demands, but Adolphe, unlike Corneille's heroes, has been swept away by emotions that have radically altered his relations with fellow-males and have left him submerged in what the twentieth century would term depression.

In this, Adolphe resembles other Romantic heroes. If Lamartine published the first 'Romantic' verse in 1820, prose-writers had anticipated him. Chateaubriand's René also wanders the world, is also a lonely and melancholic figure. So all-pervasive was this melancholia perceived to be in the early decades of the nineteenth century that it was given its own name, the 'mal du siècle': the affliction of the century. Clearly, contemporaries viewed it as arising from local, even temporary, conditions. It has been suggested that it sprang from the anxieties of an aristocracy displaced from its leading role, and, for a somewhat later group of writers, from the loss of hope brought about by the collapse of Napoleon and, with him, France's imperial ambitions. A more psychoanalytic interpretation has also been proposed: that the 'mal du siècle' arose from the depression of a generation that had lost its 'fathers', that is, the king and the nobles guillotined during the Terror. At the time, indeed, the execution of Louis XVI was overtly presented as parricide in some quarters. A quite different explanation has been put forward by the critic Margaret Waller in *The Male Malady: Fictions of Impotence in the French Romantic Novel* (1993). She argues that in the early nineteenth century women novelists were coming to the fore, writing best-sellers that aroused professional envy in their male fellow-authors. These compensated, and tried to attract female readers, by presenting 'feminized' heroes who would be gentler, more passive and more languishing than their fictional predecessors, and in some cases by adopting a pose of 'mal du siècle' themselves; in other words, commercial competition entered the picture, albeit unconsciously in some cases.

No doubt early nineteenth-century melancholia had many overdetermined causes, and in any case may not have been as widespread as contemporary and subsequent commentators suggested. Be that as it may, René was the archetypal French Romantic character. The novella itself originally formed part of Chateaubriand's defence of Christianity, *Le Génie du christianisme*; this title means both 'the genius of Christianity' and 'the spirit of Christianity', a usefully promotional ambiguity. Romanticism in France was thus, in its founding fictional text, intertwined with a reaffirmation of Catholicism. (Conservative Catholic opposition to Revolutionary ideologies was rediscovering its energy in these years.) One reason for the wildfire success of Romanticism was that it could serve the needs of both believers and non-believers, of both 'right' and 'left' political agendas; for the moment, let us look at the former. The new emphasis on individualism, combined with a liking for the Gothic that harked back to tales of medieval valour and solitary questing knights, meant that Romanticism could sit easily with a longing for the re-establishment of 'old orders' and with reactionariness of various kinds. It could even sit with an inclination for entrepreneurship, whose ideology requires that the individual forge his own path over and against the mass; and entrepreneurship was seen as desperately needed in a France just emerging from a system that, if not exactly feudal, still lagged decades behind such economically and industrially advanced nations as Britain.

At the heart of René's story is his discovery of an incestuous attachment that his sister Amélie bears him; it is never quite clear whether René returns the attachment in more than familial ways himself. He had already been a traveller full of ennui, and after accidentally learning of Amélie's passion flees to an exotic America full of majestic forests, where he is befriended by a missionary and some native American Indians. There is a degree of open-endedness in this story. Chateaubriand stressed that Christianity could and should be understood as a religion of *feeling* and of aesthetic response – it is true because good and beautiful; he adheres to his own prescription, and, rather than overtly preaching Christian doctrine in *René*, 'wheels on' religious stage effects in emotional crises, as when Amélie is taking the veil to a background of heavenly scents, the sheltering wings of the mystic dove (the Holy Ghost), and angels flying down to the altar and up again. (The passage is full of 'seemed', 'as it were', 'one could have thought': Chateaubriand hedges his bets.) The coda to the story does bring on apparently black-and-white views as René is sternly ticked off for self-indulgence by the missionary. But this piece of sermonizing is so inadequate to the narrative we have just read that it is bound to enhance by contrast the value of René's melancholia; while René both blames and exculpates himself for his ennui and current lethargy. So a self-indulgent ambivalence reigns, and this broadened the appeal of the work.

It was path-breaking in other ways too. First, in its subject-matter: the incest taboo had of course been broached – and breached – in earlier Western literature (not only in the Greek classics but in, for example, a story by the sixteenth-century Marguerite de Navarre in which a mother sleeps with her son and has a daughter whom the son eventually, in igno-rance, marries). But narratives now increasingly exploit the topic of incest, especially that between brother and sister. This serves at the least to raise questions about the nature of family and social bonds, and also chimes with contemporary preoccupations. The evocation of incest suggests the breakdown of conventional bonds; it reinforces the absence of the father or father-figure – siblings may, indeed must, now cling to each other; and it oddly echoes a certain egalitarianism and 'fraternity': brother and sister are peers, soulmates.

Second, and not unconnected, *René*'s first-person mode sowed seeds that would germinate fully towards the end of the century. The confessional, or quasi-confessional, text in mainstream French literature is not new. It goes back to Montaigne; the epistolary novel too was essentially a first-person narrative, if in some cases staging multiple first-persons; Rousseau's *Confessions* and his beautifully cadenced *Reveries of a Solitary Walker* (1782), with its evocation of the beauties of Nature, are precursors of the early nineteenth-century 'personal' narrative. Chateaubriand was also inspired by Goethe's epistolary *The Sorrows of Young Werther* (1774). So *René* is not wholly original here; and seemingly its structure would fail to be seized with special enthusiasm by the century that follows it, which after all is now famous not for short first-person narratives but for long third-person novels and for lyric poetry. But this fictional autobiography was extraor-dinarily successful. Its form enabled it to strike out with unsettling subjects in an eye-catching perspective, and it crystallized and encouraged an inward-looking mood that would mark lyric poetry for the next hundred years. A line may even be traced from *René*'s stress on subjectivity, its interest in unvoiced and forbidden parts of the mind, to the eventual for-mulation of psychoanalysis, some of whose tenets were being groped towards in late nineteenth-century France as well as elsewhere. (The French psychologist Charcot, who influenced Freud, would use the concept of 'l'inconscient', the unconscious.) And in fact the short first-person narrative itself never went away. Quite apart from *Adolphe*, it reap-pears with Nerval's *Sylvie* of 1853 (to be described by Proust some sixty years later as a 'masterpiece' of French literature), and with other nine-teenth-century novellas.

Third, *René* was stylistically pioneering. It may owe something to the diction of Rousseau's lonely rambler, but Chateaubriand's luscious text, heavy with exclamations and sighing evocations of an immense, awe-inspiring, supposedly indescribable Nature, is image-laden to a degree that had not been seen in French prose since the sixteenth century. Even then, this is imagery of a different kind from that created by Rabelais or Mon-taigne. It is unashamedly lax in its construction of similes, of which a perhaps unfairly bad example is this description of the sunset: 'L'astre, enflammant les vapeurs de la cité, semblait osciller lentement dans un fluide d'or, comme le pendule de l'horloge des siècles' ('The astral sun, inflaming the vapours of the city, seemed to oscillate slowly in a golden fluid, like the pendulum of the clock of the centuries': 206–7).

This style marked French literature irrevocably, not least because it allowed writers to blur the distinction between poetry and prose. For, although the Chateaubriand of *René* could not have foreseen this, the questioning of poetic 'privilege', or at least the tacit permission to move lyricism into prose, would form part of a strongly politicized discussion of style that would burst on the literary scene in the 1820s. At first sight this seemed to go in a different direction: that of an attack by Hugo, Stendhal and others on the classical and neo-classical restrictions imposed on verse and verse drama in the seventeenth and eighteenth centuries. Certainly it would be absurd to claim all writers were blood-brothers here. Chateau-briand, for example, was Stendhal's *bête noire*. He hated his gushily orna-mental language and throughout his own writing career presented Chateaubriand as the prime sinner against 'natural' prose. But in retrospect we may detect a pincer movement. As we have seen, Romanticism fitted 'right-wing' or retrogressive agendas, but it would also be enlisted from the 'left' as a progressive vanguard, as the rethinking of aesthetics for a new era. Stendhal, indeed, explicitly defines 'romantic' as 'modern'. Its iconic image of the lonely original, standing out not only against a back-cloth of Nature but also from the crowd, could and did encourage an assertion of the individual's *rights*: his or her autonomy must not be deval-ued by an oppressive system that viewed the subject as merely a unit in a mass. (The burgeoning feminist movement also took advantage of this stress on the rights of the individual.) And Romantics' promotion of the faculty of imagination attached a newly spiritual value to art which suited atheists as well as believers. Aesthetic responses could bolster adherence to Christianity, but they could just as easily replace religious worship with the non-supernatural awe provoked by beautiful music, painting or literature.

The two main works advocating a decisive literary break with the past – all the better to depict 'real' history – were, then, Stendhal's pamphlet *Racine and Shakespeare* (1823, 1825) and Hugo's preface to his own play *Cromwell* (1827). Stendhal argued that drama must shake off its reliance on the classics and the model of Racine and, without anachronistic imitation, must become more like Shakespeare: that is, for one, abandoning what Stendhal, with barely disguised contempt, refers to as 'fine verse' ('beaux vers'); abandoning too the three unities, since the unity of time, restricting action to twenty-four hours, did not allow for a proper *historical* sweep. Hugo, similarly, argued that the unities were a 'cage' that made *history* 'grimace', and he proposed that poetic form was connected to stages in mankind's development: the lyric, to primitive times and 'natural' man; the epic, to antiquity and the awakening of nationhood; drama, to modern times and a self divided between material and spiritual. Therefore literature did – was obliged to – change with the times. The historical generalizations are skewed, to say the least, and Hugo was not the first writer of the century to link literary form to cultural and political context: Mme de Staël, to whom I shall return, was the innovator here. But Hugo's crucial conclusion was that modern man could no longer maintain the division between beautiful and ugly (he enlists a Christian perspective on this too): the sublime and grotesque had henceforth to be interwoven, grafted on to each other. And this would entail a change of poetic vocabulary. In his later retrospective poem 'Réponse à un acte d'accusation' ('Reply to an accusation', in the collection *Les Contemplations*), Hugo would proudly give these propositions a Revolutionary setting, claiming that in his own youth the French language 'was the state before '89', but that he had placed a red bonnet on the 'old dictionary' (the red bonnet being the headgear of the Revolutionaries) and that there were no longer to be 'commoner' or 'senator' words.

These ideas are perhaps less pioneering than their authors claim. Quite apart from Staël's precedence in one key area, elite French literature had for centuries – as is by now clear – drawn on 'low' culture, 'low' language. Even in the seventeenth century, novelists such as Furetière and Scarron were writing burlesque or grotesquely 'realistic' works that self-consciously set out to be different both from current heroic novels and from contemporary classical verse drama, with such titles as *The Comic Novel* (1651–7, Scarron) and *The Bourgeois Novel* (1666, Furetière). And we have seen that already in the eighteenth century Diderot was arguing for a new kind of 'middle-class' prose drama that would break with the classical and neo-classical programme. Furthermore, in practice Hugo and Stendhal themselves would be relatively timid vis-à-vis verse at least. Hugo's attempts to break with the conventions of the alexandrine, though greeted as scandalous at the time, are scarcely noteworthy compared to the experiments of poets later in the century; Stendhal himself would never return to his own youthful attempts to write verse plays; and, more generally, serious drama would remain in the doldrums for most of the century. What is new, however, is the clear conviction of both Hugo and Stendhal that they are setting out more than a poetics: these are manifestos. When Hugo claims 'We want free, frank, loyal verse' he is using a language of social emancipation and re-bonding. The polemical nature of *Racine et Shakespeare* and the preface to *Cromwell* turns literary 'theory' into a political weapon. Literary criticism had for a long time been interwoven with the practice of writing to a degree more noticeable in France than in other cultures – at least since the seventeenth century when the concept of 'literature' began to take shape; now it overtly robes itself in political garb. To be sure, the seventeenth century had endowed discussions of literary style with social significance: Michael Moriarty, in *Taste and Ideology in Seventeenth-Century France* (1988), shows how the concept of 'taste' had worked as an instrument of power, reinforcing the claims of an elite to superiority. But in the early nineteenth century this social manoeuvring is out in the open: Hugo and Stendhal are thrusting it into the public consciousness and robustly challenging its mode of operation. The linguistically vulgar, the dirty, the seemingly trivial – everything that could be deemed humble or low – now *must* find a place in 'literature': it is a question of egalitarianism, it is an attack on a despotism that had been no less efficacious for being subtle.

The challenge would not be taken up, let alone worked through, overnight, and both 'taste' and onslaughts on it would remain remarkably tenacious in the discussion, teaching and practice of literature. Indeed, the historian Theodore Zeldin emphasizes that 'taste' continued to be a tool for control in the later nineteenth century: it must not be allowed to spread lest important social distinctions be undermined (*A History of French Passions 1848–1945*, vol. II, 2000: chapter 8, 'Good and Bad Taste'). But Stendhal and Hugo formulated tenets that would in due course profoundly affect mainstream French literature.

Egalitarianism inspired many other endeavours, for example those of politically aware women. (See my *Women's Writing in Nineteenth-Century France*, 2000.) Feminism had seemed briefly to have its opportunity just after the Revolution, when women formed their own political clubs and when, for example, divorce was temporarily made legal. But Olympe de Gouges, who had written the female counterpart to the Declaration of Rights, 'Declaration of the Rights of Woman and of Women Citizens', was guillotined in 1793, and the day after her execution the public prosecutor Chaumette publicly declared that this same fate would befall all women who departed from the domestic role designed for them by 'Nature'. Napoleon's Civil Code relegated women to the status of minors and intro-duced so many repressive measures that some contemporaries felt women had been better off under the Ancien Régime. The fear of the 'influence' of women governed much of this: spectres invoked were the Revolution-ary women's clubs and the supposedly shadowy machinations of women in the eighteenth-century royal court. Thus French feminists were in an unenviable position compared to their counterparts in, for example, Britain, where feminism was able to hold a steadier course during the same period. Yet feminist ideas, which had been part of French culture since the Middle Ages, were not likely to disappear: on the contrary. The most powerful Utopian socialist movement of the early nineteenth century, Saint-Simonism (named after its originator the Comte de Saint-Simon, 1760–1825), held feminist tenets and believed the Messiah would return as a woman – had perhaps already done so: some adherents went to Egypt to find her. Stendhal himself was a feminist (and would be one of the few male writers to be praised as such by Simone de Beauvoir in *The Second Sex*, 1949). He admired Laclos and wrote in favour of women's education in his characteristically provocative but compassionate book *On Love*; his feminism is visible in the creation of such self-determining characters as Mathilde de la Mole and the Duchess of Sanseverina in *Red and Black* and *The Charterhouse of Parma*, and in the tenderness with which he depicts the wife trapped in marriage to a husband who regards women as machines that are always going wrong (Mme de Rênal in *Red and Black*). Above all, despite numerous modest disclaimers and in some cases the adoption of anonymity, women were publishing as never before in what has been described as an explosion of women's writing: it was not only novels that they were composing, but also verse, religious tracts, literary criticism; they were being read across continental Europe and in Britain and the United States. Stéphanie de Genlis (1746–1830), who published educational works, moralizing fiction and children's drama, is cited by Jane Austen (and later in the century by Tolstoy); Sophie Cottin (1770–1807) found particu-lar favour in the United States with a novel that showed a plucky young woman travelling from Siberia to beg the Tsar's pardon for her exiled parents, and surmounting numerous perils on the way (*Elisabeth or The Exiles of Siberia*, 1806). Napoleon is supposed to have asked for the latest novel by the witty Sophie Gay to while away the night before his second, post-Waterloo, abdication: the story may be apocryphal, but the fact that it circulated at all is significant.

On the face of it, these female authors are not always particularly 'progressive'. Their works can seem to uphold conventional views of women's role. Yet what is important is their success at the time; they were forging careers, and misogynistic commentators, sneer as they might, could not escape the fact that something noteworthy was happening. And in fact, many best-selling women's works, even the most sentimental – even those wrapping up the plot with the safest conclusions – did raise feminist issues, often without drawing attention to the fact that parts of their enterprise could be deemed controversial. The conservative Genlis herself wrote a long work highlighting women's creative and social role in the history of French writing: *The Influence of Women on French Literature as Protectors of Good Writing [Lettres] and as Authors* (1811). One of the outstanding works of this period is Claire de Duras's short *Ourika* (1824), the story of a black girl – the Ourika of the title – brought up by well-meaning French aristocrats. The climax of the tale comes when she realizes that her appearance precludes marriage with any well-born white man; she has a breakdown as a result. Ourika has been described as the first black in literature to have an agonized 'European' self-awareness. This novella, mercilessly parodied by Duras's contemporaries, reflects both feminist and abolitionist ideals; it exemplifies the bravest thinking of the time.

Thus feminism re-established itself as a subject for discussion in 'high' culture and also now became a tenet of a populist movement. And this was in part owed to the most famous female writer in French of the period, Germaine de Staël, who for the rest of the century would be looked back to as a model. Staël was a Protestant, a factor which may have contributed to her independence of mind. There was no question of Staël being modest about her feminism or seeking to voice it laterally; it blazes out in her novels and in her works of cultural criticism. For Staël indeed has a claim to be the first cultural critic of France. In her *Literature Considered in its Relations with Social Institutions*, symbolically appearing just as the new century broke in 1800, she treats literature as another 'social institution' and argues that its changing forms are inseparable from national systems of government. She makes constant connections also between literary, ideological and religious phenomena; she takes it entirely for granted that the images orienting a society issue from a variety of sources, none of which can be completely disentangled from each other. She arrived at this conclusion, and extensively illustrated it, a generation before Stendhal and Hugo.

Staël is not a concise writer. She can be clumsy and often wrong. But her sheer energy and innovativeness are astonishing, and we may attribute to envy the fact that Hugo and Stendhal did not acknowledge her originality – though Stendhal paid her the sincerest tribute: his real name was Henri Beyle, but he modelled his one-word pseudonym on her surname: Staël/Stendhal. Napoleon was in no doubt as to the power of her writing: they crossed swords on many occasions, and when in 1810 she set about publishing *On Germany*, a paean to Germanic cultures, he took this as an unpatriotic attack on his own French supremacist policies. Staël fled the country and *On Germany* was pulped – proof, if we needed it, that cultural analysis can be as threatening as a political pamphlet. But the work resurfaced and helped to create an ever-strengthening concept of 'Europe' that would combine with Napoleon's defeat in 1815 to halt France's expansionist encroachment on its neighbours.

The remodelling of hierarchies was also propelled by a newly powerful consciousness of historical mutability. Of course, great writers had since the beginning of Western literature evoked the passing of empires, the fallibility of political ambition and, more locally, the ephemerality of fashions. We have seen that historical events formed either the jumping-off point of such medieval works as the *Chanson de Roland* or their raison d'être, as with Froissart's *Chronicles*. (See above, pp. 8–10, 17.) The first book printed in France was a history – the *Grandes Chroniques de France* of 1477, a collective work by the monks of Saint-Denis. In the sixteenth century, while some works of history followed a classical model (creating 'literary' portraits of protagonists and putting speeches into their mouths), others were more pragmatic, trying to adopt a plain style and avoid obvious invention (for example, a history in Latin of the age of the Wars of Religion by the magistrate Thou, 1533–1617). The great seventeenth-century preacher Bossuet wrote histories, and, again as in the Middle Ages, historical works were commissioned during the Grand Siècle for political reasons: thus the religious historian Maimbourg wrote a government-funded hostile *History of Calvinism* (1682), which was part of the renewed campaign against Protestantism. In the eighteenth century, the dominant mode was 'philosophical history', that is, history informed by analysis and taking a long view of economic, social and cultural developments; three outstanding examples are Montesquieu's *Reflexions on the Causes of the Greatness and Decadence of the Romans* (1734), Voltaire's *Essay on the Customs and*

Spirit of Nations (1756), and, by the liberal thinker Condorcet, *Sketch for a Historical Tableau of the Progress of the Human Mind* (posthumous, 1795). At the same time, 'antiquarian history' – the publication of sources and reference books – was flourishing, and other more recognizably 'modern' histories were being written, for example Voltaire's three-volume *The Age of Louis XIV* (1751).

But this interest in history acquired unprecedented force in the nineteenth century, which became the great century of historiography. France had had its Revolution, and seen its Bonaparte instigate extraordinary events that could not be comfortably fitted into a view of mankind's destiny smoothly unfolding against a backcloth of eternity. And indeed the ground had been laid by the eighteenth century's insistence on the relativism of custom and legal systems. If these were not God-given, then they must have been created by man (or a combination of man and Nature), and therefore had a history: to unravel and understand that past was to understand how conditions could change in the future.

The philosophical tradition did survive the Revolution. It would mark many of France's most famous nineteenth-century historians: most notably in this forty-year period the statesman Guizot, who in 1829 published a wide-ranging *History of Civilisation in France*. And there were other historians, or theoreticians of history, who valiantly tried to fit the Revolution into an eschatological or theological perspective, such as the counter-Revolutionary Maistre (1755–1821), and Bonald (1754–1840), an adversary of democracy in all its forms. They argued that France had sinned, had been punished for that sin, and was still expiating it, in such works as *Reflexions on France* (Maistre, 1797) and *Primitive Legislation* (Bonald, 1802). But 'Romantic' history also started to be written – that is, history in conscious reaction against this philosophical approach, now considered too cosmopolitan and bloodless. Sir Walter Scott (1771–1832) played a part: he had a truly international career in his own lifetime, attracting readers all over Europe; he was particularly popular in France, with 'historical' novels like *Waverley* (1814), *Ivanhoe* (1819) and *Quentin Durward* (1823). So strong narrative was revived and the focus shifted from 'society' to the nation, fed by a growing interest in the medieval. Thus Barante's *History of the Dukes of Burgundy* (1824–6) aimed to tell a story, and paint a picture of the late Middle Ages full of 'local colour', rather than to explain or judge; while Thierry's *History of the Conquest of England by the Normans* (1825) interpreted medieval English history as a tale of conflict between two 'races', Normans and Saxons. Such works ushered in a golden age of history-writing, with narrative lines that could encompass the unexpected and the quirky. And the influence went in the other direction too, from history-writing into fiction, creating an overlap between the techniques of novels and those of histories that would continue throughout the century. (Here the fact that the French word for 'history' and 'story' is the same, 'histoire', comes of age.)

The same development can be seen in formal opera. Story-lines had previously been derived from the classics, such as that of Gluck's *Iphigénie en Tauride*, performed in Paris in 1779 with a plot written by the French librettist Guillard; but 'Romantic' opera, which had a direct ancestry in the operas of the Revolutionary 1790s, specifically favoured historical episodes. Romantic opera led into Parisian 'Grand Opera', whose heyday was from the late 1820s to about 1850: these ambitious works had four or five acts, large-scale casts, lavish design and, still, plots normally based on or around dramatic historical events. One striking example is Auber's *La Muette de Portici* (1828), with a libretto by the popular playwright Scribe (1791–1861); a tale of revolution set in the Naples of 1647, it was the touch-paper for a genuine revolution when produced in Brussels in 1830.

Of canonical novels, the first thoroughly 'historical' one of this time comes right at the end of our forty years: Stendhal's *Red and Black* of 1830. Stendhal was another of that group of early nineteenth-century writers who had a political career: his ranged from work in the War Ministry and in government administration under Napoleon (in whose army he also served) to a post as consul in the papal states after 1830. In this period, he is the writer who 'incorporates' history into fiction with the greatest intellectual and aesthetic maturity. If we want to see plainly (and perhaps too schematically) the novelty of what Stendhal is doing, let us return for a moment to Racine. Political power shapes the plots of Racine's plays, and history is not absent. To choose a republican issue like that of the Roman populace forcing the emperor Titus to give up his foreign queen is to present a historically based struggle, even to suggest a hidden warning to the reigning monarch about unrest (*Bérénice*, 1670). But the struggle is also a 'distant' one, and Racine stresses in his preface to another tragedy, *Bajazet* (1672), that the subject of tragedy *has* to be distant, whether in period or location, for its dignity to be retained. This aesthetic stance served in part as self-protection, guarding against the danger of appearing critical of contemporary political structures. But it conveyed a sense that the human heart is the same in all places, at all times – which contributes to the power of Racine's plays.

Stendhal's presentation of feeling could not be more different. His works imply, state or even emphasize that particular psychological reactions could have occurred *only* at particular historical and political junctures. It is for this reason that the great critic Erich Auerbach, in his survey of Western literature from the Bible to the twentieth century, hailed Stendhal as the first European novelist with a truly modern consciousness of history (*Mimesis*, 1946). Auerbach discusses the burgeoning relationship between the young noblewoman Mathilde de la Mole and the hero of the novel, Julien Sorel. Julien is an intelligent and ambitious young man of peasant family who has become secretary to Mathilde's father. But Julien would not have achieved this position if he had not read the biography of his hero Napoleon and formed the plan to rise in society through his own merit. Nor would Julien have progressed if he had not himself first made a keen-eyed analysis of post-Napoleonic France. From this analysis he has deduced that, after the collapse of a system that had encouraged talent, the only way for a poor man to advance is now through the Church. Furthermore, his attitude to the two wealthy women with whom he has affairs is shaped by his modern consciousness of himself as entirely their equal but for the accident of birth: he is a figure who is not to be condescended to in any way. As for Mathilde, she is attracted to Julien in part because she is utterly bored in her father's salon, but this boredom too has a historically locatable source. In the eighteenth century, salons were forums for lively debate; now, in the fearful atmosphere that has taken hold in the wake of the Revolution, anything resembling an interesting idea is stifled. (Mathilde's own father had to suffer what Stendhal calls 'the miseries of emigration' after the Revolution.) So Mathilde longs for something different, and, realizing that Julien is consumed by a barely concealed rebellious fire, she starts to take notice of him – attracted also by the idea that his forebears were capable of guillotining hers. 'That man, at least, wasn't born on his knees,' she thinks (I 459). When in due course this aristocratic lady begs this lower-caste man to humiliate her, to make her his slave, we are seeing not merely the melodramatic pose of a besotted young woman but a political irony that will take on its force only if we remember the historical context.

The historical vision is not, in fact, all-consuming. Stendhal's depiction of love often adheres to the French tradition I have mentioned; like Constant, he shows its almost symmetrical see-sawing: Mathilde is at her most passionate when Julien is angry with her, or affects coldness, or makes her jealous. But this very see-sawing is also moulded by Julien's post-Revolutionary sensitivities. (He even reminds himself that the heiress Mme de Rênal – a kindly woman who is falling deeply in love with him – has been brought up in the 'enemy camp'.) An especially striking confrontation occurs when, shortly after they have first slept together, Mathilde appears in her father's library, where Julien is working. She looks downcast, telling him: 'I'm horrified that I gave myself to the first comer' (I 546). Julien, furious at this humiliation, seizes a sword hanging on the library wall and makes as if to kill her. And near the end of the novel it is another wound to his class pride that makes him try to kill Mme de Rênal, who has (under pressure from friend and confessor) written to Mathilde's father that Julien is an untrustworthy parvenu, in other words a 'little nobody'. This leads to his execution – not, however, before Julien himself has informed the jury that they will convict him on *class* grounds, thus in some measure provoking them to do so because he has been politically inflammatory.

Stendhal is a wonderfully ironic novelist, and *Red and Black* is indeed full of both local and large-scale ironies, arising not least from Julien's inner contradictions. He sometimes leaps to ideological interpretations out of a susceptibility that leads him to misjudge the situation entirely, and sometimes has to force himself to play the part of the radical: at one point, it is said that he longs to quit 'his sad role of the plebeian in revolt'. But irony does not preclude focused historical insights, and there are many jokes of Stendhal's that we shall simply not grasp if we are ignorant of the politics of the period. The main action of Stendhal's second great novel, *The Charterhouse of Parma* (1839), starts in Italy at the time of Napoleon's return from Elba – the hundred days that preceded his final defeat at Waterloo. The hero's father, the marquis del Dongo, is a blinkered fool who, in the midst of his general reactionary paranoia, has always harboured the suspicion that Napoleon will make a comeback: he is right! 'Europe,' writes Stendhal, 'had the bonhomie to be surprised by this event [Napoleon's landing], which did not in the least surprise the marquis del Dongo. He wrote his sovereign a letter full of heartfelt effusions; he offered him his talents and many millions, and repeated that his ministers were Jacobins [that is, 'left-wingers'] in league with Parisian manipulators' (II 48). It would be difficult to find this funny without a knowledge of the momentous events to which it refers. And we also need some historical understanding to laugh not merely at this benighted, pompous aristocrat but also, more wryly, at the reaction against reform that he represents. For in the wake of Napoleon's first exile, the allies had put Italy under the aegis of the Austro-Hungarian empire and turned the political clock back by decades.

As well as inextricably intertwining politics with his characters' feelings, Stendhal also shows the differing perspectives they have on the past. In this too he is a great 'historical' novelist. History is as much a matter of our image of events as of the events themselves. Half-way through *Red and Black*, Julien makes a coach journey to Paris; the other two passengers discuss Napoleon and his legacy, each taking a contrasting view. No conclusion is reached. Here we have both historical insight and the calm overview of the *moraliste*, or that of the dialogue in – say – Diderot's works: not neutral, not uncommitted, but marshalling the form and spirit of the conversation to allow political issues to speak for themselves.

Red and Black marks the return of elite French literature to its full powers. After 1830, there would be a flourishing of novels and poetry that would once more place France centre-stage in the cultural consciousness of Europe.

4

Balzac and the Birth of Cultural Studies (1830–1870)

The July Revolution of 1830 ushered in a calmer period for France. Louis-Philippe would reign for the first eighteen years (the 'July Monarchy'). His regime had a constitution similar to that of the previous one, with a monarch, two chambers, and a tiny, wealthy electorate (about one per cent of the population). But this electorate expanded a little throughout the reign, and the style of the regime was less reactionary. There was greater press freedom, a growth in working-class movements, and an extension of popular education. Indeed, every post-1815 government would encourage the provision and improvement of schools, in co-operation with the Church and local authorities. The Guizot law of 1833 required each commune to provide a public school: politicians were inspired not only by humanitarian ideals but by ideas of control, hoping that the schools would give morals to the masses and stability to society.

Louis-Philippe's reign also saw huge industrial growth, including the establishment of the railways: the first French locomotives were tried out in the 1830s and soon became commercial, and the railway boom peaked in the mid-1840s. The power of a wealthy bourgeoisie was consolidated, becoming a favourite target of satirists from Stendhal to the famous caricaturist Daumier (1808–79). At the very threshold of the regime, in 1830, the satirist Monnier created the character Joseph Prudhomme, the 'typical' bourgeois. The name implies both 'Prudence-man' and 'Prude-man': he is good-hearted but blinkered, naive, pretentious and verbose. (Monnier, 1799–1877, is one of those writers who straddles different cultures; his Prudhomme would influence the depiction of the bourgeoisie in elite literature; he contributed to vaudeville and puppet theatre, acted, and illustrated his own works.) Louis-Philippe himself would be called the 'bourgeois king' in part – tellingly – because he was perceived as a consumer: he went shopping with his queen in the Paris stores, taking his purchases home in the omnibus, and carrying an umbrella instead of a sword. (The umbrella has an afterlife; it will figure in Maupassant and

Proust as the ultimate petty-bourgeois object: see below, pp. 122–3.) This 'bourgeois king' label subsumed more important characteristics. Louis-Philippe's childhood education by Mme de Genlis – rather than by a man, as was customary – had taught him several manual crafts and instilled relatively democratic principles. He believed in monarchy according to the 'Charter' ('La Charte', 1814), and his very 'bourgeoisification' was a factor in the relative steadiness of the regime.

When this regime fell in early 1848, it was partly as a result of economic difficulties; however, the trigger was significant: it was the government's refusal to allow a republican 'banquet'. Republican meetings, although forbidden, reappeared in the guise of these 'banquets'. Public gatherings, and more subtly the image of public festivities, thus continued to play a catalytic role in French society. The Second Republic that was then declared lasted until a coup d'état by Napoleon's nephew, Louis-Napoléon, at the end of 1851. This brief Second Republic was notable chiefly for its huge extension of suffrage. Whereas under Louis-Philippe about a quarter of a million men could vote, that right was now extended to ten million (still men only, of course), making France the most democratic country in the world. However, universal male suffrage would soon come under attack, and fierce attempts by the right to quell the left continued. There was a second uprising in June 1848. (These events would be depicted by Flaubert in *L'Education sentimentale*.) Finally, Louis-Napoléon proclaimed himself emperor at the end of 1852. Masquerading as a 'revolutionary', he had been elected by a huge majority (92 per cent) in a plebiscite of 1851 and by another (97 per cent) when he proposed himself as Emperor a year later; however, during the first coup he had arrested the leading legislators, and massacred, deported or imprisoned nearly 27,000 protestors. The second time there was no open resistance. Louis-Napoléon ruled as Napoleon III over the 'Second Empire' until 1870, when he was defeated (and himself captured) a few months after launching the Franco-Prussian war. His regime was authoritarian, tightening censorship of both press and literature, though there was some easing in the 1860s. He also involved France in several foreign wars (including the Crimean War) and in colonial expeditions already begun under Louis-Philippe. (See below, p. 182.) This forty-year period thus divides, more or less symmetrically, between a comparatively liberal regime (until 1848) and a markedly harsher one (from 1851 on).

The key cultural development was the enlargement of France's readership. Illiteracy was diminishing: an inquiry of 1877–9 into the number of people who could sign their names showed a real improvement. (The proportion of men signing their names had risen from 47 per cent in 1786–90 to 78 per cent in 1871–5, and that of women from 27 to 66 per cent.) With the gradual spread of education, the French language continued its 'advance' against dialects and other tongues spoken in the outlying regions, an advance helped too by improvements in communications – first by better roads and then by development of the railway network. For under Napoleon III industrialization continued its rapid progress. The diffusion of books, periodicals and newspapers was also dramatically expanded by a technological revolution that both coincided with the growth in the reading public and stimulated that growth. The early part of the nineteenth century brought in changes in those printing and paper-making industries largely concerned with the special requirements of newspaper production, but these changes in turn affected books and periodicals. The main innovation in printing technique was the inked roller press. As for paper, this had hitherto been made by hand and was very expensive. Now it could be produced much more cheaply and rapidly by machine, and the rags from which it had traditionally been made were supplemented on a massive scale by such new materials as esparto grass and wood-pulp. This cheaper paper meant that extra thousands of copies of a work could be produced at low price, and allowed a spectacular increase in the number of books published during the Second Empire.

If diffusion of newspapers was improving, the nature of the press was changing too. Under the Restoration (1814–30) a number of periodicals had been founded, including many devoted to literature; they provided outlets for novels, short stories, poems and literary criticism. This trend continued after 1830: particularly significant in the literary sphere was the *Revue des deux mondes* (founded in 1829), which published such writers as Hugo, Vigny, Musset, Balzac and Sand. But, important as these periodicals were for literary life, the growth of the newspaper press was crucial. It would provide much larger sources of income for writers. A milestone date is 1836: in that year there appeared simultaneously two new papers, *La Presse* (*The Press*) and *Le Siècle* (*The Century*), selling at only half the price of existing journals. Newspapers were already deriving some income from advertisements, but these new ones counted on being able to sell more cheaply because their larger circulation would attract considerable advertising revenue. Emile de Girardin, founder of *The Press*, declared in the first number: 'the advertisements [annonces] will pay for the newspaper'. 'In other words,' says Lough, 'the modern newspaper was born' (295). Balzac, in his 1837 *César Birotteau* – the first 'business novel' of French literature – is already talking of those who were brilliant enough to understand and harness 'the influence of journalism and the piston-effect that a repeated item produces on the public' (218).

To attract custom, the editors decided to publish novels in the *feuilleton* of their papers, that is to say the 'serial section'. (Throughout almost the whole of the nineteenth century, newspapers were smaller than those we are used to; they had only four pages, the bottom of which was separated off to form the *feuilleton*.) Again, Girardin led, but others were quick to follow, and after 1836 all major Parisian dailies included serialized fiction. Novelists could therefore earn money from two sources – by publishing their works first in a newspaper, and then in book form. In statistical terms the *roman-feuilleton* was the dominant literary genre of the nineteenth century, and for many authors the distinction between 'elite' and serialized fiction was artificial, since the serial was the form in which their books initially appeared. Thus the relatively new historical penchant of narrative, which strove to resemble the forward-moving chronicle, was supported by the onward impetus that serialization lent to fiction: the drive to a teleological (goal-directed) presentation of narrative time was over-determined during this period.

Although the circulation figures of newspapers were modest by today's standards (in 1846 *Le Siècle* had 32,885 subscribers, the largest number), they were read much more widely than simply by subscribers: by family groups, in clubs and in *cabinets de lecture*. These latter were commercial lending libraries which had mushroomed in the 1820s and served the needs of those who could not afford books; by 1835 there were 500 *cabinets de lecture* in Paris alone. (They faded away after 1860, with ever cheaper newspapers and mass reprints further reducing the price of reading-matter.) To begin with, newspaper readership remained largely middle-class, but would soon expand with the appearance of novelists like Sue, author of the best-selling *Les Mystères de Paris* (1842) and *Le Juif errant* (1844–5) (*The Mysteries of Paris*, *The Wandering Jew*): this latter increased subscriptions to the newspaper serializing it, *Le Constitutionnel*, by 20,000. The period 1842–8 was the high point of the *roman-feuilleton*; it was dominated by Alexandre Dumas with such works as *The Three Musketeers* (1844) and *The Count of Monte-Cristo* (1844–6). Dumas (1802–70) is probably the most internationally famous French novelist of any period. Like the great Russian poet Pushkin, he had black ancestry: his grandmother, Marie-Cessette Dumas, was a black slave-girl. He was politically on the left, strongly supporting the republican cause in 1830. Like other novelists of the time, Dumas started by writing for the theatre; however, unlike the young Stendhal, whose ambition to be the nineteenth-century

Molière had come to nothing, Dumas, his finger on the pulse of his epoch, began with melodramas and vaudeville sketches, and would be sensationally successful. His first theatrical triumph had come in 1829, with a splashily staged historical drama, *Henri III and his Court* (again testifying to the popularity of rewritings of 'history'). Dumas's plays continued to tap into and feed contemporary mind-sets – indeed obsessions – with such plays as *Antony* of 1831, whose daring tale of adultery provided a suitably Romantic frisson, and with his tragedy *The Tower of Nesle*, 1832, which fanned the fascination with an exoticized Middle Ages. It was, however, with his serialized novels that Dumas achieved his literary and social reputation. His prolific output gained him a huge readership, and his best-known novels have continued to attract modern audiences, being repeatedly adapted for popular serialization, cinema, television and children's cartoons.

The world depicted in *The Three Musketeers*, and the tone of its narration, give a snapshot of attitudes not universal in mid-nineteenth-century literate France but evidently significant: the work's status as a best-seller makes it a litmus test. Despite Romantic interest in the medieval, the seventeenth century, in which *The Three Musketeers* is set, is still viewed as a high point for the nation: glamorous – yet permissive, for the action takes place shortly before the accession to the throne of Louis XIV; Dumas relies on a picture of (to quote him) 'the strangely easy morality of that gallant epoch' (331; translation by Richard Pevear). The musketeers can feast in Rabelaisian style, can be wild and independent, and the king (never very clearly portrayed, but obviously ineffectual) can command loyalty without provoking troublesome questions about absolutism. There is a keen but sardonic interest in religion, with Catholicism, Protestantism and finally Puritanism played off against each other (particularly in the figure of the villainness Milady); as a whole, the work is anti-clerical. Catholicism comes off worst – not only in the casting of Cardinal Richelieu as wily serpent, but also in the novel's depiction of the siege of the Protestant town La Rochelle. This siege, which took place in 1627–8, led to the reduction of the town's population from 27,000 to 5,000 through casualties, famine and disease. 'Poor fools!' is Athos's comment on the starving Protestants, as he empties a glass of 'excellent Bordeaux': '"As if the Catholic religion wasn't the most advantageous and agreeable of religions! All the same," he went on, after smacking his tongue against his palate, "they're brave folk"' (533). Linguistic and literary developments are reflected in the novel too. Aramis tells d'Artagnan that he has begun a poem in lines of one syllable:

'It's rather difficult, but the merit of all things lies in their difficulty . . . I'll read you the first canto; it's four hundred lines long and takes one minute.'

'By heaven, my dear Aramis,' said d'Artagnan, who detested verse almost as much as Latin, 'add the merit of brevity to the merit of difficulty, and you'll be sure your poem has at least two merits.' (322)

Although Latin and Greek, and composition in verse, continued to be taught in prestigious schools, forming a fundamental part of the training of almost all male poets of the century, in this nineteenth-century view of a seventeenth-century exchange we are perhaps seeing the death-throes of Latin in its long struggle against the vernacular. Or, at any rate, we are seeing a triple kick neatly administered to the prestige of the ancient classics, to that of the seventeenth-century ones, and to verse itself. D'Artagnan's sarcastic comment promotes the long and 'easy' prose read.

In two other respects, this novel typifies its period. First, Milady is the *femme fatale* who, evil and seductive from the start, finally becomes a kind of witch, a she-devil; since other women in the novel are barely characterized, it is this female hate-figure who captures the imagination. Second, *The Three Musketeers* is not merely swashbuckling – it is also amusing. Comedy is created by the farcical or absurd situations in which the musketeers often find themselves, and by their own foibles or odd behaviour, but still more important is the droll economy with which Dumas evokes these. The humour is part of the work's success, and reflects an aspect of their culture in which French people still delighted and which had been scarcely dented by the sorrowful sighing of Romanticism.

It was thus during these four decades that the market and journalism came to play a central role in all kinds of French fiction; and with serialization the production of best-sellers relied as never before on interaction with the public. Indeed, Sue changed his plots as he went along to suit expectations, as Prendergast shows in his aptly titled *For the People by the People? Eugène Sue's 'Les Mystères de Paris'* (2003). Nevertheless, the formulae laid down by the early serializing novelists continued to please and would be replayed throughout the century in variations of the *roman-feuilleton*, variations which herald among other developments the space-traveller, the detective and the comic-strip superman. This fiction told tales of heroic investigators penetrating the dark underbelly of the big city and braving the criminal fraternity in order to right the wrongs of the oppressed (Revolutionary ideals and the norms of melodrama live on here). The career of Verne (1828–1905) was launched in this mid-century, most notably with *Journey to the Centre of the Earth* in 1864 (*Round the World in Eighty Days* would follow in 1873); his male-oriented, 'scientific' novels would become the most translated in the world. In due course the cinema would take inspiration from the *roman-feuilleton*, and we can even detect in it the origins of the television soap.

In spite of these new sources of income, and in spite of the fact that, from Napoleon's regime on, authors benefited financially from copyright laws protecting rights of property in their work, one also finds in this period gloomy accounts of the poverty-stricken state of the writer. These did reflect a harsh reality for some, but for others the image became part of a cultural polemic that sought to make the modern nation think about the role of art. Vigny (1797–1803), for example, represents in his 1835 play *Chatterton* a young English poet's suicide as the inevitable product of a materialist society caring nought for literature. In his preface he declares that beings like Chatterton, belonging to 'the exquisite, powerful race of great and inspired men', need '*do nothing*' in order to do something with their art (Vigny's italics). Such a being must do – Vigny here repeats the word 'nothing' – nothing useful or day-to-day, so that he may have time to listen to the harmonies forming slowly in his soul, which the coarse noise of positive, regular work interrupts and infallibly banishes. ' – He is the Poet.' And many mid-century writers would take up the theme. Also in the 1830s, the poet Gautier (1811–72) aggressively argues that art must exist for its own sake ('l'art pour l'art') and must not be useful: 'everything that is useful,' he declares in the preface to his novel *Mademoiselle de Maupin* (1835–6), 'is ugly'. And some twelve years later, Balzac, while stressing that the artist must work at his art if he is not to be poverty-stricken, suggests in *La Cousine Bette* (1847) that some 'lazy' day-dreaming, some wandering in the city, even the extravagance of some expensive 'folly', may be important to him: from these will emerge his creative ideas (79–81). (The descendants of these 'do-nothing' artists are Baudelaire's *flâneur* and, eventually, the lyric 'I' of Apollinaire's 'Zone': see below, pp. 91–4, 128–9.)

Two aspects of this polemic are telling. First, Vigny and others are implicitly urging state patronage. (And Vigny does defend the poet's utility for the ship of state, which he guides by contemplating the stars.) Although some governmental rewards and allowances continued during the nineteenth century, these ran counter to the historical evolution in the position of the writer: away from patronage and towards what he or she could earn from publishers or the theatre. Many writers, Balzac among them, felt that this was no improvement. In practice the writer had had to transfer his flattery from a minister or king's mistress to a publisher, newspaper proprietor or theatre manager.

What is also important, however, is the appropriation by Vigny of an aristocratic status for the poet. Clearly, he needs the 'leisure' associated with the daily life of the Ancien Régime nobility. This appropriation of aristocratic status combines with the wish for continuing patronage in such later comments as Flaubert's: 'the writer is supposed to be freer and nobler because he no longer receives allowances from the great. His entire social *nobility* now consists in being a grocer's equal. What progress!' (letter of 1872 to George Sand, *Correspondance*, vol. 6, 458). Gautier's stance too ('useful' equals 'ugly') is more political than it seems: it is a hit at the bourgeois and industrialist ethos of production, a hit launched from a position of cultural superiority – from a cultural 'aristocracy'.

Thus, although tension had existed at least since Renaissance France between creative individuals and the communities to which they looked for support, in this unease we find a complex culture at a defining moment in its development. The artist still embraces, to a degree, the egalitarianism of Revolutionary ideals and even a kind of 'citizens' work ethos'. Yet he wishes to have the status, indeed the life-style, of a new nobility. Then again, he assumes the mantle of the historian who includes in his purview momentous national and international events, but he is ever more aware that history is made from 'below' as well as from 'above' – from the impact of social and industrial change on ordinary life, as well as from battles won or lost and the succession of monarchs. What class does he belong to?

Arguably, it was these new perceptions of social and artistic interrelations that gave birth to cultural studies. From one perspective, cultural studies would not see the light of day for another 120 years – in Birmingham after the Second World War, with Richard Hoggart's and later Stuart Hall's Centre for Cultural Studies. From another perspective, they had already arrived in eighteenth-century Italy with Vico's 'cultural constructivism'. (See especially his *The New Scientist* of 1725.) Staël is another forebear (although she was concerned mainly with state institutions). But if we are looking for the European writer who first – and still perhaps most fully – explored the relationship between class, art, artefacts, commerce, power, and the representations of all these, it is to Balzac that we must turn as the 'inventor' of cultural studies. And we need not, as some commentators have, believe that this exploration is necessarily an anxious process. In the hands of Balzac and many writers of this period, the unease we have noticed, and deprecatory comments about modern society, are often belied by – or at least sit alongside – zestful evocations that are allegedly 'realistic' but also unashamedly draw attention to the fact that they are fabricated. It is almost as if we are seeing a new kind of carnival – a celebration of nineteenth-century 'social imaginaries' that can be pleasurably hyperbolic. (For this phrase, see Charles Taylor, *Modern Social Imaginaries*, 2004.) Thus, when Crevel, the parvenu of *Cousin Bette* – a cleverer Prudhomme – is searching for a word to describe the wonderfully sexy seductress of the novel, he finally hits on a bang-up-to-the-minute railway metaphor: 'She's a proud locomotive, a woman like that' (309). And what now has the power – who now 'understands' the way France is going? Why, respectively the economy and the bourgeoisie, of course. Crevel launches into a paean to money (he is lecturing Baroness Hulot, a member of the now outdated minor nobility created by Napoleon):

> You're wrong, my dear angel, if you think we're ruled by King Louis-Philippe, and he knows it too! He knows, like all of us, that, superior to the Charter, there's the holy, venerated, solid, agreeable, gracious, beautiful, noble, young, all-powerful hundred-sou coin! Now, my lovely angel, money demands interests, and it's always on the look-out for them. (306)

The words 'gracious', 'noble', are still redolent of social prestige, but they have flitted into another sphere thanks to this joyously absurd character. And the boarding-house in which much of *Old Goriot* (1834–5) is set is also described with an imaginative energy, a poet's use of metaphor, alliteration and even rhyme, that make it too sit half-way between a material 'reality' and an exuberant fantasy.

All this, however, rests on sharp analysis. Balzac admired Stendhal, and like him shows how major historical events change the most intimate feelings. For example, the plot of *Cousin Bette* hinges on the infidelity of Baron Hulot to his wife. Hulot is inclined to affairs, being 'imbued with Directoire ideas about women' – an inclination interrupted for many years by his attachment to his wife. Then, however, Napoleon falls and Hulot, who had been in the imperial administration and entourage, becomes bored. 'Unoccupied from 1818 to 1823, Baron Hulot had embarked upon active service with women. Mme Hulot dated the first infidelities of her Hector to the grand finale of the empire' (35). Thus, as in Stendhal, politics affect the very nature of sexual desire. Balzac also explores the moral complexity of modern economics. Hulot's womanizing brings his family to the brink of financial disaster, and the reader follows the trajectory blow by blow until the end of the novel; but, very near this end, Balzac suddenly provides a quite different perspective. An ex-mistress of Hulot's, the actress Josépha, tells him that she prefers a 'spendthrift' like him to 'those cold soulless bankers, who're supposed to be virtuous, who ruin thousands of families with the railways that bring *them* gold but just base iron for the credulous. *You*'ve only ruined your own family' (343).

Balzac's grasp of the economic forces driving his nation was such that Marx would say it was to his novels that he turned for an understanding of these forces, rather than to economists of the time. But it is not solely macro-economics that Balzac depicts. In his works, consumer durables such as furnishings demonstrate both wide changes and the images people have of them (Crevel understands he may have a chance to seduce Baroness Hulot when he sees her faded curtains and shabby furniture, the sign of equally fading finances); and Balzac also shows how lives are altered by minor economic developments and the twists and turns of local industries. Bette, the poor relation, had earned her living making the lavish embroidery that Napoleon favoured for military and administrative uniforms. This taste of his provided a 'sure business'. But on his downfall, business collapses and an embittered Bette is reduced to sponging off her relatives the Hulots, with disastrous consequences.

For historians of the book trade, the emblematic Balzac novel is *Lost Illusions* (1837–43). This follows the fortunes of the young poet Lucien de Rubempré. He leaves the provinces for Paris, where he eventually succumbs to the lure of gutter journalism and hack-writing. Meanwhile his friend David Séchard is inventing new plant-based paper which will bring down the price of paper, hence of publishing. The novel describes the play of nineteenth-century market forces on the writer, who without the willpower to make sacrifices will be seduced and controlled by the commercial needs of publishers; it details the industrial changes taking place in book production; and it memorably evokes the thirst of the book business for pot-boilers. The virginal paper made by David in the provinces is an economic fact and a symbol at the same time – the symbol of a blank sheet that will be sullied in the capital. In this capital, Lucien is being told that verse is virtually unsaleable. His own poetic work has, it is true, been accepted for publication. But it has a title which, though corresponding to certain Romantic tastes, now verges on the antiquated: *The Archer of Charles IX*. (Charles IX ruled from 1560 to 1574.) For his publisher, at least, it risks seeming hopelessly outmoded. He tells Lucien: 'We've reserved the right to give it another title, we don't like *The Archer of Charles IX*, it doesn't whet the reader's appetite enough, there are lots of kings called Charles, and there were dozens of Archers in the Middle Ages! Now if only you called it "The Soldier of Napoleon"' (420). This ironic masterpiece demonstrates Balzac's comprehensive yet creative insight into the relationship between journalism and elite literature and, more widely, into the economics of mid-nineteenth-century French culture.

And yet, even amid what many saw as a frenzy of greed, France had not forgotten that the arts could secure it an international reputation. As we have seen, rare poets were still able to earn some sort of living from occasional state patronage: royal allowances, ministerial pensions, prizes awarded by local academies, did help some, including women poets. The outstanding example of a state-supported poet was Hugo (1802–85), awarded a royal pension for his *Odes* of 1822 that enabled him to marry; by the age of twenty-three his stature was such that he was invited to the coronation of Charles X (1825). In his youth, Hugo had moved in conservative circles. But, as the last chapter showed, he had already begun to connect modern practice in the arts with revolutionary principles, and he shifted towards republicanism and liberalism thereafter. His 1832 play *Le Roi s'amuse* was censored for its depiction of a cruel François I; and he had in 1829 published a powerful novel against capital punishment, *The Last Day of a Man Condemned to Death*. (Stendhal, George Sand and many other writers were also against the death penalty, but it is salutary to remember that great artists may sometimes have no impact whatever on prevailing social attitudes, for capital punishment would not be abolished in France until 1981.)

Hugo's meteoric rise to fame culminated with the first performance of his *Hernani* in October 1830. This play, whose experiments with verse-form reflected (rather palely) the anti-Classical principles of his earlier preface to *Cromwell*, resulted in fisticuffs between his followers and defenders of Classicism. The Romantic avant-garde would henceforth be in the dominant position. What is remarkable is the depth of feeling – the fury – acted out through a public spectacle; the participants were in no doubt as to the seriousness of the break with tradition and its political implications. And this break is reflected also in Hugo's two most famous novels, which span this period – *Notre-Dame de Paris – 1482*, published in 1831, and *Les Misérables* of 1862 (begun in 1845). *Notre-Dame de Paris*, in the very person of its hunchback hero Quasimodo, enacts the aesthetic principle that art must search for a new power in discord. On Quasimodo's first appearance, Hugo writes that he is a 'strange exception to the eternal rule which demands that strength, like beauty, is the result of harmony' (61). But Quasimodo is not merely ugly, he is plebeian, as are, of course, the 'wretched ones' of *Les Misérables* – a work whose status is now so unassailable that its French title is retained throughout the anglophone world. ('Le misérable' has the double meaning of 'wretchedly poor person' and 'scoundrel' – a syllepsis provoking us to reflect on the distinction.)

As for Hugo's non-dramatic verse, this cannot all be subsumed under the heading of 'radical'. It strikes the twenty-first-century reader as sometimes bombastic, sometimes cloying. But the grandiose rhetoric through which Hugo proclaims the quasi-sanctity of the poet is more political than may be apparent. It is not simply a Romantic presentation of the writer as solitary seer but can be located in a long-standing tradition of France's pride in its artistic prowess; it is an affirmation of the 'cultural capital' he and he alone can bring to his society. And even those poems that are most intimate or domestic – that evoke, for example, poignant or happy family affections – are doing something more novel than we might now realize, so much do we take their premises for granted. For Hugo's 'promotion' of the child contributes to a gradual but important evolution in French (and European) society. Thinkers and politicians were at last recognizing the formative role of childhood and the rights of this other category of 'lowly' creatures. Starting in the eighteenth century (a landmark work is Rousseau's *Emile*), this development gathered pace in nineteenth-century France. (The French had to borrow the word 'bébé' from English in the early nineteenth century – its first attested written use is 1841; they had no word for 'babe-in-arms'.) Aspects of literature which nowadays we may dismiss as mawkish in fact played a part in legal and educational reforms designed to protect children and further their interests. (In England, Dickens is a case in point.)

Hugo did appear to veer once more towards the right in the late 1840s, fooled by Louis-Napoléon's supposedly revolutionary youth into supporting him for the Presidency of the new Republic, and himself being elected in 1849 to a conservative Assembly. Here, however, isolated from both the left and the right, he reasserted his liberalism: he made impassioned speeches about poverty, universal suffrage, freedom of the press, lay education and capital punishment; and by 1851, he was openly opposing the government of the future Napoleon III, fleeing to Belgium to avoid arrest. He published a virulent pamphlet, *Napoleon the Little*, denouncing Louis-Napoléon, and moved to the Channel Islands in 1855, where he remained with his family until the emperor's abdication in 1870. During these years of exile Hugo wrote, among other great works, *Les Châtiments* (*Punishments*), a collection of satirical poems. Satire in the strict sense – the desire to arouse indignation – was thus still part of the armoury of famous writers, even if it does not blaze out with the potency of a Voltaire. Hugo's popularity remained high, in part because his fiction pleased contemporary tastes, achieving a unique blend of Romanticism and 'Realism'. He continued to support liberal causes after his return to France, and when he died in 1885 his state funeral was attended by two million people and delegates from every country in Europe. Hugo's writings could be contradictory, but from his earliest works he had emphasized the social responsibility of the writer, and he interpreted his own life as exemplifying a collective, historical self. Today his contribution to the rethinking of poetic forms is recognized as colossal. It was a contribution inseparable from his political views, whether these governed the promulgation of aesthetic 'hybridity' or the choice of particular historical topics.

One of Hugo's approaches to these topics was to see historiography as an amalgam of erudition and folk-lore; that is to say, 'facts' combine with a picture of those facts, and with their local re-interpretations, to produce our representation of the past. Such amalgamations are particularly evident in the poet Nerval and in the most famous woman writer of the century, George Sand.

The brilliance of Nerval (1808–55) would not be recognized until the twentieth century, when Proust would describe his novella *Sylvie* as a 'masterpiece of French literature'. In both verse and prose, Nerval creates a multilayered chronology and fuses images of the self with figures from myth and local legend. He does so with a delicacy and subtlety apparently far removed from direct political concerns. (Indeed, he adjusted in his sonnet 'Horus' an overt reference to Napoleon's symbol the eagle, changing 'The eagle has already passed, Napoleon calls me' to 'The eagle has already passed, the new spirit calls me'.) But Nerval could not have written *Sylvie* (1853) or the exquisite sonnets of *Les Chimères* (*Chimaeras*, 1854) without the Enlightenment, and without a strange offshoot of the Enlightenment, Illuminism. Illuminism, a current of philosophical and religious thought popular in the late eighteenth century and the Romantic period, proposed that all created being was symbolic of the divine, and that all religious thought-structures express the same truth ('syncretism'); for some adherents, Christianity was a perversion. Illuminism stressed the freedom of Man, at the centre of the great chain of being and charged with the restoration of the lost harmony and unity of the universe. For Nerval himself, it heralded socialism, and shortly before *Sylvie* and *Les Chimères* he published a work called *The Illuminated, or the Precursors of Socialism* (1852), which brought together portraits of the representatives of Illuminism.

Thus Nerval's works too are marked by an egalitarianism that, however idiosyncratically, embraces social structures – and animate, indeed inanimate, matter. (His early poem 'Vers dorés', 'Golden lines', has decidedly 'ecological' overtones.) The more difficult sonnets of *Les Chimères* implicitly enact syncretism by bringing together different belief systems: Nerval's supple constructions suggest that they co-exist on an equal footing, in the mind at least. Thus the narrator of the most famous sonnet in the collection, 'El Desdichado' ('The disinherited one'), asks himself: 'Suis-je Amour ou Phébus? . . . Lusignan ou Biron?' ('Am I Love or Phoebus? . . . Lusignan or Biron?'; Nerval's ellipsis). Here, figures from Latin and Greek myth overlap with two from medieval and local French legend, Lusignan and Biron. This co-existence is not necessarily a peaceful one: it does not lack tensions and internecine struggle, particularly between polytheism and Judaeo-Christian monotheism. In another sonnet, 'Delfica', the narrator deprecates Christianity as 'severe' and expresses a yearning for the return of pagan religions; while in 'Antéros', an angry protagonist engages in a mortal fight against Jehovah. In a century in which Catholicism had once more become the state religion, but in which atheism and anti-clericalism were still strong, this is not without its political charge.

A political charge shapes the tale *Sylvie* too. Here, the narrator becomes suddenly rich as the result of an unexpected stock-market rise in his bonds – reflecting, as in any Balzac novel, the caprices of a powerful capitalist system. However, his new fortune inspires him not to create a luxurious life in Paris, but to return, if only temporarily, to his native Valois region: the Loire area that, as he remarks himself, used to be the locale of the French monarchy, a place where 'for more than a thousand years the heart of France has beaten'. At the same time the narrator evokes – both humorously and wistfully – country customs and festivals; the most ecstatic moment of the novella is the memory of a young woman related to the Valois dynasty singing at one of these festivals: 'we thought we were in paradise'. Thus, Paris is being displaced in favour of a rural region as well as an older 'capital'. This is no mere pastoral idyll but a quiet reminder of the diversity of France during a century when seemingly unstoppable changes were once again imposing 'unity' and threatening to crush the local: among these changes were industrialization and the aftermath of Revolutionary attitudes that had wanted to 'annihilate' patois in order to create a nation-wide French citizenry. (See below, p. 102.)

Nerval shared with George Sand (1804–76) a keen curiosity about folksongs and popular traditions. These two writers are the key speakers on behalf of the regions in nineteenth-century French literature. Sand's interest in the rural has often been misinterpreted. Because three of the best-known works in which she promotes it are short and (deceptively) simple, for years they were deemed books for children (*Devil's Pond*, 1846; *Little Fadette*, 1848; *François le champi*, 1848). And the longer works in which she explores provincial customs and art-forms, such as *The Master Ringers* (1853), tended not to be discussed. It is now, however, beyond dispute that a factor in this relegation (and that of her other works) was misogyny. Although Sand was praised by many prominent French and European writers during her lifetime, and although George Eliot adopted her 'George' as a tribute, she was lampooned and insulted, even becoming a hate-figure for some contemporary male authors, a sort of literary 'Milady'; after her death she was rapidly demoted, and for a century was largely ignored by critics. During the last thirty years she has, however, been rescued – not only by feminist scholars. In the mid-1960s, the critic Georges Lubin began to publish a magisterial edition of her correspondence, which over succeeding decades (and as post-war feminism was reaching its peak) forcibly reminded the late twentieth-century educational establishment of her perspicacity and wit. But besides misogyny, one probable cause of Sand's hasty downgrading was the continuing tension between Paris and the provinces: it was only too easy to dismiss as sugary and outdated works that lovingly depicted rural communities, their story- and music-making. Nerval's and Sand's sympathetic evocations of rural life are, in fact, a counterblast to that much more salient image of 'Paris, capital of the nineteenth century' that the period has bequeathed to us; Sand is here, like others, revaluing the 'lowly', that which could be dismissed as backward and stupid. Still more dangerous for some, at least, were the guilds Sand describes. For *The Companion of the Tour of France* (1840), another of Sand's 'country' novels, depicts not only rural experiences of art and music but also workers' political associations. Like many intelligent women of the period, Sand had socialist and utopian ideals from which her feminism cannot be separated. (Another is Flora Tristan, grandmother of the painter Gauguin, who published her *Workers' Union* in 1843; this proposed a local insurance system for workers to protect them in times of illness. It is likely that Marx read this work; he was based in Paris and studying French socialist thought at the time of its publication.) The leading historian of nineteenth-century French feminism, Claire Goldberg Moses, has indeed argued that the reason for the stop–start development of French feminism in this period – contrasting with the steadier growth of Anglo-American feminism – was that, from the beginning of the century on, it was associated with the Left; hence, when the Left was suppressed, so too was feminism (*French Feminism in the Nineteenth Century*, 1984).

How do these revaluations of life among the proletariat or peasantry – a million cultural miles from the salons – and this new interest in the supposedly 'stupid' fit with that strand running through French culture almost from its beginnings: the foregrounding of wit? Female writers of the time are humorous themselves; many were after all the daughters and grand-daughters of the famously witty *salonnières*. The greatest critic of the century, Sainte-Beuve, said of the writer Sophie Gay (1776–1852) that a whole book could be published called *The Wit of Mme Sophie Gay*. But salons were in decline, and some nineteenth-century women writers even suggest that French men are over-inclined to promote 'wit' and to see nothing beyond it. It had become mere flippancy in Staël's character the Count d'Erfeuil (*Corinne*, 1807); others, later in the century, talk of the incurable French tendency to 'raillery' and ridicule that serves to hinder the serious-minded or the unconfident. (See above, p. 36.) Similar strictures had started to appear in Rousseau. This did not mean that the high valu-ation placed on wit would vanish. But social and conversational sparkle is increasingly enlisted in gender and culture 'wars', and Proust would cast a disparaging eye on salon 'one-liners' early in the following century.

Flaubert's character Emma Bovary is revealing here. No *salonnière*, she is stuck in the provinces, and the last intellectual quality she could be deemed to possess is wit. The wit comes from the narrator. Through his famous 'free indirect style' and his all-pervasive irony, Flaubert simultane-ously conveys Emma's vague thoughts and yearnings and renders them beautiful, implying her stupidity and demonstrating his own artistic control. *Madame Bovary* (1856–7), and Flaubert's other fictional works (*Sentimental Education*, and the later *A Simple Heart*, 1869, 1877) are the apogee of self-conscious cleverness in nineteenth-century prose. Are they, too, part of the 'women-debate', now that of the nineteenth century? Perhaps not, for the hero of *Sentimental Education* is male; one of those unheroic men who were peopling fiction from *René* on, he is as blinkered in his way as Emma and the saintly maidservant of *A Simple Heart* are in theirs. So although feminist critics have detected misogyny in *Madame Bovary*, it is perhaps more fruitful to see this renowned novel as bringing nineteenth-century ambivalences up to the surface and playing with them.

Thus, Flaubert's Emma does have imagination. She dreams scenarios fuelled by her reading of Romantic novels – scenarios of, say, husbands entirely clad in black velvet who know all about equestrianism and pistols. But the scenarios are impossible, the imagination second-hand. Emma is yearning for an upper class that has been glamorized by her and will in any case remain for ever closed to her. At stake here is the stereotyped image. By the time Flaubert wrote *Madame Bovary*, advertisements had been appearing in the press for twenty years, and the engraving and other kinds of print were starting to reach a mass market. Although Flaubert's main focus is the power of fiction to shape desire, he also alludes to the visual. Emma reads fashion magazines (101) and in the miniature of herself that she gives her lover Rodolphe, her eyes are cast sideways, a pose she must have learned from other pictures (one that even the crass Rodolphe judges to be in poor taste, 206). And Emma displays what Marx would soon call 'commodity fetishism': that overspending on fine clothes that contributes to her downfall. The energy Emma undoubtedly possesses is thus devoted almost entirely to the fulfilment of mediated desires. So thoroughly does imitation govern her behaviour that in the end the reader is left wondering what Emma's core desires are, or if she even has a core. Mediated or triangular desire had long been a motif in French literature, and Stendhal had already highlighted the role of reading in its formation; but Flaubert, bringing it centre-stage, for the first time expresses the role of mass (as opposed to popular) culture in individual psychologies – mass culture here comprising both best-selling novels and advertising.

Flaubert also exemplifies the nineteenth-century stress on the 'humble', but differently from Hugo, Nerval and Sand: indeed he incurred the reproaches of Sand for his 'cynicism', and later those of Henry James for depicting characters of mediocre intelligence. This is the nec plus ultra of an interest in the lowly, and it drags the reader into its net too, for like Emma we want something more successful and magnetic from our novels than – Emma.

Yet there is something else going on here. First, Flaubert, in an unusually direct passage, says that just because Emma expresses her innermost feelings by way of the tawdry, through 'the emptiest metaphors', that does not mean she does not feel; and he goes on to identify her with 'us' all:

> for no one, ever, can give the exact measure of their needs, their conceptions, or their sorrows, and . . . human speech is like a cracked cauldron on which we beat out melodies for bears to dance to, when we should like to move the stars to tenderness. (196)

Here, our readiness to latch on to cliché and imperfect images becomes part of the human condition, in no matter what century; but perhaps only the nineteenth century could create a writer who would voice this clumsy adherence to representations so poignantly and forcibly. Second, Flaubert, despite the 'we', *is* promoting art. With every word we read, we know, consciously or unconsciously, that Emma could not have expressed her own thoughts thus. The bourgeois, the provincial, retain their despised dullness yet are in some sense transfigured – as is the medium of prose, no longer the poor cousin of poetry. Indeed, Flaubert, in a letter of 1852, wrote to his mistress Louise Colet that verse had had its day and that now was the time for prose to display its full potential. So art is still capable of being 'noble' and giving 'value', however 'ignoble' or 'valueless' its subject. It is a nobility that has been taken away from the aristocracy, and a value that oddly chimes with, yet is different from, the criteria of the market – chimes, because the market wants prose fiction; different, because this is 'art for art's sake'.

Like Nerval and Sand, Flaubert also chips away at the hierarchy that elevates the urban above the rural. Even if he is depicting a provincial 'désert' that seventeenth-century writers would have recognized, Paris is no better. In the hero of *Sentimental Education*, written at the very end of this period, we find as it were an Emma Bovary with her dreams fulfilled: now she is male, she has money and she is living in the capital. But what we get is Frédéric, the vacillating and inactive protagonist, infatuated with a married woman he does not really want to possess: she too is desired because she is a mediated image and supposedly unattainable. In this novel, which Flaubert intended as the 'moral history' of a generation, the city loses its radiance: capital of the nineteenth century, perhaps, but also a site of mass ransacking, then inhumanity from the regime (for these are the aspects of the 1848 revolution and the 1851 coup d'état that Flaubert foregrounds). The husband of Frédéric's beloved is a vulgar art-dealer – in *this* Paris, art is now a commodity like any other, and there is a descent in the course of the novel from the original work to mechanical reproduction, loathed by Flaubert. The capital is, finally, a symbol of the wandering and confused mind. Frédéric is a *flâneur*, a stroller through the city, but he is either pursuing an ineffectual agenda or is a gawper played upon by circumstance rather than the keen-eyed poet of Baudelaire's urban 'mooching'.

Baudelaire's works are almost exactly contemporaneous with Flaubert's most famous ones. *Madame Bovary* was first published in serial form in 1856, *Les Fleurs du Mal* (*Flowers of Evil*) in 1857, while *Sentimental Education* and Baudelaire's collected prose poems were published in 1869. These prose poems had been appearing individually throughout the 1860s in literary reviews, and inhere in that decade. For these were the main years of the 'Haussmannization' of Paris – the transformation of the capital under Napoleon III that made it the Paris we know today. (Baudelaire composed some of his verse poems too in the early stages of Haussmannization.)

Baron Haussmann was prefect of Paris from 1853 to 1869. He direct-ed the demolition of the overcrowded central quarters of the city and constructed a system of rectilinear boulevards (for example Saint-Michel and Saint-Germain) which for the first time bound the city together as a structural whole. Haussmann widened and straightened the streets in part to prevent the building of barricades and to enable soldiers to quell revolts by spraying protesters with grapeshot; cobblestones were removed to deprive insurgents of ammunition. Other innovations included the radiating circles of the Place de l'Etoile (now Charles de Gaulle); new bridges over the Seine (for example, Alma, Invalides and Solférino); the transformation by landscape gardening of the Bois de Boulogne and the construction of new parks (Monceau and Buttes-Chaumont); and the creation of a modern sewage and water system. New wings were added to the Louvre, and the Halles Centrales – the covered markets – were completely rebuilt. Haussmannization divided Paris into a preponderantly middle- and upperclass west and an overwhelmingly working-class east; ironically, this redistribution of population is thought to have contributed to the insurrectionary Commune of 1871.

Haussmann's reconstruction governs the setting of Baudelaire's verse poem 'Le cygne', 'The swan'. The narrator remembers Paris as it was: 'Le vieux Paris n'est plus (la forme d'une ville / Change plus vite, hélas! Que le cœur d'un mortel)': 'Old Paris is no more. (Ah, truth to tell, / Cities change faster than the human heart!)'. He evokes the heaps of rough-hewn column-capitals, shanties and intermingling bric-à-brac that used to characterize this part of the city, and remembers a menagerie from which a swan had escaped. Trying to find water in dried-up streams, the swan longed for its native lake; and the narrator, once more in the present, returns to the image of a changed city, now still more elegiacally: 'Yes, Paris changes! But my wistful woe / Remains! For me, all becomes metaphor: / Faubourg and palace – old, new – come and go; / Weighty, my memories of what is no more. / / And so, here by the Louvre, my thoughts, obsessed, / Turn to my swan of flailing wing, and who, / Like exiles – lordliest and lowliest – / Yearns with an endless grief'. The narrator recalls other exiles: Andromache; the consumptive black woman missing her native Africa; 'those now and forevermore bereft! / Those who suck Sorrow's teat, she-wolf benign, / Midst showers of tears! Those wizened orphans left, / Like faded flowers, to wither on the vine!' The last words of the poem are: 'I think of seamen, long marooned, forgot; / Castaways, slaves . . . and many more, alas!' (Translation by Norman Shapiro.)

Here, then, neither Paris nor the changes imposed on it are glorious. The capital represents a century overshadowed by mourning and the horror of civil strife. Paris, as it both was and is, painfully evokes loss after battle (in the figure of the widowed Trojan Andromache), as well as father-less orphans – perhaps the generation that lost its 'fathers' during the Terror. It is, too, a place of inhumanity to animals and to the blacks con-quered in France's colonial adventures. 'The swan' is a first example of the complexity of Baudelaire's depiction of Paris and the way he incorporates into it different 'archaeological' and affective layers. No longer just the focus of all 'civilized' French life, here it is equally the historical centre of suffering and a troubled meeting-point of classical and modern, old and vulgarly new.

Baudelaire does evoke much else besides the urban. As the reference to Andromache suggests, Greek and Latin literature infuses this extraordinar-ily dense poetry, as do allusions to a former France and even its transition to a revolutionary phase. One poem, for instance, conjures up the bored king of a rainy country, his bed blazoned with the *fleur-de-lis* of the French monarchy, who cannot be entertained even by the spectacle of his people dying in front of his balcony ('Spleen: Je suis comme le roi d'un pays plu-vieux . . .'). But – at the risk of oversimplifying his work – we can single out Baudelaire as the artist of Paris par excellence. An entire section of the verse collected in *Les Fleurs du Mal* is called 'Parisian Tableaux' (it is in this section that 'The swan' appears), and the title of the prose poems is *The Spleen of Paris*. Flaubert turns the capital into a symbol of both desire and fatuity; Balzac depicts it as a sea or a monster that utterly changes psychol-ogy; but Baudelaire goes still further, and in numerous poems makes the city not only a locus of collective memory but also a metaphor for all perception. In piercing, sardonic, exquisite verse and prose, Baudelaire renders the capital both ugly and lovely, and – more explicitly than any of his contemporaries – links it with a modern beauty. In his critical writings too Baudelaire is the proponent and the prophet of a specifically urban aesthetic, one that can incorporate the accidental meetings and startling incongruities of the large city. Particularly in his essay 'The Painter of Modern Life' (1863), he presents the city as a source of material for the artist among the crowds, a place where there can exist a sort of aesthetic 'democracy': a site that, being man-made, represents art itself (as opposed to 'Nature', which Baudelaire despises – unlike those eighteenth-century thinkers who praised the 'noble savage'). In a letter to his editor prefacing *The Spleen of Paris*, Baudelaire claims that he has created a work that can be 'cut up' howsoever artist, publisher, reader wish; 'take away a vertebra, and the two bits of this tortuous fantasy will join up again with no diffi-culty'. He has wanted, he says, to describe 'modern life, or rather . . . *a modern and more abstract life*' (Baudelaire's italics), and to create the 'miracle' of a poetic prose – musical but 'without rhythm or rhyme, supple and jolting enough to adapt to the lyrical movements of the soul, the undulations of reverie, the sudden shocks of consciousness' (Baudelaire uses the word 'conscience', which in French means both 'consciousness' and 'conscience'). And he then says that this ideal is born 'above all from the frequentation of enormous towns', from the 'criss-cross of their innumerable connections' (6–7).

The 'urban' poet is urban or urbane as much in his attitude as in what he describes: ironic, off-hand, even self-deprecating. For the contradictions of the poet's relationship with his society also reach a climax in Baudelaire. The poet is like a city street-performer, a mountebank, an old clown. He is there to provide *entertainment* in a public space. This picture both mockingly echoes a centuries-old view of art (now a bourgeois one) and simultaneously reinforces the pride of the artist. Nineteenth-century society may judge his art to be a sideshow; it is indeed a fabrication, in some sense a 'fraud'; but it alone in the cityscape creates meaning, pleasure and beauty.

Baudelaire's aesthetic marks the transition from the Romantic to a radically new poetic stance, and his influence on subsequent poets both inside and outside France has been immense. (Among foreign poets who took a lead from Baudelaire were Swinburne, Rilke, T. S. Eliot and Wallace Stevens.) Paris was already the hub of European art; Baudelaire's vision made it stand for post-Revolutionary creativity in all its contradictions. It is Baudelaire who inspired that famous phrase of Walter Benjamin's: 'Paris, capital of the nineteenth century'. Here, then, is the apogee of French 'centralization' and cultural prestige, with its excitements and ambitions held in an equivocal balance with its self-confessed failures. Baudelaire, the maker of modern European poetry, could have existed only in France and more specifically in Paris – Paris both ancient and 'reformed'.

He could also have existed only in a France that was succumbing to the lure of exotic goods and to Orientalism. Many of Baudelaire's most luscious poems summon up foreign trade, Eastern goods; these sit side by side with the ordinary accoutrements of the bourgeois home, as in 'Le Flacon', 'The flask': an old flask that still emits its evocative perfume is as likely to be found in a 'casket from the Orient' as in a dusty black wardrobe. 'La Chevelure', 'Tresses', turns the beloved's hair into an 'aromatic forest' in which live 'languorous Asia and burning Africa'; the narrator smells coconut oil, and will sow rubies, pearls and sapphires in her 'mane' (the word used, 'crinière', can mean a lion's as well as a horse's mane). Commerce plays, indeed, a surprisingly large part in Baudelaire's imagery. Both the verse and prose versions of his 'L'invitation au voyage' ('Invitation to a journey') evoke a mist-covered land of rare flowers and sleek bourgeois prosperity; in the prose version, this land is more obviously Holland. Holland – specifically Rotterdam, long one of the greatest ports in the world – was the European centre for sea trade from the Far East. It was also the home of flower speculation: the narrator tells the beloved that 'the alchemists of horticulture' may search as long as they like, may propose prices of sixty or a hundred thousand florins 'to find someone who can resolve their ambitious problems! As for me, I've found my *black tulip* and my *blue dahlia!*' (Baudelaire's italics). Capitalism, as we have seen, flourished later in France than in those other successful imperialist powers Britain and – precisely – Holland. In order to maintain its affluence, and to bolster the consumerism essential to its mushrooming economy, France had to conquer far-off countries. A self-serving middle-class passion for the Oriental, both naive and greedy, gave impetus to business at the same time as it allowed creative writers to bathe their subjects in Eastern mystery. In the most complex authors, celebration of these strange riches often co-exists with irony directed at the incursions of the imagination into 'foreign parts'.

Between 1830 and 1870, then, poetry began to reach for a new ambiguity, while the novel was perched on the one hand between a high point of prose achievement, and on the other the demands of the market. What, meanwhile, was going on in that other supremely popular art-form, the theatre? Here we must look a little more closely at the history of censorship in this period. Under the July Monarchy (1830–48) very few cases were brought for infringement of the censorship laws; only about four a year (for non-periodical and non-theatrical publications) were heard between 1835 and 1847. But once Napoleon III was in power and consolidating an oppressive administration, republicans were again silenced; offenders against the censorship laws were deprived of the right to trial by jury. It was under Napoleon III that the heavy hand of the censor fell on *Madame Bovary* and *Les Fleurs du Mal*, prosecuted in 1856 and 1857 respectively for supposed immorality. That of *Madame Bovary* was thought to lie in the erotic nature of its heroine's religious devotion, while *Les Fleurs du Mal* was deemed to show an obscene and irreligious 'realism' (involving, for instance, lesbianism, sadism and blasphemy). The key issues judged subversive by the regime were, then, female desire, unorthodox sexuality and attacks on religion. But the strength of resistance can be seen in the acquittal of Flaubert and the relative leniency of the treatment of Baudelaire (ordered to remove only a few offending poems and pay a small fine).

Theatre, however, was feared by the authorities more than other literature, hence subjected to more censorship. As a collective, public experience,
it could be seen as a potentially direct and immediate incitement to sedition. For example, the July Revolution was followed by a torrent of plays,
banned under the previous regime, that glorified Napoleon, attacked the
Church and breached accepted standards of morality. The government
then took to banning plays after they had been put on stage – as we have
seen, for instance, with Hugo's *Le Roi s'amuse* in 1832. All Hugo's protests
were in vain. (The play would not have its second performance at the
Comédie-Française until fifty years later, that is, not until monarchy had
disappeared for ever from the French constitution.) And in 1835 theatre
censorship was officially brought back. Briefly suspended after the 1848
Revolution, it was re-established in 1850, and for the next twenty years
the censors would be extremely vigilant. They insisted on numerous and
diverse changes to plays that were eventually performed, and banned others
completely. (For example, a proposal in 1864 to put on Musset's *Lorenzaccio*
of 1834 came to nothing: this drama revolved around the Florentine hero's
murder of a tyrant duke.) Even supporters of the regime like the playwright
Augier encountered difficulties over supposedly immoral characters and
situations.

In principle, the regime's anxiety was not misplaced. Theatre audiences
were growing and to some extent becoming more democratic, in part
because of the extension of state education. The rising commercial and
manufacturing class looked to the stage to provide distraction from its
humdrum life while reflecting its concerns about money, property and
social mobility. From the Second Empire onwards, the railways brought
provincial visitors and foreign tourists to Paris, swelling the theatre-going
public and the demand for spicy entertainment; Haussmannization led to
a boom in theatre building (for example Châtelet, 1862); and the constant
demand for new plays led to hundreds of co-authored comedies, farces and
vaudevilles, some of which might in theory have had the potential to be
inflammatory.

But in practice the authorities had little to fear. Whether consciously or
unconsciously, dramatists generally toed the political and cultural line.
These decades were not a high point for French theatre, which – despite
some bold experimentation late in the century – would not recover fully
until the 1950s: then the Theatre of the Absurd would once more put
French drama on the world map. Nevertheless, these nineteenth-century
plays are often skilful, catering to the taste for neat, almost 'symmetrical',
structures that are in evidence from very early on in French writing (and

that were seen in, for example, the eighteenth-century Marivaux's plays); thus Scribe, a dominant dramatist of the period, was acclaimed for his 'well-made' plays. It is this mid-nineteenth century that exported to England and other countries the 'French farce', which moved away from the vulgar comedy of its predecessors in response to the new bourgeoisie's aspirations to respectability. Theatre did, however, retain some power to tease conventional attitudes, as we see from the other main dramatist of the time, Labiche, who (with collaborators) wrote more than 170 plays between 1837 and 1877. Labiche's earliest comedies reflect the improvisatory techniques of popular vaudeville, but his later farces are both better-plotted and pay more attention to contemporary mindsets; they poke fun at middle-class attitudes to wealth, possessions and marriage – even, sometimes, at benighted attitudes to women. (Women themselves, as we know from memoirs, contributed to play-writing too: many of them will remain forever anonymous, since association with any aspect of theatrical production was still considered disreputable for females; but Delphine de Girardin, wife of the press baron Emile de Girardin, was a well-known dramatist of these decades, and a few others, overcoming strong social pressures, staged plays in their own names.)

The multitude of plays written by Labiche and others once more demonstrates the overwhelming liking for amusement and wit that marks French culture. Where there is mockery, this can feed into a certain complacency (as with the appreciation of parody): 'We are so sophisticated that we can laugh at ourselves'. (See above, p. 57.) Numerically, comedies far eclipsed high-minded plays, and by the mid-century Romantic drama was in decline. Thus one of the most successful theatres in this period was the Théâtre des Variétés, which specialized mainly in vaudevilles; the Théâtre des Bouffes-Parisiens also enjoyed great popularity with the light-hearted operettas of Meilhac and Halévy, set to the music of Offenbach (for example *La Belle Hélène*, 1864). Certainly, some serious plays (and operas) could find favour. Augier wrote 'bourgeois' drama which, if not in the vein that Diderot had hoped for, did raise sometimes disturbing questions about rank and – say – money-marriages. Dumas *fils*, the illegitimate son of Alexandre Dumas, wrote *The Lady with the Camelias* (first performed 1852), which implicitly criticized society's attitudes to prostitution; it would provide the plot of Verdi's *La Traviata* (1853) and in the twentieth century that of many films, the most famous being Greta Garbo's *Camille* (1936). And French opera itself flourished in this period (Berlioz and Bizet are the most famous names) – indeed composers of all nationalities vied to have works performed at the Paris Opéra, Paris being for most of the century the musical as well as the literary and artistic centre of Europe.

But the theatre market itself was dominated by clever, safely flippant, plays. And an incentive to keep on the right side of the regime lay in the fact that substantial financial rewards came from writing for the theatre, not just because of its popularity but also, paradoxically, because in 1829 a prototype trade union had been formed by and for dramatists, the Society of Dramatic Authors and Composers. It was to prove a much tougher guild than the equivalent one for non-dramatic authors (the Writers' Society ['gens de lettres']). In theory it should have been able to protect playwrights who courted controversy, but to guard its members' financial interests it exercised iron control over them and their output. It exercised the same control over theatre managements, forcing them to 'pay out'; so risk-averse managers tended to opt for plays by established writers that they knew would be successful. Thus, thanks to their Society playwrights were in a strong financial position, but the Society's efforts, combined with the nervousness of managers and of the regime, led drama – that public form par excellence – into stagnation. From 1830 to 1870, it was fiction, poetry and aesthetic criticism, rather than the theatre, that offered genuinely provocative and multifaceted insights into the culture.

5

Republic, Reaction and the Murder of Taste (1870–1913)

Seemingly, many nineteenth-century writers believed that a burgeoning mass culture must militate against an equivalent blossoming of 'high' art. Yet the four decades from 1830 to 1870 had seen an almost unparalleled concentration of French works now judged canonical. That forty-year period is comparable only to the still more extraordinary twenty years which, two centuries earlier, produced so many masterpieces of French classical literature. We might conclude that the wide dissemination of popular art-forms may well also contribute to elite culture and that, if this seems to be suffering momentary lapses or dilution, adverse factors other than the market are coming into play. This question arises here, for the four decades from 1870 on would be somewhat less fertile. The figures who stand out for today's literary establishment are Rimbaud, Zola and Mallarmé. Rimbaud and Zola are internationally renowned, and their impact on European literature still resonates in the twenty-first century, but it is perhaps only Mallarmé whom traditional critics now single out from these decades as a genius comparable to such immediate predecessors as Stendhal, Balzac, Baudelaire and Flaubert.

This is not to over-generalize about the period. Numerous writers were experimenting between 1870 and 1913, and Claudel and Gide, for instance, were setting the tone for bold cultural moves. The young Proust and Valéry were finding their feet; and this was a time of extraordinary vitality in the visual arts. But the period started, at least, with a political instability more traumatic than anything in the nation's history since the Terror and Napoleon's defeat at Waterloo in 1815. For this last third of the nineteenth century began with two major political disasters: the Franco-Prussian War and the crushing of the Paris Commune. Napoleon III foolishly declared war on Prussia in the summer of 1870 (the official excuses were a dispute over the candidate for the Spanish throne and a diplomatic snub). France suffered a series of humiliating defeats, and Napoleon III himself was captured at Sedan on 2 September. Two days later, a republic was declared in Paris, but Prussia then besieged the city until January 1871. Parisians endured horrific hardships until the French capitulated. The government that was then established negotiated with Prussia, and in the Treaty of Frankfurt (May 1871) France agreed to pay a heavy indemnity to Prussia and to give up large parts of two coal-rich provinces, Alsace and Lorraine. (Although France recovered them through the 1919 Treaty of Versailles, these areas are still effectively bilingual.) The defeat would have lasting repercussions, not least an anxiety about German technological and demographic superiority that would affect the cultural sphere too, as we shall see.

Meanwhile, the siege of Paris had a long-lasting political impact even once the capital was relieved: the sufferings Parisians had undergone, combined with financial demands made on them by the new government, led in March 1871 to the uprising known as the Commune de Paris. The government and many wealthy Parisians left the city: thus the Commune was essentially a proletarian insurrection that became a counter-government. Its leadership was collective, and its actions were a blend of the immediate (aimed at relieving hardship, such as free redemptions from pawnshops) and of far-reaching policies, for example the introduction of free, compulsory, secular schooling, bans on night work, and the co-operative takeover of abandoned businesses. Similar insurrections elsewhere (in Marseille, for instance) took their lead from the Paris Commune; and it inspired the song that would become the anthem of international socialism, 'The Internationale', whose words were written by the working-class politician and Communard Pottier and set to music by another Frenchman, Degeyter, in 1888. (The song would also become the national anthem of the Soviet Union until 1944.) But the Commune was soon destroyed by Thiers, the first President of the Third Republic. Thiers, who fondly considered himself a military genius, had hatched his plan for subduing a potentially rebellious Paris back in 1848, and relished the chance to put it into action. He asked the Prussians to release a number of prisoners-of-war so that they could be used to help crush the Commune. The repression killed more people than had the Terror: 20,000. Unarmed civilians, women and children were shot dead. 50,000 additional Communard suspects were tried; many were sent to the penal islands off French Guiana; thousands of others fled into exile. The name of Thiers is still anathema to Parisians today.

A republican constitution was not finalized until 1875, and then by a majority of one. It was only the rivalry between competing Royalist factions that forestalled a monarchist majority. This Third Republic would go through many crises (including attempted right-wing coups in 1877 and

1889), but the centralized administrative system would remain in place and the Republic would survive until the fall of France in 1940. Its success is demonstrated by the fact that the idea of France as a republic is now firmly entrenched in the minds of most French people. Indeed, this image of 'republican France' has been central to Pierre Nora's recent analysis of the contemporary nation's identity. (Between 1984 and 1992, Nora edited a path-breaking series of essays by historians and cultural commentators called *Les Lieux de mémoire, Sites of Memory*.) Many symbols of France that we now take for granted were launched under the Third Republic. The Eiffel Tower, for example, was constructed in 1889 to commemorate the centenary of the 1789 Revolution. Ironically, it was the centrepiece of an international trade show – the opposite of Revolutionary ideals. But many succeeding painters and writers (for example, Robert Delaunay and Apollinaire) would figure the Eiffel Tower as a symbol of modernity, a modernity which in France is thus inextricably linked with the honouring of both Revolution and Republic. Other symbols of France adopted by the Third Republic were the Marseillaise as an anthem; the tricolour flag; the motto *Liberté, Egalité, Fraternité*; and the busts of 'Marianne' still to be seen outside many town halls. Marianne is the female personification of the Republic, and anti-republicans have often referred to her as 'la gueuse', 'whore'. She originally bore a resemblance to Liberty in the painter Delacroix's *Liberty Leading the People* (1830), but feminists have been dismayed by her successive incarnations as Brigitte Bardot and Catherine Deneuve. This renewal of Marianne is scarcely to be interpreted as a gesture of defiance to the right wing; it more likely testifies to the persisting high valuation of 'sexiness' in French culture, although the most recent face, that of the chat-show host Evelyne Thomas, is perhaps (on the most optimistic reading) a sign of a greater interest in personality.

The Third Republic established that the President was to be a symbol of national unity while real power lay with the National Assembly; it would usher in other profound changes, re-establishing the manhood suffrage laws first brought in briefly in 1849, allowing women to advance in important spheres, and extending education. Since Germany's victory in 1870–71 was attributed to intellectual and scientific superiority, German universities became the model for reform of the French higher education system. Provincial faculties were developed, partly in response to the needs of local industry; scientific research institutions were founded; and both arts and science faculties expanded to bring in large numbers of full-time students – among them, at last, women. *Lycées* (grammar schools) were created for girls in 1880, though the curricula for boys and girls would follow divergent syllabuses until the 1920s. The 'Ferry Laws' of 1881 and 1882 (named after the statesman who introduced them) made primary education free and compulsory. Here Ferry was in effect filling gaps in an already steadily expanding system. His laws sprang too from the republican belief, evident in reforms earlier in the century, that education could and would not only spread social progress but also build the nation: schools would continue to break down local loyalties and form French citizens. This programme still, remarkably, involved France's language. Dialects and patois had proved tenacious, testifying to an irrepressible desire for regional autonomy. Before the Revolution, only a quarter of residents of France spoke standard French as their first language. Revolutionaries, as well as earlier rulers, had considered that a single language would help achieve their political ideals: the violently emphatic title of one report submitted five years after the Revolution was significant: *On the need and means to annihilate* ['anéantir'] *different kinds of patois and make the use of French universal.* The author of this 1794 report, Henri Grégoire, a notable advocate of the rights of Jews and blacks, saw the measure as a path to democracy. Other motives came into play too: twenty-five years of military conscription under the Revolution and Napoleon had gathered young men from all corners of the country and obliged them to learn basic French so that they could understand and communicate orders. Now, like Grégoire, Ferry had democratic ideals in mind. He banned the unofficial languages of France from public documents and schools and made their use punishable. Thus did linguistic centralization continue to make its mark.

One of Ferry's achievements was to put Third Republic education on a solid financial footing; another, perhaps the truly novel one, was the enforcement of state neutrality in religious matters (*laïcité*). Education must henceforth be secular. From the 1840s on, the Catholic Church's hold on education had been steadily expanding, a development that had been deprecated by republicans even before the Third Republic: in 1850, the Loi Falloux had given the Church the power to supervise primary school education, and from the early 1870s a number of new Catholic educational institutions were founded, appealing to the nobility and to right-wing bourgeois. Republicans reacted with alarm, perceiving these as dangerous; indeed, one of the difficulties besetting the Third Republic would be a wider struggle between the Church's view of the State and the secular perspective. Thus, anti-clericalism was a linchpin of republican educational policy. Civic instruction replaced religious, and state school teachers had to be lay people. This emphasis on non-religious education was backed by the ever-growing understanding of advances in science. Catholics, for their part, denounced the 'atheist' schools and built up their own. But in 1904, a law was passed against education by religious bodies, and when, in 1905, the Loi Falloux was repealed and the Church was disestablished, priests' salaries dropped by half. In the heated political atmosphere after the Dreyfus Affair (see below), republicans attempted to eliminate even private Catholic schools. This state–Church – or 'ordinary citizen' versus clergy – conflict was not new. It had been represented in medieval and sixteenth-century literature, and more recently, on the nineteenth-century educational battleground, it had been echoed in Flaubert's clerics, who struggle to instil religious learning into classes of communicants. In both *Madame Bovary* and *A Simple Heart*, Flaubert slyly showed groups of children repeating the catechism like parrots, 'taught' – in *Madame Bovary* at least – by a priest whose intelligence is as limited as his spirituality. But the combat reached a new pitch of intensity in the early decades of the Third Republic. Only fervent believers remained attached to the Church, this 'hard core' preparing the way for a Catholic revival during the first half of the twentieth century. (Religious adherence and practice have once more declined since then.)

The political upheaval of this period that would become, lastingly, its most notorious one was the Dreyfus Affair (1894–1906). This gave existing Right–Left divisions schismatic proportions. Captain Alfred Dreyfus was a Jewish officer serving with French Military Intelligence. In 1894 he was found guilty of spying for the Germans and sentenced to life imprisonment on Devil's Island, one of France's harshest penal colonies. Over the next few years, the discovery of new evidence led many to realize that a shocking miscarriage of justice had occurred. The real culprit was identified in 1896 – a French Army major named Esterhazy. But he was acquitted in 1898; French counter-intelligence officers fabricated false documents designed to secure Dreyfus's conviction for treason. Zola's article 'J'accuse' of 1898 was a turning-point, leading to Dreyfus's retrial in 1899. However, he was again found guilty. By now, the choice was between him and the Army's honour, which – anti-Dreyfusards argued – must be protected even if Dreyfus was innocent. This vile line of reasoning (*la raison d'Etat*) held that because the state was more important than the individual, it was morally justifiable, even mandatory, to sacrifice an innocent person rather than admit that government prosecutors had erred (as with Guantanamo). Dreyfus was in due course 'pardoned', but not fully exonerated until 1906. (He re-enlisted in the army, fought for France in the First World War, and was awarded a medal for bravery in combat.)

Beyond the immediate and proven case of Army corruption and establishment wrong-doing, the Affair became a significant social symbol. It
was not just *raison d'Etat* that prolonged it. At this time anti-Semitism
was part of the glue that held together the Faubourg Saint-Germain (that
is, an aristocracy that by now lacked any real power). Those adhering
to caste-inspired notions of nobility were inclined to want to believe
in Dreyfus's guilt because he was a Jew. There were honourable excep-
tions. (Proust would later give a change of heart to his fictional characters the Prince and Princesse de Guermantes, who independently of
each other become convinced of Dreyfus's innocence.) And religious
affiliations themselves did not always dictate allegiances: among pro-
Dreyfusards were the Catholic poet Péguy, among anti-Dreyfusards
were the atheist poet Valéry. (Other pro-Dreyfusards apart from Zola
himself included the young Proust; other anti-Dreyfusards were the
Catholic poet Claudel, the right-wing novelist Barrès, and the cartoonists
Forain and Caran d'Ache.) But generally speaking the Affair was used by
the right wing to attack Jews, freemasons, Protestants and republicans,
while pro-Dreyfusards passionately clung to Enlightenment ideals of
justice, tolerance and transparency. The Affair contributed to the formation of the right-wing party Action Française in 1899, and to those of the
moderate left Radical Party (1901) as well as the Socialist Party shortly
after (1905).

All these events figured in French literature; and arguably the cruelties
of the Franco-Prussian War and of the Commune's destruction marked
the very tenor of imaginative writing – more profoundly than had the
1830 and 1848 revolutions, more obviously than had the Terror with its
(relatively) oblique after-effects such as melancholia in literary heroes.
The Commune was chronicled and 'fictionalized' by a number of writers,
for example by Vallès (1832–85), a left-wing journalist and newspaper
editor who in semi-autobiographical novels combined satire, sensationalist
comedy and disturbing pictures of a hand-to-mouth existence. In *The Insur-
gent* (posthumous, 1886) the hero first resists the absurd patriotism of the
Franco-Prussian war, then becomes involved in the Commune. Vallès was
sentenced to death after the Commune but escaped to England, where he
remained for nine years. Also punished, by deportation to New Caledonia,
was one of the Republic's most striking female writers, the radical Louise
Michel (1830–1905), who in her memoirs describes the bloodbath of the
Commune's suppression. The ideals of the Commune mark the poetry of
Rimbaud (he is thought to have visited it briefly): in both verse and prose
poems, he expresses sympathy for the poverty-stricken (in, for example,

'Les pauvres à l'église', 'The poor in church'), and he sometimes evokes hopeful and implicitly egalitarian futures.

Maupassant (1850–93), one of Europe's greatest short-story writers, participated in the Franco-Prussian War, and it forms the setting for a number of his tales, for instance *Boule de suif* and *La Mère Sauvage* (*Ball of Lard, A Savage Mother/Mother Sauvage*). The mother of this latter story – called 'la mère Sauvage', hence the double meaning of the title – is billeting four young Prussian soldiers, treating them with almost maternal care, 'for,' says Maupassant, 'peasants do not really entertain patriotic hatreds; that is only for the upper classes' (106). The soldiers in exchange do her filial good turns. But she receives news that her son has died at the front. She sets fire to her house, having ensured the young men cannot escape, and in reprisal is shot by their Prussian colleagues. The title of the tale suggests that war returns 'naturally' kindly women to a primitive state when their sons' lives are at stake. Maupassant is, to be sure, exploiting stereotypes of womanhood, but he does so in order to create narrative shock. He is generally deemed the master of that sting in the tail characteristic of good short stories; in his tales, the final volte-face is frequently inseparable from a sudden sense of 'the pity of it all'. It may be the pity of war, or, say, the pity of a wasted life, of human cruelty to animals. Maupassant's short-story structure is complex, then: his abrupt reversals rely on a stab that is part pleasure, part discomfort; part piquancy, part – precisely – sting. It is significant that this form reached a peak of mastery in an author writing shortly after the violence of the early 1870s.

Violence is also more evident than utopianism in the works of Rimbaud (1854–91), the young prodigy who in his late teens (mainly 1870 to 1872) composed a body of extraordinarily original verse and prose poems. He can be credited with the invention of free verse in the early 1870s (with the poems 'Marine' and 'Mouvement'.) Rimbaud's background was relatively humble (by comparison with earlier nineteenth-century poets, many of whose names carry the noble particle *de* – Alphonse de Lamartine, Alfred de Vigny, and so on). The Prussian invasion of 1870 disrupted local life; Rimbaud repeatedly ran away from home, and in September 1871 embarked on a stormy erotic relationship with his older fellow-poet Verlaine (1844–96). Rimbaud was an innovator in so many respects that it could appear crude to focus on hypothetical links between the immediate historical context and his iconoclasm. This iconoclasm springs at least in part from the energy and frustration of a brilliant adolescent who sees through social and cultural hypocrisy, and from a powerful personal vision of a divided self. And the iconoclasm can also be seen as not so much a response to 1870s France, more as a theatrical summum of aesthetic developments that had started three generations earlier, with Hugo's recommendations to mix sublime and grotesque. Thus Rimbaud gives Venus an 'ulcer on her anus' (in 'Vénus anadyomène', 'Venus rising from the sea'); he mockingly chides poets for their overuse of lilies and other flowers; he attacks elderly bourgeois men (decrepit patriarchs); he evokes slobber and vomit in beautifully written verse; and in famous letters he claims that 'a long, immense and reasoned derangement of all the senses' will allow the poet to become a visionary and to understand that '"I" is another' ('JE est un autre': Rimbaud's capitals). All this may, on a conservative view, be interpreted as a re-statement of a crucial nineteenth-century literary evolution, expressed now with the vehemence of the adolescent. But the impatience and raw feelingness enable Rimbaud to take forward the evolution with a new shockingness that does chime with the period. One of his earliest and still most popular poems (because 'easier' than the rest) is 'Le dormeur du val', 'Sleeper in the vale', which portrays a soldier lying peacefully in the grass – the surprise (as with Maupassant) comes at the very end: 'He has two red holes in his right side'. Words like 'bleeding' recur, and the narrator of one of his obscure prose poems, the *Illuminations*, declares: 'I alone have the key to this savage parade' ('Parade'). The French word 'sauvage', which Rimbaud uses here (like Maupassant in the short story just mentioned), can mean both 'wild' and 'barbaric'. The ambiguity works well for the poetry of a writer who presents himself as an 'untamed' being endowed with insights into the cruelty of his society. He enters another world whose main link to the conventional one is language itself; to gain this entry, he must kill off 'taste'.

It must be killed also by Zola (1840–1902). Highly influential both in France and abroad, Zola was at first scorned by the literary establishment, for, like Rimbaud's, his iconoclasm is more overt and confrontational than that of pre-1870 writers. Yet he too has predecessors: his overarching idea of writing the history of a Second-Empire family in a many-volumed group of novels – an inspired marriage of fiction and chronicle not seen since the Middle Ages – was unlikely to have come to him without Balzac. Balzac had grouped his own fiction under the heading of *The Human Comedy*, had woven it together with recurring characters, and had declared his aim to be the 'secretary' of his society and to write the 'history of customs' ('history from below'). Now Zola creates the *Rougon-Macquart* series (1871–93). The Rougons are the upper-class side of the family, the Macquarts produce the bourgeois and proletarian characters. This was a 'roman-fleuve' ('river-novel'), a form that would become ever more popular in the early-to-mid twentieth century: it ambitiously bound the fortunes of individuals or families to changes in society. The 'river-novel' would appear in England too, for example Galsworthy's *Forsyte Saga* (1906–21), but it found a particularly congenial home in France.

Another of Zola's claims to innovation was his proposal for 'scientific' fiction (set out most plainly in his essay *The Experimental Novel*, 1880). Here he was influenced by the critic and historian Taine and his deterministic formula of 'la race [heredity], le milieu [social setting], et le moment'. But experimental science was the chief model. Zola's main premise was that the novel could be scientific because it would examine the workings of environment and heredity on characters. They would be placed in an as it were fictional 'laboratory' by a writer who would then sit back and watch the results. And Zola's own practice involved the painstaking gathering of documentation as part of the process of drafting his works. However, arguably none of these aspects of Zola's work or even theory is 'scientific'. The idea that man is shaped by his environment dates back at the least to Montesquieu in the eighteenth century. Both Balzac and Stendhal, as we have seen, were revolutionary precisely in their incorporation of social conditions into their characters' thoughts and intimate feelings; Zola's 'Naturalism' is not so distinguishable from their 'Realism', their stress on historical causality. Furthermore, Zola asserts at one point in *The Experimental Novel* that to understand the impact of people's surroundings will 'in the end resolve all the problems of socialism' (76): he himself therefore clearly sees this as an enterprise belonging to political inquiry and to what we now call the *social* sciences. Similarly, his documentation is more akin to the sociologist's investigations than to those of a scientist working in laboratory conditions. As for heredity, Zola uses this as and when it suits his aesthetic purposes, invoking it at moments to create a sense of inevitability and doom (as with the Macquarts' tendency to alcoholism), but elsewhere seemingly forgetting about it. Heredity becomes an expedient tragic mechanism not very different from the curse of the House of Atreus.

What Zola's credo therefore testifies to is less the potential of the novel to be scientific than the power of the image of science during this period. Positivism, with its emphasis on political evolution and on empirical science, was adopted as the 'philosophy' of the Third Republic. (It had been launched by the thinker Comte in his *Cours de philosophie positive, Course in Positive Philosophy*, 1830–42, but its stress on the verifiable would not gain widespread acceptance until this last third of the century.) In recent years, scholars have, in the wake of Foucault, studied the unfortunate use of so-called science in this period to incarcerate 'misfits' thought to be 'undesirable elements'. But the heightened prestige of science also fed into the democratic ideal of an 'objective' pool of knowledge that should be available to all. (It is part of Louise Michel's sense of herself as a 'new woman' that she attends lectures on biology, even if she is horrified by the vivisection that she there witnesses.) As we have seen, the respect accorded to science also bolstered the anti-clericalism that entered into the post-1870 restructuring of education. Thus Zola's project became that of a Third-Republic citizen; further, to claim that the novel could be scientific was to remove art from the arena of the religious: it had never been entirely free from this since Chateaubriand's *Spirit of Christianity* of 1802 and the Romantics' figuring of the artist as a semi-divine creator.

Scientific inquiry and a stress on the 'natural' were, too, part of the Impressionists' enterprise. They flourished between 1872 and 1886 but their impact was much longer-lasting. Not only did the Impressionists take painting out into the open air and away from studio settings of 'classical' subjects, they also used the latest scientific discoveries about colour to inform their techniques. (Cubists, similarly, would borrow another science, that of geometry, to innovate.) Zola championed the Impressionists – a stand it is easy to overlook in the face of his earthy descriptions of farting and dirty linen, which can seem leagues away from the delicate stippling and pastel shades of a Monet. He did not fully understand all the concepts behind the Impressionists' practice, but he saw that they were breaking with a notion of 'suitable' presentation, and in some choices he and they converge – for the Impressionists are as likely to paint 'humble' objects like haystacks, rainy city streets and bundles of asparagus as Rouen Cathedral. (And when Monet does paint Rouen Cathedral, that is more to suggest how it varies in different lights and from different angles than to celebrate it as an unchanging model of architectural beauty.)

The continuing drive to represent and transfigure the lowly lies behind Zola's most important technical innovation: his adaptation of free indirect style (the form of reported thought or speech that Flaubert had used to express clichéd imaginings). Zola now merges slang and vulgar formulations with the more dignified register and compassionate tone of the narrator, thus enacting afresh Hugo's recommendations. Also innovative is Zola's portrayal of crowds and communities, which creates an epic sense of 'masses' – even masses on the move. His novels are in this sense truly political. They can sometimes seem to be demoting the individual, the 'rounded' character, but with hindsight this too can be hailed as a pioneering attempt to incorporate into literature the politics of the collective, and as an important step down the road which would lead to Brecht's 'alienation' effect. Still more radical are his plots. The violence Zola depicts in such works as *Germinal* (1885), a novel about a miners' strike, is in one light part of the greater post-1870 willingness to depict physical cruelty. But he brings something quite different too. He is important as the first major French novelist to figure conflict between labour and management: *Germinal* stages an industrial proletariat. The title *Germinal* itself, referring to the Revolutionary calendar and expressing too a picture of new growth, could have occurred perhaps only to a novelist of Zola's courage who was writing after the Commune and in a freer political ambiance than any so far seen in France.

Earning a huge income from his sales, Zola can be difficult to pigeonhole socially: some of his attitudes both to fellow-writers and to the working class align him with the affluent bourgeoisie, and traces of this show in his fiction. But he was also admirably independent-minded: he set the example for the emergence of the modern public 'intellectual' who is unafraid to speak out on political issues, and himself helped to create the same liberal awareness that he then reflects in his works. Zola is an outstanding example of mutual imbrication, indeed symbiosis, between the creative individual and the culture that surrounds him.

Violence and vulgarity find other ways into French literature in these decades. One straw in the wind is the tenor of Feydeau's farces, which dominated 1890s theatre. The farces of the earlier Labiche evoked a relatively tolerant, 'ordinary' world; across the Channel, English Victorian farces of this later period have a comfortable geniality; but Feydeau's world is far less cosy: it is cruel and frenetic. In other writers, assaults on linguistic seemliness are accompanied by images of killing. Eloquence, a plank of young French gentlemen's education for centuries, is dispatched – in recommendation at least – by Verlaine thus: 'Take eloquence and wring its neck!' ('Art poétique', in *Jadis et naguère*, 1884). The opening word of Jarry's play *Ubu Roi* is 'Merdre!', a combination of 'meurtre' ('murder') and 'merde' ('shit'). Jarry (1873–1907) was still at school when he wrote it (it was first performed as a puppet play in 1888), but like the works of the young Rimbaud it was destined to have an extraordinary afterlife, in fact to launch the revivification of French theatre. Its stage premiere in 1896 caused an uproar, not perhaps comparable to that surrounding Hugo's *Hernani* in 1830, but still provoking members of the audience to walk out. Both its subject-matter and its style were outrageous. Ubu, the hero of the play, is a tyrant obsessed with power and money who orders arbitrary executions: the play, though not directly historical, has uncomfortable political insights at its heart. As for the style, the opening 'Merdre' was not the only respect in which the play's language offended. Its characters have names like 'Bou-grelas' and 'Bordure', the former suggesting the word 'bougre' (weaker than the English 'bugger' but still impolite), and the latter combining 'ordure' with 'bords', 'boundaries' – boundaries are being crossed. The seventeenth-century La Bruyère's strictures against the tastelessness of two sixteenth-century predecessors use the word 'ordure': Marot and Rabelais are 'inexcusables d'avoir semé l'*ordure* dans leurs écrits'(82; my italics): 'inexcusable for having sown filth in their writings'. These late nineteenth-century attacks constitute a newly ostentatious murder of that persistent class concept, 'le goût'. (See above, p. 65.)

For even now the French liking for refinement, and for acknowledge-ment of the culture, were not so easy to dislodge. Jarry himself plays knowingly with echoes of past French writers, including Racine. From 1893 on, the theatre director Lugné-Poë developed anti-naturalistic tech-niques not to shock but in order to heighten 'suggestiveness' in drama. And the Belgian poet, dramatist and essayist Maeterlinck (1862–1949) pub-lished plays in the 1890s that were, like *Ubu*, originally puppet-plays but – unlike it – create static, dream-like 'dramas of inaction'; if they break with prevailing theatrical conventions, they preserve a certain delicacy. The most famous of these was *Pelléas et Mélisande* (1893). Maeterlinck, more acceptable than Jarry, was widely recognized at the time as an inno-vator: his *Pelléas* was turned into an opera by Debussy in 1902 and he was awarded the Nobel Prize for Literature in 1911.

This period was, indeed, as interested in the elaborate as in the cruel, and some critics have brought these together in the link between 'torture' and the 'tortuous' appearance of such overtly decorative forms as *art nouveau*, which peaked in popularity between 1880 and 1914. (Its most public manifestations are the entrances to the Paris metro, designed by Guimard in 1899 and 1900.) Convolutions, writhing, could represent a form of anguish, but a well-wrought one. Here, the novelist Huysmans (1848–1907) illustrates important trends. Already in his early work of 1874 *Le Drageoir à épices* (*The Spice-Box*) he was experimenting with non-Natu-ralist forms; the most famous of his novels would be the 'Decadent' *A rebours* of 1884 (*Against Nature*). Its hero des Esseintes, in his dislike of a new democracy and banal mass consumption, retreats from society; but he is just as disaffected with the aristocracy. 'Then again, the nobility had decomposed, was dead; the aristocracy had drifted [versé] into imbecillity or filth [ordure] . . . It was wallowing in the mud of lawsuits that made it equal in turpitude to the other classes' (262). The tale is ostentatiously ornamental, exaggerated in both content and style: in his home, des Esseintes creates semi-sensory, semi-imaginary worlds reliant on the assemblage of diverse (and lengthily detailed) accoutrements – perfumes, for example; the effect is as often one of consumer fetishism as of an artistic extravaganza. One of the culminating moments comes when des Esseintes studs a tortoise's shell with jewels; the over-aestheticized creature dies. (The French for 'tortoise' is 'tortue', only one letter short of 'torture'.) Another crowning stroke is des Esseintes's trip to London; he ends up in an 'English-style' eating-house in Paris, peopling it in imagination with characters from Dickens, then visits an 'English tavern'; he proceeds no further, deciding that the fabricated representation of England is as good as, if not better than, the reality (162–79).

This novel was to be characterized by the English poet Symons (1865–1945) as 'the breviary of the Decadence'. However (as with Gautier's proclamation of 'art for art's sake'), it can be forgotten that Decadence was originally linked not with an 'effete' refusal of harsh realities, but with anti-Establishment politics. Novels by the socialist Lombard or the anarchist Mirbeau present Decadence as a regeneration, a blow against a mediocre bourgeoisie. Decadents intended to create a new language and new forms partly in order to turn the 'masses' away from consumerism. To this end, they used up-to-date publishing techniques of large-scale printing, reproduction and distribution. But these attitudes and procedures were dangerously double-edged; and Decadence fell rapidly into such stereotypes as the dreaming hero frustrated by the mob and the *femme fatale*.

Huysmans's art criticism followed a similar trajectory, moving from art and architecture that celebrated technological advances and modern urban life to a focus on artists who depicted dream (or nightmare) and mysticism, such as Moreau, Redon and Rops. By the 1890s, Huysmans was also embracing a reactionary and nostalgic Catholicism (ignoring an embryonic modernizing movement within the Church): the perverse cruelties of his earlier writing were transformed into a cult of suffering female martyrs and saints. Huysmans's transitions have been interpreted variously. They have been seen as a refusal of democratization and an escape into a fantasy-world whose imagery is consonant with a right-wing politics; or as the well-judged recognition of a turn in the market – a market that was starting to tire of Naturalist 'rationalism'. In effect Huysmans's inconsistency is all those things, and the (to us) bizarre combinations that resulted – lip-service to a reformist 'educational' programme, fear of women and of the masses, a wish for innovation yet a taste for the artificial, even to the point of deathliness – enact key paradoxes of the culture of the Third Republic.

They are enacted too in the most audacious female novelist of the period, Rachilde (1860–1953). Women had comprehensively benefited from the Third Republic. They were not only 'consumers' of an expanded educational system, but also 'providers': the great increase in primary schools meant that many now went into teaching careers, achieving in these circumstances, at least, financial autonomy. And divorce became legal once more in 1884, albeit on terms which favoured men. The feminist movement gained strength and confidence after 1870, and international congresses were held in France, the 1878 one hosting representatives of eleven foreign countries and the 1889 one receiving favourable mention in more than six hundred newspapers round the world. The 'new woman' was jettisoning her corsets and taking up such sports as cycling. And women were once more making their mark in literary circles. George Sand had often retreated to her country refuge in the Berry. But now salons began a last brilliant resurgence as centres of intellectual exchange, for example that of the gay poet and essayist Natalie Barney; and the bisexual Colette (1873–1954) was breaking fresh ground with her titillating Claudine novels (1900–3) and her scandalously independent life-style. Yet there was also a strong reaction against the 'new woman', and Rachilde indicates this ambivalence, long-standing and now surfacing in Third-Republic incarnation. Her novels and plays combine morbid eroticism with a sardonic attack on gender boundaries, as shown by such titles as *Monsieur Vénus* (1884 – written when she was only twenty-four) and *La Marquise de Sade* (1887). They provoke in the reader both disgust and the sense of a hilarious dissolution of taboos. *Monsieur Vénus*, for example, depicts necrophilia and explicit female masturbation. Not that this latter is presented as a social emancipation (Rachilde would in 1931 publish a work called *Why I am Not a Feminist*). Nevertheless, it is probably a first in French writing outside the (admittedly porous) boundaries of pornography. Rachilde's hyperbolic gay characters no doubt also emboldened Gide and Proust in their own later depictions of male and female homosexuality. Finally, Rachilde played a significant role in the literary culture of her time. As the wife of Alfred Vallette, who edited the influential periodical *Le Mercure de France*, she helped to shape not only editorial policy but also critical opinion, with her extensive reviews of contemporary fiction. (The *Mercure de France* published work by, for example, Jarry, Rachilde's protégé. Surprisingly long-lived, it gave birth to a publishing house in 1894 and survived until 1965.)

So far, then, the literature of the Third Republic is a mixture of violent iconoclasm on the one hand and dreamy passivity on the other – contradictions which could sometimes appear to be mere symptoms of confusion. However, Decadence developed into, or shaded off into, 'Symbolism', whose keenest-eyed adherents express a maturely complex response to late nineteenth-century tensions. The 'Symbolist group' is less cohesive than has sometimes been thought, but its broad aim, in both painting and litera-ture, was to counter Naturalism by creating scenes, figures and objects loaded with a significance that was not readily definable but was powerful enough to take the viewer or reader to the unconscious mind. These scenes, figures and objects were Symbols. In technique, musical models were the ones to emulate. Thus the same Verlaine who called for elo-quence's neck to be wrung wrote, from the mid-1860s on, verse whose intensive sound-patterning is designed to create a mesmerizing musicality, and whose content, though sometimes piquant, is more famous now for its indefinable, wistful languor. 'Symbols' were, in the hands of the best practitioners, haunting and (as with Decadence) as likely to be fearful as beautiful: grinning spiders or severed heads in the lithographs and paint-ings of Redon and Moreau; abandoned, haunted rooms and paralysed swans in the poetry of Mallarmé.

But Mallarmé (1842–98), often hailed as the quintessential 'Symbolist', is *sui generis*. There is no comparable writer in Europe of this period, let alone France. With Mallarmé, more than with any other author of these decades, one may hesitate to draw close connections between the indi-vidual's writing and contemporary culture and politics – yet these connec-tions do exist. Mallarmé's major works appeared from the mid-1870s on. Their linguistic daring is truly unprecedented, and so exceptional that still, some hundred years after his death, he remains for many readers utterly baffling. Thirty years earlier, Dumas's d'Artagnan had given vent to a dislike of brief and difficult verse, almost as if his creator foresaw this apogee of a reaction against the 'easy read' (see above, pp. 78–9); and Proust, in *A la recherche du temps perdu*, would hold Mallarmé's verse up as the example of an art with which an older generation of 'ordinary' litera-ture-lovers by definition could not feel comfortable – which they might even fear (II 782). Most of Mallarmé's poems are indeed brief, and within them units of sense are even briefer, sometimes almost momentary. He dislocates sentences in such a way that words seem to hang on the ends of verse-lines, unconnected with anything surrounding them; he presents glimpses of images that appear visualizable, only to snatch them away again. He evokes grief with pictures of helplessly immobile beings or deso-late shipwrecks, but simultaneously his verbal games plunge us into a hedonistic network of echoes and puns so that we do not know if we are seeing tragedy or the simulacrum of tragedy. Similarly, he creates scenes of haunting sensory beauty while his wordplay suggests that these are purely products of the sexual drive and the conceptualizing mind. Let us take a few examples from only two works of the mid-1880s, first his most famous sonnet 'Le vierge, le vivace et le bel aujourd'hui', and second his 'Prose pour des Esseintes' (a longer poem this time, but each line is only eight syllables and each verse only four lines).

In 'Le vierge, le vivace' the central figure is a swan caught in ice; its long neck strains to be free but never will be. Exceptionally, I reproduce here the whole sonnet and its translation: we shall not understand what happened to later French literature, and what is still happening in the early twenty-first century, if we have no immediate sense of how Mallarmé works on the page.

> Le vierge, le vivace et le bel aujourd'hui
> Va-t-il nous déchirer avec un coup d'aile ivre
> Ce lac dur oublié que hante sous le givre
> Le transparent glacier des vols qui n'ont pas fui!
>
> Un cygne d'autrefois se souvient que c'est lui
> Magnifique mais qui sans espoir se délivre
> Pour n'avoir pas chanté la région où vivre
> Quand du stérile hiver a resplendi l'ennui.
>
> Tout son col secouera cette blanche agonie
> Par l'espace infligée à l'oiseau qui le nie,
> Mais non l'horreur du sol où le plumage est pris.
>
> Fantôme qu'à ce lieu son pur éclat assigne,
> Il s'immobilise au songe froid de mépris
> Que vêt parmi l'exil inutile le Cygne.
>
> (Will lovely, lively, virginal today / Tear us with a wing's drunken blow / This hard, forgotten lake haunted in snow / By the sheer ice of flocks not flown away! // A swan that was remembers it is he / Hopelessly yielding for all his fine show / Because he did not sing which way to go / When barren winter beamed its apathy. // His neck will shake off that white agony / Space deals out to the bird that will deny, / But not earth's horror where the plumes are clamped. // A phantom whose brightness assigns him to this place, / He stiffens in the cold dream of contempt / Donned amid useless exile by the Swan.) (Translated by Keith Bosley; some changes.)

The sonnet is full of phonetic replications that at times reinforce the main 'picture' and at other times go their own way, forming such strong patterns that these appear almost to determine the meaning – for example, the *v* and *i* sounds that appear in 'vierge' (virginal), 'ivre' (drunken), 'hiver' (winter), and elsewhere. Furthermore, the French for 'swan' is 'cygne', an exact homophone of 'signe', 'sign'; so are we simply looking at the large Sign that is the poem and the series of signs within it? This juggling of different thought-systems, and the need to entertain simultaneously both anguished and linguistically playful readings, stretch the mind like nothing else in French literature. Similarly, 'Prose pour des Esseintes' (a reference to Huysmans's hero) evokes a marvellous island, home to a multitude of irises. The French for 'irises' is 'des iridées', an again exact homophone of 'désir, idées' ('desire', 'ideas') – with which Mallarmé does indeed rhyme the phrase. Is this a representation of a physical response to a 'lovely flower', or is it – is all art – a creation made up of a blend of desire and ideas?

Mallarmé's verse is uniquely adventurous, beautiful and profound. But even it can be thought about in a cultural context. He himself (like some other writers of the period) defined his enterprise in contradistinction to Wagner's using specifically national terms: 'If the French mind [l'esprit français], strictly imaginative and abstract, therefore poetic, throws out some brilliance, it will not do so thus [ce ne sera pas ainsi]' (from 'Richard Wagner: rêverie d'un poète français', II 157). The self-aware structure and wit, the liking for visual as well as aural patterns in the poem's layout, do have their place in a French tradition whose history I have been tracing throughout this book. More immediately, we can link the flickering pictures and the broken-down, then regenerated, syntax with the ambitions of Impressionism and Pointillism, and also with the slightly later emergence of Cubism (1907 on). Triumphant wordplay would come to be the hallmark of some of the most adventurous twentieth-century French writing: even if most of Mallarmé's contemporaries did not understand him, he would influence the endeavours of many successors. And if we look only at the characteristics of French literature in these four decades from 1870 to 1913, resemblances emerge here too. Mallarmé, like his fellow-writers, evokes physical violence with words like 'déchirer', tear, as in the second line of 'Le vierge, le vivace' where we do not know if it is we who will be torn, or if the new day is going to tear open a hard lake *for* us – the syntax creates ambiguities, and what is happening to the syntax is intellectually violent too. Another of Mallarmé's sonnets evokes battle, with the first two words suggesting an insoluble dichotomy: 'Victorieusement fui', 'victoriously fled': is this military victory, or is it a rout? Yet another mentions mastery, but it is that of an absent Master; his salon is empty and his 'trinket' is 'abolished' ('aboli bibelot', in 'Ses purs ongles'). Since other important works of this period refer, whether ironically or directly, to the Franco-Prussian War, and to a futile grasping after power and commodities, it is perhaps not too absurd to see here a thematic kinship with, for example, Maupassant, even with *Ubu Roi*.

Mallarmé was in certain lights an elitist, expressing a distaste for mass culture that we could expect from this period that made Zola's novels best-sellers and allowed the market an ever-tighter grip on literary production, yet during which some writers – not only Mallarmé – chose to target only a tiny fraction of the public. Thus Mallarmé (or his poetic persona) suggests that an aim of the poet's might be 'to give a purer meaning to the words of the tribe' (in 'Le tombeau d'Edgar Poe'), while in 'Prose pour des Esseintes' he cites a monotonous, lying 'game' that could represent nonpoetic 'entertainment'. And one of his ambitions was to realize a supreme 'Book' ('Le Livre') whose pages would be shufflable – not an experiment the market would have seized, addicted as it still was to the teleological unfolding of plot! 'Le Livre' would be an ultimate mechanism for symbolizing the interchangeability of intellectual phenomena and for making an ungraspable, creative world in some sense intelligible.

This is, however, a side of Mallarmé that might equally be seen as quasi-educational (as with some of his Decadent colleagues). And like certain nineteenth-century 'democratizing' predecessors, he revivifies popular trades and culture in such lesser-known (but still exquisite) poems as his 'Chansons bas' ('Low songs'). In his prose poem 'Réminiscence' the narrator identifies with the fairground performer, like Baudelaire with his mountebank. (This part-serious, part-mock self-deprecation marks Picasso's Harlequins and sad Pierrots too.) Nor did Mallarmé write exclusively for the few: he straddled a variety of literary forums, being a reviewer, a reporter, a translator, a lecturer, and most strikingly the compiler of a fashion journal that celebrated *haute couture* – but if we think of the links forged during the period between 'decorativeness' and Symbolist art, this is not so startling. Mallarmé's imagination was also seized by advertisements, whose layout, according to Valéry, played a part in the structure of his visually boldest piece, the picture-poem *Un coup de dés jamais n'abolira le hasard* (*A Dice-Throw Will Never Abolish Chance*, 1897). This is set out across double pages like a landscape painting, but also uses the white spaces of the paper, and different fonts, to create the impact and unexpected visual links that would be offered by a skilfully arranged advertisement – except that here is no invitation to buy soap but a wild, sorrowing yet majestic evocation of a shipwrecked 'master' looking to the constellations.

Mallarmé became an almost priest-like figure for younger and contemporary authors and artists, who attended his famous Tuesday gatherings (the 'mardis'). He was a communal model (however self-selecting the community) in a way that neither Baudelaire nor Rimbaud was. This period saw the development of another kind of communal model, 'l'intellectuel', whom I have already mentioned briefly in connection with Zola; the first attested use of 'intellectuel' as a noun is at the end of the nineteenth century. This figure would play, and still plays, a special part in France's culture.

It has been argued that 'intellectuals' took on their status at this time for historically locatable reasons. The intellectual did have precursors: the *philosophes*, as we have seen, specifically took it on themselves to construct critiques of social systems with a view to changing these. They presented themselves as spokesmen – as thinking citizens with the right to pronounce on matters of political urgency. (And the *philosophes* have their own forebear in Montaigne, who sees it as his right to 'go anywhere' in the moral, imaginative and social worlds that variously compose his sense of self.) Other predecessors were the Romantic writers who felt no discontinuity between their role as visionary or prophet in matters of the imagination on the one hand, and as political agent on the other. We have only to recall Hugo's lyric verse and its co-existence with his political career, his social novel *Les Misérables* and his satirical collection *Les Châtiments*. Thus, by 1870, writers had for at least a century enjoyed not only public prestige but – albeit inconsistently – the power to intervene. But something different did happen after 1870: numerous developments consolidated the intellectual's status. The growing cult of science led to fame for savants like Louis Pasteur. The spirit of democracy played its part, since the modern intellectual could not exist without press freedom. Continuing improvements in printing technology and transportation (roads and railways) contributed to ease of circulation, meaning that the nation's discussions were no longer confined to the salon; and an explosion of small literary magazines during the Third Republic created a network that enabled intellectuals to view themselves as a group.

The Dreyfus Affair had a role too, being viewed often as an 'affair of intellectuals': certainly, intellectuals were central to the debate, and saw themselves as national symbols, both sides claiming to represent 'the true France'. The newly visible position of French Jews also crystallized thoughts about 'the intellectual'. Noted Jewish scholars like Durkheim and Bergson were viewed as pillars of the republican establishment, as 'official' intellectuals who, favoured by newly democratic educational policies, had acquired renown via the university system. For Jews themselves, the emergence of the modern intellectual, who espoused rationalism and 'universality', was a means by which to integrate into the mainstream of French society. But the Affair allowed attacks on 'the Jewish intellectual' to be stridently elaborated in the guise of 'argument' by such anti-Semitic writers as Maurras and Barrès, who presented the Jew as the prime symbol of a disliked modernity.

And issues of sexuality that came to the fore also carried a high charge. French intellectuals in the main defended Oscar Wilde, yet were none the less sensitive to charges of effeminacy; thus avant-garde intellectuals shared with their opponents a common discourse of masculinity. A common discourse but not a common perspective: during this period two visions of honour emerged, that of the military hero who symbolized physical courage and the cult of the army; and that of the intellectual hero, who incarnated moral courage.

This phenomenon of 'l'intellectuel' was, then, the culmination of a long-standing and peculiarly French attitude to political thought, while at the same time it was period-specific. Intellectuals would remain important to France, and without recourse to their history it is difficult to understand fully the self-declared role and rhetoric of later twentieth-century French writers. The enshrining of the intellectual also signalled the end of the ferocious onslaught on the bourgeoisie that had characterized much nine-teenth-century literature. 'Bourgeois' attitudes would still be taken to task in the rest of the twentieth century – in such works as Sartre's *La Nausée* – but it is as if the heart has gone out of the assault, since almost all writers would now emerge from this class, would have access to higher education, and could in theory construct a public persona for themselves. Even if the bourgeoisie would keep its stranglehold on the means of production, authors could no longer identify it so readily with philistinism and oppression.

6

Despair and Optimism (1913–1944)

The turn of the century had brought a sense of confidence. Writers were moving away from the 'miserabilism' of much nineteenth-century literature. Not only the Third Republic's political progress but also the marvels of technology played a part – for painters as well as authors. Already, such works as Monet's multiple versions of the *Gare Saint-Lazare* (1877) had rendered beautiful an invention that was changing people's lives, the steam engine. The domestic harnessing of electricity was transforming daily living. The techniques of photography (invented and developed in France in the early nineteenth century) were rapidly improving, and the creation of the lightweight camera meant that amateurs could record images on a regular basis. The telephone had started to take its place in the home from the early twentieth century on; test airplane flights had succeeded in 1903; and the first ever public film-screening had been shown in Paris in 1895. Optimism, belief in creativity, and the urge to experiment are so unmistakable in the art of the immediate pre- and post-war periods that we cannot help identifying 'inventiveness' with 'inventions' in these decades at least. Yet at the same time, during and after the First World War (1914–18), Europe was struggling with the terrible trauma of the slaughter: thinkers throughout the West expressed their shock and dismay. In France, foretastes of the war itself had come with the Franco-Prussian conflict, its long aftermath and more recently the murder of the Socialist leader Jean Jaurès in 1914. (Striving to organize resistance to the rush into war, he was assassinated by a right-wing activist.)

France seemingly recovered quickly from the war, buoyed up in part by the victory over Germany and a settlement that the almost universally short-sighted observers deemed fitting revenge for France's defeat in the Franco-Prussian War. Furthermore, the Third Republic remained in place; at obvious levels, therefore, stability was regained. France soon rediscovered its highly creative twentieth-century élan and would maintain it during the twenty-two years after the First World War, 1918 to 1940. In these two decades, however, the divisions between Left and Right that had crystallized round the Dreyfus Affair became ever more acute, and although for some of the period a broadly left-wing government was in power, the right-wing party Action Française grew increasingly strong and influential. The French Communist Party was founded in 1920, the fascist-leaning party the Croix-de-feu (Cross of Fire) in 1927. In 1934, the year after Hitler came to power in Germany, there were right-wing demonstrations in Paris, countered by an anti-fascist general strike; two years later, the left-wing Popular Front came to power under the Jewish prime minister Léon Blum. He introduced numerous reforms, such as paid holidays, a forty-hour week, the raising of the school leaving-age to fourteen, and collective bargaining. Although Blum soon lost power (1937), his reforms remained in place and his government has acquired legendary status in left-wing circles.

By now it was clear that another pan-European war was looming; after the eight-month 'phony war' of 1939–40, France was invaded by German forces in 1940, to its own shock, and remained under occupation until 1944. In *Suite française*, French reactions to the invasion are described both feelingly and ironically by the Jewish writer Irène Némirovsky, who would herself be arrested by the French police and die in Auschwitz in 1942. For during the Occupation, French anti-Semitism, never far from the surface as (most recently) vicious attacks on Blum had shown, emerged once more. (See below, p. 137.) The south of France remained free from occupation by German troops but was still under the rule of the government based at Vichy and headed by Marshall Pétain, who had reached an agreement with Hitler. De Gaulle broadcast to 'Free France' from London and numerous brave Frenchmen and Frenchwomen joined the Resistance.

Among the many remarkable writers publishing during this rich period were the poets Claudel, Valéry and Apollinaire, the novelists Gide, Malraux and Mauriac, the playwright Giraudoux, and the philosopher Sartre. The poet Saint-John Perse (1887–1975), who has somewhat dropped out of view, was recognized abroad: his *Anabasis* of 1924 was translated into English by T.S. Eliot and he would win the Nobel Prize for Literature in 1960. This was, too, the period that gave birth to Surrealism, with such writers as Breton and Eluard bringing the 'wilder' side of late nineteenth-century literature to a climax and shaping crucial aspects of mid- to late twentieth-century French and European culture. It was also, most notably perhaps, the period in which Proust (1871–1922) published his great novel *A la recherche du temps perdu, In Search of Lost Time*. The first volume appeared in 1913; publication was then interrupted by the war, but resumed in 1919, and although Proust himself died after the publication of the fourth volume, the rest of the work continued to appear posthumously, the seventh and last volume being published in 1927. *A la recherche* therefore straddles fourteen years – nearly half – of this period, and its influence continued to mark the rest of it. That influence has been extraordinary in the longer term also, and Proust's reputation is higher than ever in the twenty-first century.

For decades, Proust's encyclopaedic interest in his culture was underestimated or simply ignored. He was portrayed as a bard of nostalgia, a refined successor to the elite writers of the nineteenth century; his long sentences – which many found rebarbative – were held to be a recreation of multilayered perception as interpreted by the innermost self. This view was espoused particularly in Britain, where Proust's 'in-grownness' was implicitly or explicitly opposed to British 'vigour'. But in France too it had adherents, and occasionally came close to a picture of the hysteric, even the 'Jewish hysteric'. Long sequences of *A la recherche*, for example those dealing with male and female homosexuality, were ignored or played down, the focus being mainly on Proust's descriptions of 'nature', his depiction of time and the psychology of his narrator. And in the thirties, the critic Albert Feuillerat tracked down some proofs that showed, in part, what the original novel would have been like – for Proust had expanded it hugely during the interruption provided by the four years of the First World War; according to Feuillerat, these proofs demonstrated that the war had embittered Proust, and that his most biting comments and character-portraits – as well as his depictions of a widespread bisexuality – were not in the original plan, were not the 'real' Proust, the lyrical Proust. Feuillerat wrote clearly and persuasively, and was no doubt responsible for the continuing tenacious refusal of critics to confront the politically and culturally troubling sides of the novel. But the manuscripts, typescripts and proofs of *A la recherche* came into the public domain in the early 1970s, acquired by the Bibliothèque Nationale in a last-minute intervention by the French Government – they were about to go to the United States; this hesitation, then decision, by the French state suggests that it was the 1960s that were the cusp for Proust's reputation, itself a significant fact. At any rate, these documents showed that Feuillerat had been proceeding according to fallacious premises, and that, although Proust's early plans could not have foreseen the First World War, social issues were always part of the project. (See my *Proust's Additions.*) With hindsight, we can see that Feuillerat's blinkered commentary was of his time – that it belonged to that section of French society and of the academy that chose to ignore the threats hanging over Europe, and that preferred to interpret this tragi-comic and troubling masterpiece in as tame and reassuring a way as possible.

From the 1970s on, ever more critics have been at pains to point out the historical and political insights of *A la recherche* and the ways in which these intertwine with its aesthetic. Just as we can say that Balzac 'invented' cultural studies in the nineteenth century, so we can say that Proust reinvents them for the twentieth. Indeed, as well as being France's first great modernist novelist, Proust is its last great 'Balzacian', curious about all aspects of its history and culture. A new scholarly edition that came out in the late 1980s shows how curious, with careful notes explaining virtually every factual reference (1987–89). The inspiration for this new edition itself can be linked with the growth of 'cultural history' in France. (See below, p. 170.)

It would take the rest of this chapter, indeed a whole book, to describe the cultural historian in Proust in any detail. Here, I point to a few indicative aspects under six broad headings: Proust's use of contemporary technology, appurtenances and settings; the politics of the Third Republic; deeper social structures; the development of the arts, and their usage in social interaction; the historical role of Proust's style; finally, the artist's income and his or her place in the community.

All the major technical developments of Proust's time figure in both the plot and imagery of *A la recherche*: the use of electricity for domestic lighting, the telephone, the airplane, the motor-car. Proust suggests that these innovations, as well as changing our experience of time and space, sink deep into the hiding-places of our psyche. He also celebrates France's continuing achievements in *haute couture* and cuisine, dwelling on characters' dress and the family servant's cookery, and assimilating the practice of these two crafts to the process of composing the novel or any work of art. Baudelaire had already extolled such 'artificial' activities as cooking and dandified dressing: they are truly *human*, thus comparable to art. But Proust incorporates them still more ostentatiously into his practice and theory, and though he does not say they have a special place in French culture, most readers knew and know they do. More humbly: when the narrator's friend Bloch refuses to carry such a 'flatly bourgeois' object as the umbrella, he becomes part of a relatively new focus on the amusing accessories of a growing stratum of society – that of the 'petits fonctionnaires' who figured, for example, in Maupassant's short story *The Umbrella*. The umbrella had been the symbol of the 'bourgeois king' Louis-Philippe, but it has now become a subtler indicator, that of post-1870 white-collar life. Office workers cannot afford carriages to shelter them from the rain, but must nevertheless arrive at work looking respectable. So the umbrella is now essential to many levels of the middle class, and the lower middle-class Bloch's rejection of it makes him look merely silly – not only an old-fashioned Romantic who loves storms even if they soak him to the skin, but also an 'arriviste' – which he is. Proust's settings are 'period' ones too. Thus the ghost of Haussmann is present in his Paris. The Bois de Boulogne, to which the narrator refers with piercing nostalgia at the end of the first volume *Swann's Way*, was, contrary to what twenty-first-century readers might suppose, not a long-standing Parisian beauty spot but a site of Hauss-mannization, as were the Buttes-Chaumont that, later in the novel, become a focus of the narrator's anxiety over the whereabouts of his partner Albertine. As in Baudelaire, the 'fixtures' of the narrator's yearnings and personal memories shift not just because his mental world is shifting and time is passing, but also because they are part of a material Paris subject to the dictates of planners – scarcely the stuff of an immemorial, ahistorical landscape.

The politics of the Third Republic are treated with the same deftness. Perhaps the keenest political irony is the one underpinning large swathes of the novel: the young narrator's snobbish admiration of the aristocracy. But the narrator is a Third-Republic boy! It is generally accepted from internal indications in the novel that the narrator was born in about 1880 – but even if he shares Proust's own rather earlier birth date of 1871, he is still of that modern nation in which democracy has the upper hand and the nobility is in terminal decline. The critic René Girard has pointed out that the irony attaching to the narrator's fantasies of god-like beings all around him could work – could be, precisely, ironic – only in a period when belief in God, or gods, was seen as outmoded (*Mensonge romantique et vérité romanesque*, 1961). Part of Proust's comedy will pass us by if we ignore the fact that the young narrator's activities are not only naive but also dated. 'Old rank' did still count for something in the Third Republic: Michael Lucey, in *Never Say I* (2006), points out that when Colette performed at the Moulin Rouge with her female lover, an aristocrat nick-named 'Missy', newspapers of the time were more shocked by the breach of class etiquette than by the lesbianism thus publicly revealed; but, as this very performance proved, the nobility's dignified prestige was a façade everyone knew to be false, even if they tried to pretend otherwise.

There are still more obvious political and cultural critiques to be found in Proust. He condescends to France's colonial exploits past and present: for example, a holiday-maker at the seaside town of Balbec has had himself declared king of a tiny isle of Oceania (that is, the islands of the Pacific Ocean, many of which were under French control): he looks both foolish and pretentious as a result. Proust is also well aware of the feminist debates of his time. In a telling aside, he shows the narrator's mother underestimating her own intellectual judgement *because* she is female: 'her feeling that being a woman . . . she lacked, *so she thought*, the necessary literary competence' (III 230); and discussions of schooling among the narrator's female friends (in the form of the absurd literature essay-titles they are set) show that Proust was alert to the educational reforms now opening up opportunities for women, and to the still rather feeble form that their syllabuses could take. This 'little band' of girls in fact constituted one aspect of the novel for which Proust was long and often pruriently criticized. The narrator meets them at the seaside town of Balbec; among them is his inamorata Albertine. The young women are noisy and physically energetic, and disport themselves without chaperones. For years critics claimed that this behaviour was typical of young *men* of the time, and thus proved that the band was a thinly disguised literary transposition of adolescent youths. Recent histories of women have, however, drawn attention to the emergence of the 'new woman' at the end of the nineteenth century. As we have seen, she did indeed practise sports, and she went out alone. So Proust is not creating females who are 'really' males, but is reflecting back to his reader a change in the culture; and there is an again ironic tension between the deliberately old-fashioned lyrical title of the relevant volume – *A l'ombre des jeunes filles en fleurs*, *In the Shade of Blossoming Girls* – and how these modern girls actually conduct themselves.

Proust looks too at class divisions and the barbarity of war. Baudelaire had depicted a ragged family staring at a luxurious café, its well-to-do clients sitting outside, in his prose poem 'The eyes of the poor'. Proust takes up this picture. But he is writing after Zola, after the 1889 Exposition Universelle celebrating the 1789 Revolution, and perhaps after the 1917 Russian Revolution itself (the date of the passage in question is post-1914 and possibly post-1917). Now he places a restaurant window between the poor onlookers and the affluent diners. He suggests that the window may not offer indefinite defence: 'a great social question, to know if the glass partition will always protect the banquet of marvellous beasts and if the obscure people watching avidly in the night won't come to pluck them from their aquarium and eat them' (II 41–2). The insertion of the glass emphasizes the fragility of the class-barriers, and the shock of 'eat them' is as violent as anything in *Germinal*. Brutal also is the description of trench warfare by the narrator's friend Saint-Loup: '[I've] got into the habit of seeing the head of the comrade who's talking to me suddenly ploughed apart by a torpedo or even severed from his torso' (IV 333).

Thus Proust signals the violence inherent in social structures and is explicit about that of national conflicts. More widely, he picks out the scapegoating mechanisms of communities. At the beginning of the fourth volume, *Sodom and Gomorrah*, the narrator launches an extended comparison between the plight of the gay in a homophobic society and that of the Jew in an anti-Semitic one; the comparison will recur throughout the novel. Proust's treatment of both gays and Jews has made some readers uneasy, starting with Gide, who reproached Proust for making his homosexual characters – or some of them, at least – grotesque. It is true that Proust, or rather his narrator, shows not only the overwhelming pressures of a prejudiced society but also the pitifully strange habits into which it can force the objects of that prejudice. Proust often makes these habits ridiculous. What he is doing at these points is making the narrator a conduit for the contradictions of his culture: drawing attention to such contradictions is a central part of what great art does. Here Proust is in the tradition of the *moraliste* – he who, as we have seen, remarks on the odd behaviour of mankind without judging it – rather than in that of the moralizer who preaches a particular course of action. And in this respect, Gide himself is rather more the moralizer, construing it as part of his writer's mission to proselytise on behalf of gays – about which, more later.

A la recherche has much to say, too, about the social impact of the arts. Proust makes thought-provoking comparisons and contrasts between different areas of cultural awareness (for instance, seeking out the value of 'bad' as well as 'good' music); and he considers the public assimilation of new artistic phenomena, implicitly advising against the blurring together of historically separate endeavours. That is, we should give their full value to past artistic revolutions as well as to present ones, while also appreciating continuities:

> No doubt it is easy to imagine, in an illusion analogous to that which makes everything on the horizon uniform, that all the revolutions that have taken place until now in painting or music nevertheless respected certain rules and that what is immediately in front of us, impressionism, search for dissonance, exclusive use of the Chinese scale [that is, so-called 'defective' musical scales], cubism, futurism, differs outrageously from what went before. (I 522–3)

These comparisons and contrasts are often put forward by way of simile and metaphor. Thus Proust likens the 'spread' of bisexuality – or what his characters perceive as a spread – to other cultural developments. Here is his great gay character the baron de Charlus wondering why a hetero-sexual man would want to sleep with a boy: "'I'm pretty old-fashioned, but I don't understand," he said in the tone of an old Gallican talking about certain forms of Ultramontanism, of a liberal royalist talking about Action Française, or of a disciple of Claude Monet about the cubists' (III 811). The narrator's analogy – between sexual experimentation, extreme ideologies and Cubism – brings together both the fluidity and the schisms of Third-Republic consciousness. Proust also slyly incorporates into his aesthetic judgements, and his character-comedy, contemporary debates about iconic figures such as Wagner and Zola. Wagner takes us to new heights, says his narrator, but as with the stunning technical achievements of the air-plane, the 'powerful snoring' of the engine may 'somewhat prevent us savouring the silence of space' (III 668). Zola, and other artists, are exploited in cultural battles which anticipate the novels of Nathalie Sarraute and the analyses of Bourdieu. (See below, pp. 146, 170.) So Mme de Guermantes's claim that Zola is a 'poet' is true in certain lights, but is deployed by her mainly in order to stun one of her salon habituées (II 789). The sister of the snob Legrandin performs conversational acrobatics that allow her to change her position on Poussin and Chopin once she learns that Degas and Debussy respectively like them (III 208, 212). In other words, Proust's keen eye picks out both aesthetic developments and the use to which these are put, cultural capital being earnestly wished for even by those who have plenty of the other kind of capital.

Proust's very style, too, while profoundly original, has a cultural history. It displays both the elegance and the robustness, sometimes earthiness, that go back to the Middle Ages. (As the snob Legrandin bows low before the wife of a local landowner, a bow described in a string of delicately bal-anced clauses, the rippling of his buttocks betrays a fleshy baseness, 'bas-sesse': I 123.) Proust also takes his place in that line of French writers who highlight the social function of set phrases and overblown speech; while glorying in a hyperbolic recreation of these, he opposes them to the 'truer' language of the great writer. For Proust, such clichés and verbal inflation include parliamentary rhetoric and the stereotyped mouthing of newspa-pers, particularly in times of national crisis such as war. Thus the writer's efforts – more accurate than the unthinking, defensive language that springs out at moments of pressure and more honest than the chauvinistic sloganizing of journalists – can be counted as socially oppositional. So Proust is the heir not only of the Flaubert who sought the 'mot juste' but also of the democratic and would-be educating Decadents of his own youth. This quasi-democratic attitude is to some extent reflected in the gentle, open-minded musings of the narrator's friend Saint-Loup as he ponders the combined clichés and heroism of working-class soldiers in the trenches; the narrator, on the other hand, is at his fiercest when describing the efforts of war poets who, instead of placing themselves 'at the level of events', fall back on such trite and well-worn phrases as 'blood-stained dawn' (IV 333). They are blunting the dreadful significance of the slaughter. Lastly, with Proust we see the final triumph of 'poetic prose'. Proust is sometimes held to be the greatest prose writer France has ever had. But this is 'great prose' of a special kind: not the subtly probing, laterally figurative, prose of Montaigne; not the lapidary, biting prose of La Rochefoucauld or Voltaire. Flaubert, with his alliterative and image-laden writing, is Proust's closest predecessor: both authors knew they were composing fiction in an epoch when opting for prose over verse was, in the ways I have already brought out, a political as well as an artistic choice. In his style, as in other respects, Proust is of a particular era, while at the same time sublimely surpassing every other prose writer in it.

And what of that question to which we have necessarily kept returning: the income of the writer? Lough, while not denying the obvious – that some twentieth-century writers could still gain vast earnings from their works – asserts that 'the golden age of the professional writer' was more or less over by 1914 (370). By 'professional writer' he means those who, like Hugo, appealed to both the elite and the rest of the populace. Where does Proust sit? Personally wealthy, he was able to devote himself to the arts and to writing in part because he never had to earn a living. His private correspondence, while at times focusing on the ups-and-downs of the stock market and on his own financial position, provides no evidence that he was ever seriously in danger of impoverishment. Yet the narrator of *A la recherche* does refer a great deal to money, either actual or metaphorical: its use in the consolidation of relationships; the ways in which the possession or lack of it shapes interaction between the classes; the fluctuation of investments as a symbol of other kinds of instability. And at the end of the novel, when the narrator declares he will now write his work, commerce puts in an appearance. He makes the famous statement that his readers would be, 'according to me', 'les propres lecteurs d'eux-mêmes': 'the readers of themselves, my book being only a kind of magnifying glass like those the Combray optician used to offer to a customer' (IV 610). The optician relies on his customers for a living. Yet the tone is low-key: 'according to me', 'only'; this is no sales-pitch – the optician simply 'offers' his wares for trial. Perhaps the bourgeois narrator can dispense with a publisher's contract, perhaps he hopes for it: we do not know. But he rapidly goes on to present his future achievement as one that will become part of the image-making, the story-telling and the internal checks of a community. Whether it will be a financial success is so unimportant that, the matter having been vestigially broached, it simply fades out.

> De sorte que je ne leur demanderais pas de me louer ou de me dénigrer, mais seulement de me dire si c'est bien cela, si les mots qu'ils lisent en eux-mêmes sont bien ceux que j'ai écrits . . . (IV 610)
>
> (So that I would not ask them [my readers] to praise or denigrate me, but only to tell me if it is so, if the words they read inside themselves are indeed those I have written . . .)

Yes, with this the narrator is claiming a right to cultural capital, but modestly so; there is something much more generous here than we have witnessed in other characters' culture-wars, and gentler than we shall find in Bourdieu – something, also, that goes beyond the division between 'elite' and 'popular' writing. The future novel is presented as a means to self-knowledge for a culture, as an offering that respects its diversity and may begin to close up its schisms.

Other writers of the time find their own ways of negotiating this diversity, and of reflecting yet distancing themselves from social developments. Three writers in whom the interweaving of 'modern' and 'old' is particularly striking are the poets Apollinaire and Valéry and the playwright Giraudoux.

Apollinaire (1880–1918) did not grow up in France, but his formative years coincided with those when 'free verse' was burgeoning (from the 1890s on) – free verse, with all the loaded social connotations of 'free'. And Apollinaire apparently embraces the present. In the very first line of his collection *Alcools* (1913) he declares: 'A la fin tu es las de ce monde ancien' ('In the end you're weary of that old world': from 'Zone', the opening poem). His verse structure is unconventional and he abandons most punctuation; he embraces technological innovation, indeed to a point that can be disturbing, as in his famous and probably unironic celebration of the 'fireworks' of the First World War, and his narrator's exclamation 'Ah Dieu! que la guerre est jolie' ('God! war's a pretty thing', in 'L'adieu du cavalier': *Calligrammes*, 1918). But elsewhere sarcasm enters the picture of 'progress' and battle; shells merely 'fart' in the spare and sober 'Mutation'; his narrator laments the death of friends in battle as elegiacally as the *Chanson de Roland* did centuries earlier; and in such poems as 'Le pont Mirabeau', with its ballad like-refrain, Apollinaire brings together ancient and new: 'Vienne la nuit sonne l'heure / Les jours s'en vont je demeure' ('Come night chime hour / The days go by I remain'). Similarly, in that opening poem of *Alcools*, the Eiffel Tower is a shepherdess looking over her flock, the bridges 'bleating' with cars while herds of buses moo; Apollinaire artfully combines pastoral with urban, the traditional with the symbol of republican modernity. This smoothing-over of divisions is the beginning of an ambition to heal, through play, a cultural and political rift.

Valéry (1871–1945) is less deliberately provocative than Apollinaire: one will not find billboards figuring in his poetry, and he 'old-fashionedly' uses traditional verse forms throughout his collection *Charmes* (1922). But he is more disturbing. While exploiting subjects rooted in an older Western culture – Narcissus, Greek temples, the Serpent of the Garden of Eden, sun, sea and death – he treats these with such irony and dexterous symbolism that they simultaneously become modern. The poems of *Charmes* are atheistic, proposing that the unique spark in the cosmos is man's consciousness – nothing more; they are self-reflexive, suggesting connections between the major combats of life and the construction of the very poem that we are reading. ('The rower', for instance, is both 'about' the painful process of dying, with the narrator effortfully rowing upstream to return to his source, and at the same time 'about' the intelligence struggling to delve into its own being.) Valéry's alliteration and assonance are so overt that there are moments when his poems become a glorious swirl of sound which (as with Mallarmé) seems to dictate the meaning. The verse thus both creates an illusion of verbal 'music' and highlights the arbitrariness of communication systems, beautifully as well as quizzically. Here is a brief extract from Valéry's own favourite lines, a description of sunset from 'Fragments du Narcisse' (I give a literal translation but this in no way conveys the cumulative force of the echoing vowels and consonants in the French):

> Puis s'étendre, se fondre et perdre sa vendange,
> Et s'éteindre en un songe en qui le soir se change.
>
> (Then stretches, melts and loses its grape-harvest, and is extinguished in a dream into which the evening changes.)

Valéry was a polymath, and an intellectual in the Third-Republic sense. In voluminous notebooks (the 'Cahiers'), he compiled thoughts on diverse branches of knowledge, and he commented on political events in collections with such mock-hesitant titles as *Quasi-Political Essays* and *A Look at Society Today* (*Regards sur le monde actuel*). It was Valéry who wrote the famous judgement on the First World War, a *moraliste*'s judgement: 'We civilizations know now that we are mortal' (in 'The Spiritual Crisis', 1919).

Giraudoux (1882–1944) too is of his period, finally excessively so: unable in the end to retain the independence of mind of many fellow-authors. His plays, like those of later twentieth-century playwrights and like Valéry's poems, return to classical subjects. Part of his achievement is to give these an oddly contemporary dignity. One impulse here is perhaps 'How can we educated writers retain the privileges of our knowledge while at the same time affirming our adaptability?' – an adaptability still important for commercial success in the theatre. Thus Giraudoux's delightfully witty *Amphitryon 38* (1929) is so called because it is supposedly the thirty-eighth rewriting of the Amphitryon myth. The title proclaims the cultural self-consciousness of the play, as do its deliberate anachronisms (such as a women's magazine-style interview with Leda about her congress with Jupiter); its heroine Alcmene resolutely refuses to believe in the gods. Jupiter has slept with her disguised as her adored husband Amphitryon, and tells her they have just spent a 'divine' night together, but her reply is not to his satisfaction: 'Your adjectives are pretty weak this morning, darling!' (IIii). The cliché 'divine' is just that, a trite word without meaning in this post-religious society. The same skilful modernity governs Giraudoux's best-known play, *The Trojan War Will Not Take Place*. This stands the expected ending on its head yet fulfils it, at the same time pleading for no new conflict to take place – for already, when this play was written (1935), a new war with Germany was on the horizon. Other ambivalences are apparent in both *Amphitryon 38* and *The Trojan War*. Giraudoux's female characters are strong and intelligent, validating post-1870 feminist strains of French thought; at the same time, they are charming in a mode emanating from that other tradition of 'courtesy', gallantry, that allowed women to have intellectual qualities – but only so far. Giraudoux reflects his culture in more sinister ways too: that appeal for peace in *The Trojan War* was part of a Germanophilia that in his case would go so far as to support Hitler. In 1939, the year he was put in charge of France's propaganda services by the weak prime minister Daladier, he claimed, in a work called *Full Powers*, that Jewish refugees to France were physically abnormal and were eliminating the rights of the French, and stated: 'I am fully in agreement with Hitler in proclaiming that policy attains its highest form only when it is racial' (*Pleins pouvoirs*, 65–6, 71–6). The extreme Right in France was able to make its voice heard through some of the country's cleverest writers: Giraudoux was not the only one.

Part of the appeal of Giraudoux's plays was that they preserved the virtues of popular nineteenth-century boulevard theatre. Lightness of touch, comic misunderstandings, neat plots, above all skilful repartee, were still agreeable to French audiences. Certainly, his drama lacks the formidable innovativeness of other theatrical forms such as the Ballets Russes, which gripped the cultural elite of Paris between 1908 and 1929, or the extreme experimentalism of the director and playwright Artaud (1896–1948; see below, p. 152). Indeed, the tension between elite and popular forms of literature becomes yet more salient and complex in this period. This is in part due to that decline of the 'professional writer' already mentioned. Prizes and honours were still being bestowed upon notable authors and would multiply as the twentieth century went on. (In this period, for example, Colette and Rachilde were made Officers of the Legion of Honour – 1920 and 1924 respectively – and Proust won the Goncourt Prize in 1919, beating a 'war novelist' and hence causing some indignation.) These awards acknowledged challenging literature, and led to financial boosts for authors whose sales increased thereby. But the twentieth-century proliferation of honours and privately funded literary prizes served almost as compensation for the withering away of state patronage. It was as if France wished to retain publicity for its literary culture without the expense of allocating a proper income to practitioners.

And commercial competition with elite literature was now coming from varied sources. The reformed working conditions gradually taking hold, and extended by Blum's Popular Front government of 1936, meant that the working class had more leisure to enjoy new cultural forms. Whatever the reason, many talented and creative Frenchmen (for these semi-professionals were almost all men) were turning to cinema, whose birth-place had after all been France. Film and literary culture have always both enriched and vied with each other in France. From its beginnings with Louis Lumière in 1895, French cinema had progressed to the imaginative films of Méliès, whose *Journey to the Moon* (1902) created striking illusions with special effects. It soon produced outstanding works: Gance's eight-hour silent film about Napoleon in 1926 (we note the hold of history and of this major symbolic figure, still, on the public imagination); Buñuel's and Dalí's shocking *L'Age d'or* (1930); and Jean Renoir's *Le Crime de M. Lange* (1936), *La Grande Illusion* (1937) and *La Règle du jeu* (1939) – these last four all with strong anti-religious or political themes. The versatile Cocteau, active in many media including poetry and ballet, was also a major film-maker. Cinema was the most prestigious new medium, but others too were rising in public esteem. France had a long and distinguished lineage of witty cartoonists, most notably the nineteenth-century Daumier; but now the story in cartoons, or comic strip ('bande dessinée'), reached a peak of achievement with the Belgian Hergé's creation of Tintin in 1929. (The speech-balloon had been introduced in 1925 in Saint-Ogan's *Zig et Puce*.) And photography – again, as we have seen, a French invention – was used everywhere to promote both consumer goods and political messages, especially during the Occupation.

Perhaps paradoxically, then, France's excellence in diverse media shaped its interwar literature. Professional rivalry, as well as polarization between Left and Right, arguably strengthened the need of novelists across the ideological spectrum to reach the concerns of ordinary people as well as of intellectuals, and to write suspense-filled fiction. For many it was a matter of survival. It was during these decades that the Catholic novel flourished, with Mauriac and Bernanos writing such accessible and gripping works as *Thérèse Desqueyroux* (1927) and *Diary of a Country Priest* (1936). They themselves descended from the 'Catholic Renaissance' that had begun in the early twentieth century, with such distinguished writers as Péguy (1873–1914; he was killed in the First World War) and Claudel (1868–1955). Claudel himself was not likely to appeal to a mass market. His reputation rested upon powerfully declamatory plays, for example *The Tidings Brought to Mary*, 1912, and the experimental *The Satin Slipper*, written 1919–24 and originally considered unperformable: Cocteau is said to have remarked of it: 'It's lucky he didn't put on the pair!' But Mauriac and Bernanos were aiming at a wider readership, as was Céline (1894–1961). Like Giraudoux, Céline is a disturbing case. His *Journey to the End of the Night* (1932) creates the illusion of an appeal to a proletarian audience. Céline's style is full of argot, like Zola's; the difference is that now we have a first-person narrator, and one whose onslaughts are cutting and sustained: onslaughts on pretentious habits of thinking, and on those who send poor men to their deaths in battle. Parodies of high-mindedness, and swoops into vulgarity, create a tense and innovative work. Yet the cruel zest, the Swiftean revulsion, in this novel foreshadow a descent into real cruelty, and into disgustingness: only five years later, Céline was to publish a violently anti-Semitic pamphlet, *Bagatelles for a Massacre* (1937), and two others followed. The distinguished American critic Wayne Booth, in *The Rhetoric of Fiction* (1961), would argue that no prose style is 'neutral' – there is always an implicit moral charge, but in all novels that are judged 'great', that moral charge leans towards compassion and tolerance; in a wide survey of Western literature, he singles out Céline's *Journey* as the paradigm of a work which, if taken seriously by the reader, 'must corrupt him' (383). It is, at the least, noteworthy that French culture, along with its immense contribution to Western liberal values, also in the 1930s produced the author who would be condemned outright by this fair-minded critic.

On the Left, Malraux wrote two famous 'committed' novels well before Sartre argued for 'committed literature'. These are again gripping ones: *La Condition humaine* of 1933 and *L'Espoir* of 1937, set during respectively the Chinese Revolution and the Spanish Civil War. (Malraux himself commanded a Republican air squadron during this latter conflict.) In these novels, characters try, often with desperation, to find a meaning for their lives in political action; the structure and style borrow from those of newspaper reporting, with short telegrammatic reports succeeding each other, almost layered in collage manner; and the impact of the cartoon is perceptible in physical descriptions that seize upon single facial features or parts of the body with a caricaturist's eye. There is, indeed, a headline-grabbing aspect to Malraux that can disconcert, but it is less surprising if we bear in mind that the novel is necessarily – and yet again – carving out a new public and commercial role for itself.

These efforts were also interwoven with the continuing attempt to define and re-assert the function of the intellectual. Malraux could scarcely have been so bold as to include in his fiction meditations on the meaning of life if not for the continuing status of this figure. The very title of *The Human Condition* speaks for the confidence of the intellectual. Not even Shakespeare called any of his plays *The Human Condition*. The essayist and critic Benda (1867–1956) made significant contributions to the current debate about the intellectual, even if in retrospect he can be seen as hotly pursuing an outdated agenda. He attacked the philosopher Henri Bergson for his interest in flux and mobility, and such writers as Gide and Valéry for what he deemed their obscurity. And in *La Trahison des clercs, Betrayal by the Thinkers* (1927), he lambasted modern intellectuals for abandoning contemplation and 'pure' analysis and for going down social or crusading paths. His swingeing arguments are testimony to the more general fact that French interest in the intellectual was public and sustained; but his book had an effect opposite to the one intended, in that it crystallized for writers the reasons why they *should* be involved in public affairs. Gide himself (1869–1951) is a case in point. He wrote political essays as well as literary-critical ones, and his novel *The Counterfeiters* (1926) blends formal experimentation with an exploration of the role the novelist may have in the lives of those around him. *The Counterfeiters* gives no easy answers, seeming at times to favour an 'art for art's sake' approach but elsewhere making its central character – a novelist – look questionable for espousing this. More provocatively than in any work since Balzac's, literature in this novel is given a role like that of money: they are necessary, but ungraspable and symbolic, linchpins in social and economic exchange. For *The Counterfeiters* implicitly compares counterfeit currency to the circulation of that other great 'fabrication', the work of art. In another less comfortable area, Gide the elite writer can coincide with Gide the proselytizer: not in his celebration of gay sex – an essential and liberating task – but in an apparent unawareness that paedophilia exploits its victims. (See below, p. 180.) This marked *The Immoralist* of 1902 and still shows in the somewhat glamorized novelist-hero of *The Counterfeiters*, a figure to whom teenage boys flock. The heady role of the prestigious intellectual can carry certain dangers and, without agreeing with the testy Benda, we can see these dangers in interwar France more clearly than at any other time.

Perhaps the most fruitful conjunctions of this period between intellectual, artist and political activist came in the appearance of Surrealism from about 1924 (the publication date of the Surrealist Manifesto). Taking its cue from Freud (whose works began to be more generally known in France from 1926 on), Surrealism pioneered new types of composition – notably 'automatic' writing, which relied on free association – and at the same time claimed that the revolutionariness of these would transform readers' lives. In theory, then, Surrealist writing would mediate between the personal and the political. Many Surrealists – including the poet and theoretician Breton (1896–1966), author of the Manifesto, and the poet Eluard (1895–1952) – were Communist Party members, if only briefly. (However, the distinguished poet, novelist and journalist Aragon remained a Communist after all the other Surrealists had left the Party.) They championed 'liberty' in all walks of life and thought: the simultaneously political, cultural and aesthetic affect of this word endures.

Other Surrealist emphases can be interpreted as a re-invention of nineteenth-century ones – but this incorporation of earlier concerns into modern ones contributes to the excitement of their venture. They focus on the city, especially Paris (Baudelaire); on chance (Mallarmé); on the marvellous (Nerval, Rimbaud); on the everyday (Balzac) – this was now a gateway to novel experiences of time and fresh epiphanies. Another successful Surrealist enterprise was the fusion of art forms. For more than a century, writers had made both informal and formal efforts to bring the arts closer together, in – say – novelists' and poets' allusions to painters and composers, and in their own attempts to create 'word-paintings' and 'musical' poems. Symbolism had more self-consciously reached out across the music/literature boundary. But no movement before Surrealism so determinedly and publicly bestrode different media. Painters and film-makers were among those who responded to this literary development, both in France and across Europe (Paris was still home to many non-French artists).

Arguably, Surrealism's strong push to be political and to engage with other arts once more had some source in rivalry with 'popular' media. The Surrealists' attitude to photography is a case in point. Breton claimed that surrealist painting developed in part because the perfecting of photographic techniques invalidated any remaining ambition simply to reproduce 'reality'. However, photography was not only perceived as 'competition' but was also welcomed by the Surrealists, who used photographs and photomontage in their journals (Breton himself includes photographers' images in his quasi-autobiographical *Nadja*, 1928). They soon saw that the photo did not merely copy: it could be manipulated to make 'reality' strange and disorienting. Here, then, we see a joining of forces rendered almost imperative for the birth of avant-garde literature – undertaken both from a celebration of the progressive and from an unspoken sense of necessity.

Under the Occupation, some left-wingers did continue to publish. Sartre brought out his major philosophical work *Being and Nothingness* in 1943, and in the same year staged a play in Paris, *The Flies*, whose mythical setting lends itself to an exploration of choice and determinism in the most general terms, but which takes on its full import only in the immediate political context of acquiescence and rebellion. The hero Orestes comes back to his native city of Argos to find its inhabitants in thrall to guilt about the past (the murder of his father Agamemnon); his sister Electra, apparently bolder, turns out to be no less a slave of this fixation. The guilt is represented by the flies plaguing Argos and by a showman-like Jupiter. These are the visible threats; but the real enemy is the internalized remorse of the Argives – their self-flagellation. Orestes kills his father's murderers (his mother Clytemnestra and her second husband Aegisthus) and departs, taking the flies with him. This 'god-sanctioned' remorse was intended by Sartre to reflect a reality of occupied France: the Catholic Church, while limiting the influence of Nazism and giving some their only available hope, at the same time promoted a view that the Occupation had been visited upon the French because of their sins. This is represented even more directly in Camus's *La Peste* (published shortly after the war, in 1947): his Catholic priest Paneloux thunders from the pulpit that the plague is sent by God to punish the inhabitants of Oran, the plague-stricken town; his certainties start to weaken when he sees a child dying of the disease.

But self-reproach was not the only response to the invasion. In his book about the Occupation, *Marianne in Chains* (2003), the historian Robert Gildea stresses that many French people, far from resisting the Germans, welcomed the demise of the Republic. It allowed them to further their own material ambitions as well as to blame Third-Republic politicians for the defeat of France in 1940. They were happy too to persecute free-masons, Communists and Jews, also held responsible for France's so-called decline. The Republic was seen as a radical and socialist mafia: revenge could now be taken by the Vichy regime. Furthermore, the Occupation was made easier for the Germans because a number of cultivated French-men saw them as cultural compatriots. 'For many,' writes Gildea, 'the Germany of Goethe and Beethoven was never quite eclipsed by the Germany of Hitler'. Some occupying officers were fluent in French or were descended from French stock; and, 'despite the hereditary enmity between the French and the Germans . . . , there was a counter-current of mutual respect based on the common sense of military honour shared by veterans of the 1914–18 war, a common European civilization, and some-times a common religion too' (52–4, 67, 415). We can trace the sense of a shared civilization – indeed of Germany as a cultural inspiration – back to (for example) Staël's *On Germany*, Nerval's translations of Goethe, and the cult of Wagner, still strong in the early twentieth century. These contradic-tions are evoked in the 1942 novella by Vercors, *The Silence of the Sea*. Vercors was the pseudonym of Jean Bruller (1902–91). Under the Occupa-tion he co-founded a clandestine publishing house, the Editions de Minuit; its first publication was his own novella, and it would also publish forty-three other texts by such authors as Aragon and his partner, the novelist Elsa Triolet, both of whom were in the Resistance. In *The Silence of the Sea*, an educated German, billeted with a girl and her grandfather who never speak to him, expatiates on his love of France and French literature; finally he realizes that Germany wants to destroy France, and in expiation sacri-fices himself by volunteering for the Russian Front.

Collaboration and resistance did then manifest themselves in cultural domains. Although much popular activity under the Occupation was purely escapist (for instance, cinema-going or semi-secret dances), nine-teenth-century operas such as Donizetti's *La Fille du régiment* and plays such as Péguy's *Jeanne d'Arc* (1897), when staged, elicited patriotic reactions from their audiences. Other icons of 'Frenchness' acquired new resonance under the Occupation, re-affirming the national culture. The statue of Rabelais in Chinon, for example, was nearly removed for smelting down, but was saved in deference to a sentiment that clearly wished to affirm a certain distinctive and communal exuberance through this symbolic author. But that 'Frenchness' had its sinister side. Anti-Semitism was not simply confined to an upper-class glee that the 'Jewish' Third Republic was finally overthrown. Some heroic individuals did warn Jewish neighbours to escape or kept them in hiding until the Liberation. But working-class people and local officials alike scarcely dissented from the 'Aryanization' of local commerce (that is, the appropriation by Gentiles of businesses owned by Jews, including those who had served in the First World War), and almost none protested against the arrest of Jews destined for concentration camps. Indeed, an enthusiastic Vichy Government rounded up Jews for deportation to the camps so promptly that the Nazis complained they were not yet ready for them; and after the war underground anti-Semites in the Church sheltered a number of Nazi war criminals in monasteries until they could be spirited away to Argentina – where some still live today.

All these features of the Occupation – themselves a deadly demonstration of long-present schisms – would continue to affect France well after the Liberation in 1944. In public, at least, there were strong declarations of a complete break with the war years: a new Republic, the Fourth, would be proclaimed in 1946 under de Gaulle; but locally many officials simply carried on serving in town halls – it would be too difficult to find sufficiently prestigious replacements; and there was a collective silence about the deportations that would be whittled away only gradually in the postwar decades. For the shrewdest writers, there could be no question of unalloyed satisfaction. A strain of sternness, even bleakness, would be visible in French culture during the twenty-five years after the Liberation.

7

Commitment and Playfulness (1944–1968)

Literary developments in France during the twenty-five years after the Second World War were as pathbreaking as those of the interwar period, thanks in part to those writers who were prepared or able to support themselves financially rather than succumb to the lure of commercial writing, and who clung to their independence. For example, in the early stages of his writing career Beckett earned money though translations, while Ionesco trained as a teacher of French. Loyal literati helped too: thus they supported the impoverished Parisian Théâtre de la Huchette, which staged two of Ionesco's plays in the early 50s but would not become successful until 1957. So innovation in French literature of this period was backed by the elite (still in the capital). Yet side by side with the experimentation, a certain traditionalism persisted in the literature, while in politics reactionary mind-sets and persistent conflicts were simmering, ready to boil over.

To take only the issue of feminism: at last, women were able to vote in the 1945 elections. But with this went the head-shaving or hair-cropping of those who had slept with German soldiers or were suspected of having informed on fellow-citizens; these ceremonies were often accompanied by a carnivalesque glee. Certainly many high-profile male collaborators were severely punished (there were 9,000 executions in the immediate wake of the Liberation, among them that of the fascist writer Brasillach); but men who had practised a relatively low-level co-operation with the Germans, equivalent to what the women had done, were not subjected to such public humiliations.

The very eagerness with which the Third Republic's collapse had been greeted by the French right, and the fact that Pétain was condemned to death after the Liberation (though the execution was not carried out), now secured the place of Republicanism. Albeit with some manoeuvring, the Fourth Republic (originating in a referendum of 1945) moved relatively seamlessly into the Fifth in 1958; so, at the present moment, France's two post-war republics, with their total of sixty-five years, are on the way to catching up with the Third Republic's record-breaking seventy. That did not mean, however, that right-wing governments could not be returned, nor that neo-fascist sympathizers had been shamed into silence. Young right-wing intellectuals ran their own vigorous periodicals and tried to dominate the culture from as early as 1946; while the Poujadist movement, which started in 1953, harnessed images of the small shopkeeper and businessman to promote a crude nationalism. This movement would be superseded in the middle and late 1950s by the still more nationalistic one formed by the opponents of Algerian independence. For this was the period during which France would lose many of its colonies, from North African to Indo-Chinese, and perforce change its relationship with others, such as those in the West Indies – a process that unfolded smoothly in some countries, but in others was effected only through bloody battles and was accompanied, in France itself, by a point-blank refusal to understand the rights of the colonized. The most harrowing case was that of Algeria. (See below, pp. 182–3, 195–6.)

De Gaulle dominated French politics for the first two and the last ten years of this period; he was able to impose himself as President in 1958 because civil war was feared. One of his most-quoted sayings is the first sentence of his memoirs (1954–9, 1970–1): 'Toute ma vie, je me suis fait une certaine idée de la France', 'All my life, I have had a certain idea of France'; he goes on to describe his strong belief in a national destiny. That belief marked everything he did. He achieved the extraordinary feat of obtaining the status of a major world power for a vanquished, humiliated and collaborationist nation (one of five seats on the UN Security Council; one of four zones of occupation in Berlin). And it was 'in the name of France' that he appealed to the populace after an attempted putsch over Algeria in 1961: 'Françaises, Français, aidez-moi' ('Frenchwomen, Frenchmen, help me'). The comprehensive attraction of this nationalism is demonstrated by Malraux's political career path. Hitherto left-wing, he felt able to work for de Gaulle, becoming his minister for information (1945–6) and subsequently his first minister for cultural affairs (1959–69): it was in the cause of France, for the moment embodied in de Gaulle. This exceptionalism, this powerful sense of the nation – which we have seen from early on, and which also guided the (numerous) governments that ruled between de Gaulle's two stints of power – accounts for such developments in post-war France as its independent nuclear deterrent strategy.

The aftermath of the Occupation, and the threat of coups and civil conflict, encouraged 'strong' leadership in the post-war period: it was felt necessary to pull the country together, but this left insufficient formal outlet for left-wing dissent. The French Left itself was to a degree stalemated. It had unusual political strength, achieved by effective worker-student alliances since 1944; on the other hand, the stultifying leadership of the Parti Communiste by Maurice Thorez, with his Stalinist leanings, robbed the Left of much potential power in government. An eventual eruption was perhaps foreseeable. The dramatic events of May 1968 focused initially on protests against the American war in Vietnam, but these quickly spread to the living and teaching conditions of students (a far larger proportion of the age-group than in 1960s Britain), to workers' rights and to individual liberation. The demonstrations and 'street events' led to the occupation of the Paris Stock Exchange and to widespread strikes. But, astonishing though they were, the events did not apparently reflect majority views, since the Gaullists won a huge victory in elections called immediately by de Gaulle. Nevertheless, he himself was irremediably weakened, resigning less than a year later, and changes did come about: most notably, improvements for students, and more pervasively in social and intellectual attitudes. (I shall return to this; meanwhile, we may note that the events had drolly personal as well as politically hard-hitting manifestations: one famous street slogan read: 'I'm a Marxist, Groucho tendency'.) On the broadest view, the May events proved three things: that sharp divisions continued in France; that resentments were felt to have imperfect channels of expression; and that the Left was ready, still, to revolt through public action combined with spectacle.

During this quarter-century, Sartre, Camus and Beckett dominated post-war French thought and literature; this promotion of an exclusive trio was arguably a product of what universities and the literate public wanted to focus on at the time. For in the same years, but scarcely impacting on the perception of 'French literature', Simone de Beauvoir's *The Second Sex* was published, and other thinkers were emerging who have since made an outstanding international mark: Lévi-Strauss, Foucault, Lacan, Derrida. A mismatch thus exists between works that were in the glare of the cultural limelight and other more 'subterranean' currents. It was a mismatch perhaps more striking than in any other period of recent French history, and is owed to the queasy reaction of the then literary-critical establishment to 'theory', which slowed down the acceptance of these thinkers as major writers. It is therefore almost tempting to consider them in the chapter dealing with the post-1970 decades, that is, at the time of their real fame; but that would be to overlook the ways in which they were in fact interacting with their keenest-eyed contemporaries.

Let us start, however, with Sartre (1905–80) and Camus (1913–60). Both wrote works that responded to immediate post-war political concerns: the formation of the Soviet bloc, the threat of nuclear annihilation, the definition of a new humanism. Since these were a source of confusion and anguish for most Western Europeans, it is easy to see why Sartre and Camus above all seemed to speak for and to the French public and beyond. Both men had, in fact, started their writing careers with relatively apolitical works. Sartre's *Nausea* of 1939 and Camus's *The Outsider* of 1942 were similar in their presentation of a solipsistic hero endowed with little historical awareness. Sartre, it is true, had gestured towards broader issues. The Roquentin of *Nausea* gives up the writing of an aristocrat's biography in order to create a book inspired by a jazz tune – this tune is composed by a Jew and sung by a black. Thus Roquentin rejects 'nobility' and espouses culture produced by the marginalized. Camus's outsider, however, seems unconscious of any social structure other than the broad scapegoating mechanism that allows a hypocritical society to execute 'criminals'; when Arabs figure in this novel set in North Africa, it is only as hostile presences. The writer and diplomat Conor Cruise O'Brien wrote a fiery attack on Camus in a book of 1970 whose criticisms still stand: he accused Camus of writing as a white colonist who simply overlooked the reality of France's oppression of the Arabs. O'Brien asserted that even *The Plague* (1947), set in an Algerian town and posing as a politically concerned work, ignores Arabs; and that, furthermore, to allegorize the Occupation as a plague, a medical problem, sidesteps the moral issues, for after all bacilli have no volition whereas occupiers choose to occupy.

Despite the quasi-Romanticism of *Nausea*, then, the seeds of a political consciousness were more visible than in *The Outsider*. As we have seen, only four years later Sartre was to compose *The Flies* (1943): he himself claimed that the war had politicized him, and certainly almost all his post-war drama and fiction is more anchored in social exchanges and overt political dilemmas than *Nausea* (or *The Flies*, necessarily restricted because, as we saw, staged during the Occupation). Thus the trilogy of novels that came out between 1945 and 1949, *Roads to Freedom*, airs issues that would have been unthinkable for the hero of *Nausea*. To take only one: the hero of the trilogy, Mathieu, has to find money for his mistress's abortion; it is difficult to imagine this down-to-earth quest, with all its predicaments, engaging Roquentin. Characters discuss such questions as whether to join the Communist Party, and undergo the suspense of the phony war in what is, technically speaking, the masterpiece of the trilogy. This is the second volume, *The Reprieve*, in which Sartre, through a range of different characters, creates a collage (more sustained than Malraux's) of simultaneous responses to the international situation. Both the trilogy and Sartre's post-war drama, portray personal and political options as intimately interwoven, and as being, precisely, options: humans are not subject to preordained rules but are free. Sartre's philosophical works explain the complex guises in which, according to him, this freedom presents itself to consciousness – it is barely graspable, it is beset with difficulties, but it is always available to us. We encounter again the precious and loaded word 'freedom'; and, as it did for his predecessors, it includes for Sartre aesthetic freedom. He provides a theoretical and practical underpinning for the literary experiments of both his contemporaries and his immediate successors. As early as *Nausea*, he was proposing that traditional narrative line is an unsuitable tool for the depiction of consciousness. This is because a clear cause-and-effect chronology encourages us to view life as a 'story', whereas what we need is to see our own lives as fluid and ourselves, therefore, as able to change – not as cast in the mould of nineteenth-century literary characters. (Sartre is being too sweeping about previous literature here, but so are many authors who write polemic on behalf of their own novelty.)

In *Nausea* and particularly in his philosophical works, Sartre is writing for a knowledgeable and sophisticated readership. And to some extent he does so in his plays. These are more formally innovative than has sometimes been thought. The last words of *Huis clos* (*In Camera*), his 1944 drama about three unsavoury people stuck in hell with each other for eternity, are: 'Well, let's carry on' ('Eh bien, continuons'). This heralds the finale of *Waiting for Godot*, and the open-endedness yet circularity that would characterize many challenging plays written in later decades. But Sartre is as much a *philosophe* as a philosopher – he reaches out to the public, sees his mission as a partly educational one, and does not hesitate to use fiction and theatre to that end. He aims also to rivet his spectators with inherently dramatic and topical situations, such as the political assassination carried out in a Soviet-bloc country by a reluctant stooge (*Dirty Hands*, 1948) or the madness of the ex-Nazi kept locked up by his family (*Sequestration in Altona*, 1959); other topics include Cold-War tensions and torture under the Occupation. While it could not be said that Sartre favours the well-made plot – many of his plays are bedevilled by longueurs during which existential choices are explored – he always retains the wish to draw in a wide audience that comes not only from his Enlightenment predecessors but also from nineteenth-century French theatre. Thus, as well as meditative speeches, his plays deploy quick-fire repartee and such devices as mistaken identity; and *In Camera*, at least, has the tautness of the best

French drama – now a seventeenth-century tautness, for the characters' entrapment in one room closely resembles the three unities that created, in that century's theatre, an illusion of inescapable claustrophobia and crisis. Paradoxically so: the reason Sartre feels able to create these three firmly delineated characters – a heartless coward, an infanticidal coquette and a sadistic lesbian – is that they are dead; and in Sartre's philosophy it is only when you are dead that you attain your definitive personality: until then you can always change. So Sartre has here exploited the resources of his national tradition to combine instruction with aesthetic pleasure.

Sartre's work is both severe and liberating, speaking to a post-war France that felt shame and at the same time the need to embrace the future. Camus's thought was more approachable, his fiction easier to grasp than Sartre's. His 'outsider' Meursault, taken up with enthusiasm after the war, could be readily interpreted as a figure for the times: godless, frank, concentrating on the here-and-now and his own sensory pleasures. Above all, there was a certain numbness or under-reactiveness in Meursault that harmonized with both elite and popular culture. It chimed with such new literary paradigms as Brecht's alienation effect, and also with a display of cynicism, or a strong silent heroism, to be seen in the Westerns that were starting to grip France. *The Plague*, too, with its readable style and comprehensible message, appealed to a yearning to rediscover 'goodness', but in a secular or humanist mode; it offered a sober yet attractive morality. (There is no God, but we must still help each other: in Camus's famous words, 'Peut-on être un saint sans Dieu?', 'Can one be a saint without God?', 276.) But it is not only the imperialist aspects of Camus's writing that are problematic. René Girard goes so far as to claim that it was only with such late works as *The Fall* (1956) that Camus would attain real profundity, and that he was on the verge of becoming a great novelist when he had the road accident that four years later ended his life. This is because (in Girard's argument) *The Fall* at last shows a protagonist who is not Romantically self-sufficient but is aware that he imitates others. Decidedly not the kind of hero who would dive into the Seine to save a drowning woman, he prefers to skulk amid the foggy canals of Amsterdam and to relive his humiliations by cornering interlocutors in bars. He frenziedly turns these interlocutors into distorting mirrors of his own tortured consciousness. *The Fall* is a witty work, intellectually and socially complex; this is the current of French literature that places linguistic virtuosity centre-stage and weaves a knowing web that both tantalizes and entertains. And if Camus had earlier seemed unaware of racism against Arabs, he does to some extent make that omission good in *The Fall* by sketching out the deportation of the Jews with an irony that is no less mordant for being laconic.

Camus would eventually worry late twentieth-century cultural commentators. He was an undeniably weighty figure in post-war intellectual life: he was editor-in-chief of the national newspaper *Combat*, he wrote and directed plays, and he was in the vanguard of liberal opinion, upholding just causes while speaking out against totalitarianism. His popularity was in itself significant. But he was popular in part, perhaps, because he was peddling a somewhat vague programme; and perhaps, too, because he gave a reluctantly decolonizing France a signal it wanted to hear. For Camus, who with his own white Algerian background could have made a real difference had he spoken out against France's brutality in Algeria, scarcely did so: he could not bear the idea that his homeland might be turned into a 'non-French' country. Even before adopting this stance on Algeria, Camus had quarrelled with Sartre and other contemporaries. The quarrel was complex but revolved fundamentally around their charge that in his essay *The Rebel* (1951) Camus was elevating human suffering to a metaphysical level and was overlooking the economic, historical and political conditions that determined this suffering (the same is true of his wartime essay *The Myth of Sisyphus*). Furthermore, Camus, they argued, was selective in his condemnation of injustice. The judgement of posterity has increasingly sided with Camus's opponents; his political thought is now perceived as tending to the simplistic in novels and drama as well as in essays. For example, he places too much emphasis on 'the absurd' as a catch-all explanation for human behaviour. (In his play *Caligula*, 1945, the Emperor Caligula's cruelty is put down to the fact that he has seen the absurd.) And this leads Camus (until *The Fall*, at least) to duck such thorny moral problems as sadism – problems which Sartre, on the contrary, was already tackling head-on in his *Being and Nothingness* of the war years.

Many might indeed now argue that a more important thinker than Camus had emerged in the person of Simone de Beauvoir (1908–86). Her book about the history and condition of women, *The Second Sex* (1949), was a summum of French feminist thought since the Middle Ages, but pushed previous arguments further than any earlier writer had dared, and illustrated them with unprecedentedly comprehensive examples. Beauvoir also set part of the agenda for the later discipline of cultural studies; for she draws in equal measure on reported experiences and on images of women in literature. That is to say: representations are evidence as important as documentation. Beauvoir discusses a great range of women's experiences, from the infant girl's suckling at the breast to the sensations prized by lesbians; from the young girl's mode of urination to the adolescent's menstruation; from the frustrations of housework to the daughter's position as a chattel in societies ancient and modern. Beauvoir was a naturally gifted stylist and rhetorician (her use of irony, for example, is masterly); but it was her espousal of existentialism that contributed to her felicitous and renowned formulation 'You are not born a woman: you become one'. In other words, there is no such thing as a female essence to which all women conform; their 'femaleness' is created by familial and social pressures. This had been said, especially by her nineteenth-century predecessors, but 'ne'er so well expressed'. It is subtler in French: 'On ne naît pas femme: on le devient' (II 13). The loose pronoun 'on' is gender-neutral and always carries a masculine agreement; the 'le' in front of 'devient' also suggests masculinity. 'On' can be both formal and informal, appealing to registers used by different social classes. And in this phrase the word for 'is born' is a half-pun ('naît' is a near homophone of 'n'est', 'is not'). It conveys a negative: we could almost read this as 'On n'est pas femme': not only 'You are not born a woman', but 'You are *not* a woman'. 'Femininity' is thus undermined at all levels of the sentence. Arguably its lapidary and alliterative nature owes something to the rise of the advertising catchphrase. Feminism needed a slogan: here it was.

The Second Sex was soon translated into English (1953), in an unfortunately truncated version; nevertheless, the translation had an enormous impact. Indeed, the influence of *The Second Sex* was at first stronger in English-speaking countries than in France, where in many quarters it was regarded as scandalous; however, it was the work that (albeit slowly) led to the resurgence of French feminism in the 1970s. (See below, pp. 164–6.)

Sartre, Camus and Beauvoir were all what Sartre called 'committed' writers; that is, they engaged with the political issues of their day and reflected these in their writing, however variously. Meanwhile, a literary movement was developing that was, apparently, at a polar opposite to 'commitment': the New Novel. Yet, as we shall see, it was not without political implications; and significantly, the New Novelists were so closely associated with the publishing house Editions de Minuit that they were also known as the Ecole de Minuit, 'the School of Midnight'. This publisher (clandestinely founded, as we saw, during the Occupation) had, from 1948, built up a reputation for avant-garde literature, publishing Beckett from 1951 on, and then such challenging novelists as Marguerite Duras and Simon, who would win the Nobel Prize for Literature (1985). Again, then, we see in France an easy transition from left-wing politics to experimental literature.

In the early stages, the main New Novelists were held to be Nathalie Sarraute (1902–99), Robbe-Grillet (1922–2008) and Butor (b. 1926). Their novels radically deflated plot-impetus, foregrounded fantasy in the very line of the narrative, and alluded constantly to fiction-writing as well as fiction-making. Robbe-Grillet, the most startling of the three, constructs elaborate sequences of half-repeated scenes within a superficially thrilling, stylistically pared-down 'story'. Thus a detective is sent in to solve a murder (*Rubbers*, 1953); a travelling salesman peddling his wares on an island may or may not have killed a young woman on that island (*The Voyeur*, 1955); a jealous husband watches and wonders about his wife and her possible lover (*Jealousy/The Venetian Blind*, 1957 – the French title, *La Jalousie*, can mean either). But the plots, such as they are, turn to farce or at least irresolution: in *Rubbers*, twenty-four hours are somehow lost, 'rubbed out', and the detective ends up killing the victim who had supposedly died the day before. Robbe-Grillet's novels recreate *déjà-vu* and other dizzying moments when in our heads past merges with present – but slightly differently each time; and if we start to get involved with an old-fashioned excitement in his plots, it is we who are the suckers.

Sarraute, for her part, writes works in which interpersonal events – often a mere change of body-language – are the jumping-off point for an exploration of our inner sensitivities. She narrates the often comical trajectory of those reactions, buried or only half-recognized, that dictate our relations with our peers. So, if I venture an opinion on a painting and you drop your eyes, not only do I know I've said something wrong, I also feel as if I've been felled by a club. It is worse if there are witnesses: they will gather round and gaze at the fallen victim before baring their own fangs preparatory to another attack on the vulnerable fool. Sarraute's most sustainedly amusing and self-conscious novel is her *Golden Fruit* (1963), which charts the ticklish reactions to a novel called – precisely – *Golden Fruit*, and the vagaries that make it dip in and out of fashion.

Butor describes our subtle and often slow mental adaptations to either external stimuli or apparently new ideas. Often the thoughts were already there but now gradually move forward to become accessible parts of consciousness. In *Using Time* (1956) and *The Modification* (1957), the heroes' desires and sense of self change as their imaginations adjust to, respectively, a bleak English Midlands city in the course of a year, and a decisive train journey between Paris and Rome – decisive not because anything 'happens' but because during the journey the hero changes his mind, realizing he does not want to leave his wife for the mistress whom he was on his way to see. Again, the very process of composition is part of the plot.

In *Using Time*, the hero keeps a diary and gradually, as he learns English, also writes with increasing fluency in his native French, thus finding a voice (sometimes an obtrusively over-ornamented one); by the end of *The Modification*, we can assume that we have been reading an account written by the hero, or have at least read his inner 'rewriting' of himself. That self is in some sense the reader's own, since throughout the protagonist calls himself not 'I' but 'you' ('The priest on your left gets up', etc.). Furthermore, this 'you' is in French the formal and plural 'vous', not 'tu', thus implicitly addressing a community.

These bare summaries inadequately convey the disorientating experience of actually reading the New Novelists. On almost every page they whip away the most familiar guidelines of fiction, such as who is speaking, or what exactly has happened in a scene seemingly being related before our very eyes. These scenes often take the form of mini-tales recounted with verve but then, with equal gusto, replaced by another tale, the suggestion being that the previous one was merely a fantasy in the mind of a character. Who is the narrator – is there even a narrator? Where is the dividing-line between actual and imagined events: does a character really sprawl on a divan, legs in the air and yattering about everything that comes into his head, or is his retrospective embarrassment making him imagine he did so? (This is a re-writing of a more acceptable picture on the previous page, where the same character was merely sitting on the divan with his legs crossed, chatting comfortably: Sarraute, *Le Planétarium*, 1959, 150.)

The New Novelists theorized their works extensively, defining and redefining their enterprise. The most famous of their essays are Sarraute's *The Era of Suspicion* (1956) and Robbe-Grillet's collection in *For A New Novel* (1963); also remarkable for its succinctness was the statement by a lesser-known practitioner, Ricardou, that the New Novel was no longer 'the writing of an adventure, but the adventure of a writing' ('l'aventure d'une écriture'). In other words, the novel had abandoned the eventful story and had taken for its subject the process of fictional construction – individual in each work ('a' writing suggests this), but with a shared wish to evoke composition itself. It was in this period that the phrase *mise en abyme*, a term first seized on by Gide in 1889, came into prominence. *Mise en abyme* (literally, 'setting in an abyss') denotes internal duplication, a reduced model of a work contained within it as one of its parts. For example, on the old Quaker Oats packet was a picture of a Quaker holding a packet of Quaker Oats. On that packet was, of course, a smaller picture of a Quaker holding a packet of Quaker Oats. And so on to infinity. The *mise en abyme* was the order of the day, and in its apparent sophistication provided a platform from which to attack with abandon almost all previous literature. (The phrase came from heraldry: thus the sophistication is in its origins linked to an aristocratic emblem, the shield-shaped coat of arms. The 'nobility' of elite literature dies hard.)

Robbe-Grillet and Sarraute launched these attacks with particular relish: Balzac became a favourite whipping-boy. At first critics took their strictures seriously, and repeated them (almost *ad nauseam*) in their accounts of these strange works. But Butor himself came to Balzac's defence in an essay called 'Balzac and reality', and gradually a more complex view crept in. First, it was recognized that for centuries experimental writers' manifestos have tended to overstress their own novelty and denigrate their predecessors (as we have just seen with Sartre): it is part of their own search for cultural status. Furthermore, the New Novelists were not the only ones claiming 'newness'. In film, from the mid-fifties on there was the 'New Wave', in *haute couture* there was the 'New Look', in drama the 'New Theatre' (what we call the 'Theatre of the Absurd'). It was as if everything had to be new. Here again, plausibly, is that hidden embarrassment about the Second World War, the wish to break decisively with everything 'retrograde' in France's history; these writers' falsified view of the past was revealing in its very hyperbole. Second, following Butor's lead, critics pointed out that self-consciousness and self-reflectingness may be found 'even' in Balzac, and indubitably in many other recent predecessors – to pluck simply four novelists from the preceding 120 years: Stendhal, Flaubert, Proust and Gide. Indeed – critics now said – authors have displayed awareness of their own curious procedures since the beginnings of literature. In the mid-1970s the critic Robert Alter, for example, would claim that, from its origins, the genre of fiction in particular has teased the reader and played with the question of its own veracity (*Partial Magic*). It is simply that at certain junctures – of which the mid-twentieth century is one – this teasing has been more flagrant than at others. The eighteenth century is another: *Tristram Shandy*, Diderot's *Jacques le fataliste*. That is not to mention the poets who had already been proceeding with identical assumptions (Mallarmé, Valéry, Apollinaire): the New Novelists had strangely little to say about these.

To be sure, the New Novelists *were* doing something radical: the hostility and bewilderment of many readers shows that, as does the retreat from their more extreme techniques by later novelists. A fair summary might be that the New Novelists adopted self-consciousness as a badge of honour and that it became the main motor of their works. It also made the novel more overtly ludic than it had been for decades or even centuries. In the New Novelists' juggling with structure, language, character, plausibility, we can see the liking for games that has often characterized French literature and culture. But, equally, we can see a playfulness that is a product of those immediate post-war years. It is as if the novelists feel they can relax – can present a wilful hedonism in counterbalance to the more earnest lessons issued by such writers as Sartre and Camus.

The New Novel is not entirely given over to play or 'art for art's sake'. The manifestos suggest that this mode of writing can change readers' lives by changing their attitudes. Furthermore, and almost in spite of themselves, these authors do reflect historically specific concerns. The specificity can be uncomfortable. Robbe-Grillet often uses semi-pornographic, sadistic images of women to 'hook' readers before bumping them out of the fantasy: all in the service of an artful aesthetic . . . or displaying a misogyny stubbornly entrenched in a still schizoid culture? More often, though, the social insights are sharp and subtle. Sarraute has claimed that her works are ahistorical in as much as subterranean jealousies or anxieties can be detected in any community, at any time. For all that, her works dramatize a peer-group pressure that may be more likely to surface in – to use Alexander Mitscherlich's phrase – a 'society without the father': a society that gives ever less credence to the vesting of authority in one person or in an oligarchy (*Society without the Father*, 1969). France could hardly lend such credence in the wake of Pétain and the Vichy regime; as for de Gaulle, his adoption of the 'strong leader' persona was perceived as a charade by many. Furthermore, Sarraute's works are set not in some never-never land of a 'universal' psyche but – it would appear – in post-war intellectual Parisian circles. The capital still reigns. *The Planetarium* refers to recognizable areas of Paris and evokes a group that clusters round a well-known woman writer; it alludes to a French literary past (for example, the writer's first name is Germaine, as was Germaine de Staël's); and it describes an uneasy tyranny exerted by 'intellectuals' and rivalry between them. And Sarraute's later novels, while more anonymized in setting, do still make aesthetic debate the trigger for peculiarly modern forms of squirming, embarrassment, outright hostility between supposed 'equals'. Her figures of speech are also locatable. They conjure up not only 'timeless' tableaux of suspects exposed in front of a crowd of onlookers, but recent ones too: colossal statues, totalitarian systems, guards shooting escapees from towers with raking searchlights, hint at Soviet bloc and Fascist regimes. Finally, Sarraute, like all the New Novelists, draws on local currents of thought. She conjures up a psychology that adapts in response to its immediate surroundings (this adaptation is what she calls 'tropisms'), thus returning us indirectly to the eighteenth- and nineteenth-century stress on environment; she owes a debt to phenomenology, a philosophy that explores how perception *seems* in the here and now. This philosophy derives from Husserl and Heidegger and was taken up by Sartre and his fellow-philosopher Merleau-Ponty; it was an integral part of Sarraute's cultural milieu.

No more than Sarraute is Butor simply 'playing'. He puts his finger on an aspect of what would become 'cultural studies', or at least practises a form of local anthropology. His heroes pointedly register the signs emitted by the differing cultures in which they find themselves, from the red buses and red Bass beer triangles of England to the myths woven round Rome ancient and modern. Butor's works were early on said to enact an 'affectivity of geography'; these days, we would be more likely to say they enact an 'affectivity of cultural codes'. Butor is concerned to create patterns rather than delve deep into their significance. Nevertheless, in so far as fiction shapes the direction of academic disciplines, he has contributed; his two major works, not coincidentally, appeared in the same three-year span as Lévi-Strauss's *Tristes Tropiques* (1955) and Barthes's *Mythologies* (1957). (See below, pp. 155–8, 169.)

The New Novel also sardonically twins itself with one of the most popular forms of the twentieth century, being often a skit on the detective story or thriller. All three of the novelists we have been looking at incorporate the crime-story formula, sometimes directly (Robbe-Grillet in *Rubbers* and *The Voyeur*; Butor in *Using Time*; Sarraute in *Martereau* and in others that enact 'mysteries' to be turned over and over but never solved). It has been said that while the elite literature of a period will reflect that period's anxieties without mitigation, the more popular literature will equally reflect anxieties but will provide reassurance. Like the New Novel, the detective story and often the thriller rewind the chronology of narrative, starting with the end (the murder/s), and gradually unfolding the events that may have led up to the crime. But these tales finish with the air of a magician pulling a rabbit from a hat: the suggestion is: 'all puzzles are now solved', just what a public in uncertain times will want to think. The New Novels' pseudo-detections, however, pull out only fake rabbits. They lead readers up the garden path not on a temporary basis but as a permanent technique, making us wonder, finally, just what kind of comfort it is that we seek from both popular and elite literature. For in spite of all the cross-overs, the New Novel is 'high' literature, proud of its own difficulty.

One reason, no doubt, why the New Novel liked to bounce off the detective story was because of the great – and American-related – popularity of this genre in France. The detective story had a venerable history, dating back at least to the mid-nineteenth-century novels of Gaboriau (1832–73), but production had gathered pace in the interwar period with such collections as Le Masque, founded in 1927; the post-war years saw the thriller/detective-story (known familiarly as the *polar*) reach an acme. The Série Noire, founded almost immediately after the Liberation in 1945, translated and adapted English-language works like Chandler's, and produced home-grown authors at least two of whom pretended at first to be American (Arcouët and Amila); while Vian's *J'irai cracher sur vos tombes* of 1946 (*I'll Spit on Your Graves*) was a pastiche *polar*, purporting to be translated from the American and resulting in a conviction for pornography. The thousandth Série Noire title (American, as it happened) appeared in 1966. It was indeed between 1945 and 1968 that French attraction to the United States was at its height. This attraction too had a long history. Almost as 'foreign' as the Orient was the America analysed by the mid-nineteenth-century historian Tocqueville in his *Democracy in America* (1835–40). Tocqueville promoted the democracy that he saw as already well advanced in that country. Others, however – for example Stendhal in post-1830 texts – expressed a fear that 'American democracy' would dilute high artistic standards, and that in a country full of 'grocers' (that is, self-employed small businessmen) opera would disappear. This suspiciousness would persist into the twentieth century in the form of mistrust of, and rivalry with, a successful United States, which in due course would be presented as a threat to France's cultural hegemony – in certain governmental quarters, at least. The public, however, perceived no such threat. American *polars*, whether books or films, were devoured by France. One home-grown film of these years is indicative. In Godard's *A bout de souffle* (*Breathless*, 1959) the hero, a cheeky thief, flirts with the United States in the person of his girlfriend (endowed with a hyperbolic American accent), who in the end betrays him. The jazz backing, too, highlights the place in French consciousness of American culture. But Godard's great film deploys tricks that coincide with those of post-war elite literature: the heavy American accent has an 'alienation' effect; the jump cuts with their discontinuous chronology, the in-jokes for film enthusiasts, the quizzically open ending, are not dissimilar to the techniques of the New Novel. America is there, but the ironies are thoroughly French.

Exuberant games, deliberate inconclusiveness, deflation of authority were also enacted in one of France's most remarkable post-war literary successes, again a 'spectacle': the Theatre of the Absurd. As is by now clear, the revival of French drama did not spring from nowhere. It had been building up since the late nineteenth century, with Jarry's and Maeterlinck's experimental plays (and Apollinaire's *The Breasts of Tiresias*, 1918), and with pioneering productions by such directors as Lugné-Poë. (See above, pp. 109–10.) Great reformers of the inter-war years – Copeau, Jouvet, Baty and Pitoëff – had exploited the bare stage and group movement, and had revived circus and *commedia dell'arte* techniques. Influences had been absorbed from abroad: from Russia that of Chekhov, from Italy that of Pirandello. The trail-blazing *Six Characters in Search of an Author* (1921–5) had made Pirandello a household name among the Paris and Berlin intelligentsia of the 1920s, and Pirandello himself wrote excitedly to his daughter from Paris on the occasion of the first French production: 'I've truly arrived at the peak of my literary career!' Finally, the dramatist and theorist Artaud (1896–1948) had argued, in *The Theatre and Its Double* of 1938, that theatre must return to its early functions as a primitive exorcizing rite; to that end, it must abandon the fine language and intricate psychology of the Western tradition, and become a theatre of the body – of gestures, groans and cries – a 'theatre of cruelty' that would truly 'infect' audiences and enact their deepest fears and desires.

Now post-war dramatists such as the Irish-born Beckett (1906–89), the Romanian Ionesco (1912–94) and the gay convict Genet (1910–86) would further these reforms and give them international standing. French theatre perhaps needed an injection from the 'margins' at this point; however, Beckett's and Ionesco's adoption of Paris as their cultural 'home' is equally significant: it was a two-way enrichment. (Beckett's identification with his new country was such that he joined the Resistance during the war.) French drama was now at its best since its previous high point three hundred years earlier. Its concerns overlapped with those of the New Novelists, but in making them theatrical it also made them more accessible. (*Waiting for Godot*, 1952, was famously received with understanding when it played to the inmates of San Quentin jail.) It might seem paradoxical to speak of these plays, in which little apparently happens, as theatrical. But, just as broad political interests shape the New Novels, so too Absurdist plays stage power relationships, lending them a tension that was not always recognized. (In Britain Ionesco's work provoked a polemic, led by the theatre critic Kenneth Tynan, attacking the playwright for his lack of social purpose.) This staging of power and powerlessness reveals the enduring influence not only of Artaud but also of the first 'absurd' play, *Ubu Roi*. In Beckett's *Godot*, Pozzo has power over Lucky, and everyone – potentially – has power over the tramps; in *Endgame* (1957), Hamm has power over Clov and his own parents, living in dustbins. In Ionesco's *The Lesson* (1951) the teacher bullies the pupil, and his *Rhinoceros* (1960) is an allegory for the totalitarian state. In Genet, the fantasies woven round 'masters' are acted out in front of us by the servants of *The Maids* (1947), and in *The Balcony* (1956) the habitués of a brothel appear on shoe-blocks, artificially tall and exaggeratedly dressed up as figures of authority – bishop, judge, general. These plays are not historically specific in the way that Romantic drama, or Balzac's novels, were. But they do demonstrate elemental social mechanisms, those of control or would-be control, and the role these play in our fantasy lives – literally the role, for we are play-acting to ourselves and to each other as we construct these mechanisms. Post-war France no doubt needed both to escape specifics yet also to find a way of pondering political abuses.

As I have suggested, the intelligentsia needed, too, to reinstate literary sophistication as part of its recovery of faith in itself. It was well served in this not only by the New Novel but also by the eternal present of Beckett's plays – or what was perceived as such; in fact, his drama does chart move-ment of a kind: the second act of *Godot* is more anguished than the first, Hamm's mother Nell does seemingly die in the course of *Endgame*, the mound in which Winnie is buried up to her waist reaches her neck by the end of *Happy Days* (1963). But the elite wanted to recover that knowing rejection of teleology that had begun at the end of the nineteenth century; and it wanted to recapture literary playfulness not just via the narrative acrobatics of the New Novel, but in virtuoso linguistic games of a kind not to be found in Malraux or Sartre. Here one Absurdist playwright in par-ticular fitted the bill: Ionesco. Ionesco does and does not follow Artaud's programme. Does, in that his characters can defamiliarize language to a point where it resembles a mere gesture or vocalization and strings of formulae become primitive babble almost like a bird's twitterings. Does not, in that these linguistic 'gestures' allow series of words to follow rhym-ingly on from each other, whereupon other meanings emerge: 'Le pape dérape! Le pape n'a pas de soupape. La soupape a un pape': 'The Pope is skidding! The Pope has no valve. The valve has a Pope'. To link 'pape', 'dérape' and 'soupape' (Pope, skids, valve/plug) – as happens in one of the final speeches of *The Bald Primadonna* (1950) – may not be a blow struck for atheism, but neither is it ideologically innocent. Religion and patriarchs are sliding; whatever form of safety-valve or 'plug' they represented has disappeared – or at least, the connection between them is inverted and plain to see: the need for the valve or plug comes first, then the Pope fills it. Speech may have mutated into an Artaudian excrescence of the body, apparently a mere movement of the tongue, yet it cannot really lose its cultural meanings.

With the Theatre of the Absurd, especially with Beckett, a new kind of tragedy emerges, Chekhovian in origin. It no longer shows high-born or dignified characters losing status and potentially bringing down the whole body politic in their fall. Modern tragic characters may already, indeed, be at the bottom of the social heap, ignoble not noble. Nor do they undergo the lucid agony of a Phèdre; their awareness comes and goes, is often non-existent. They are not fully tragic but pathetic or tragicomic. It has been suggested that modern tragedy resides not in the loss of the transcendental (as in earlier tragedy) but in our loss of belief in the transcendental. It was post-war France that gave this loss of belief its most accomplished and magnetic expression: France, the home of Mallarmé's poetry, which some seventy years earlier had similarly created a disturbing relationship between poignancy and playfulness, and similarly left readers puzzled as to whether they were witnessing grief or an imitation of it that hovered on the verge of pastiche. So one way of looking at post-war French theatre is to see it as breaking completely with its most distinguished ancestor, classical French tragedy, but another is to see it as the apogee of that move away from the 'noble' that had been gathering pace since the 1820s.

Equally bold, yet equally redolent of longer-standing strains in French culture, were the productions of OULIPO. This acronym stands for Ouvroir de Littérature Potentielle, Workshop of Potential Literature. Founded principally by the novelist and poet Queneau (1903–76) and three colleagues (among whom was a mathematician, Le Lionnais), it also included such distinguished writers as the poet Roubaud (b. 1932), the novelist Perec (1936–82), and the Italian author Calvino (1923–85). It met initially in 1960 and its activities and output (including two manifestos) continued throughout the 1960s and 1970s. It saw the creation of literature as arising ideally from the imposition of rigid constraints, sometimes quasi-mathematical. Thus the sonnet is a good example of 'littérature potentielle', combining rigorous structure with freedom of invention. This 'potential literature' could operate in two ways: either as a set of transformational rules applied to existing literary works (Queneau reduced Mallarmé's swan sonnet to a near-haiku), or, more famously, through voluntary restrictions in the author's own work. For instance, Perec's work *La Disparition, The Disappearance* (1969), was written entirely without the use of the letter e, an omission that went unnoticed by some critics on its publication. And Roubaud's work ε of 1967 brings together the literary and the strategic pattern, its structure following the rules of the Japanese board-game *go*. The symmetrical and arithmetical have not, then, lost their power to enchant in these maze-like and jokey works. Finally, although OULIPO deliberately bypasses the Surrealists' interest in the uncontrolled, it retains from them and earlier authors a special attention paid to the ordinary. For OULIPO as for its predecessors, the everyday – the humble, we may still say – preserves both its familiarity and its capacity to show the way to something marvellous. OULIPO's masterpiece, *La Vie mode d'emploi* by Perec (*Life: Instructions for Use*), long in gestation, would burst on the literary scene with the award of the Prix Médicis in 1978. It would bring together both sides: the willing adoption of formal constraints, and access to the wondrous by way of the 'normal'. This 'novel of infinite extensions' has ninety-nine chapters which move like a knight's tour of a chessboard around the room-plan of a Parisian apartment building, revealed as it would be if its façade were to be removed at about eight o'clock one evening. Diverse, sad, quirky, labyrinthine, full of mock-scholarly appara-tus, Perec's novel would be the feeling culmination of a refinement once more staking its claim.

Post-war French literature, then, displays characteristics that could appear incompatible, yet often creatively fuse: overt political commitment; the depiction of a passive numbness or alienation; ostentatiously mirrored structures that dilute the teleological; and the figuring of 'lower-class' characters like maidservants and tramps – often semi-willing victims col-laborating in the social delusions that trap them. This literature both fed into and was nourished by the writings of thinkers who are still celebrated, and still a source of controversy, outside France. Notably, these include literary critics such as Barthes (1915–80) and Blanchot (1907–2003), also an autobiographer and novelist; equally notably, many of them write power-fully figurative and allusive prose.

We might compare Barthes and Blanchot with two well-known anglo-phone literary and cultural critics of the same period, Richard Hoggart (b. 1918) and Raymond Williams (1921–88). Hoggart, in *The Uses of Literacy* (1958), turned his critic's eye on the reading habits and domestic appurte-nances of the British working class; Williams discussed the relationship between culture (especially written culture) and prevailing ideologies in *Culture and Society* (1958) and *The Long Revolution* (1961). Both opened up fertile areas of research in the anglophone world; in particular, Hoggart's creation of the Birmingham Centre for Cultural Studies in 1964 gave birth to new syllabuses, and exported academics, all over the UK, the United

States and Australia. Yet, writing in 1992, Stuart Hall, Hoggart's successor as director of the Birmingham Centre, singled out post-war French thinkers as the key influence on later anglophone cultural studies. It has been suggested that this was in part because – although the pragmatic and down-to-earth focus of Hoggart was revolutionary, even visionary – when younger academics came to market their books, they found it easier to 'sell' theories that could be 'applicable' in any context than to analyse – say – the significance of housewives' attitudes to their children's education in Welsh mining towns. We may simply signal here that French thinkers of the same generation were starting from a different base. They were writing in and for a culture that deemed it both permissible and desirable for intellectuals to mingle philosophy with ethical and political imperatives and to do so, if wished, by way of an alliterative, assonantal and even punning rhetoric. Of course Hoggart and Williams have a political agenda, and Hoggart writes well; but both proceed in an understated way, a rather 'English' way, it is tempting to say – at any rate, understated by comparison with their zestful counterparts over the Channel, whose style can be hilariously funny, dazzling, peacock-like. These French thinkers had been reared on Huysmans, Mallarmé, Proust and Valéry, not to mention the still earlier virtuosos of language whose history I have traced through previous chapters. And their sometimes lateral or suggestive organization of argument was informed by developments in French drama, film, fiction and poetry of the time.

Thus the philosopher, historian and social and ethical debater Foucault (1926–84) was also a literary critic; the psychoanalyst Lacan (1901–81) and the philosopher Derrida (1930–2004) play with language to a degree that some readers still find outrageous. Lacan builds arguments around such puns as 'omelette/hommelette' ('little man/feminized man/scrambled man'; from *Ecrits, Writings*); Derrida's theses propose, and in their very language enact, multiple series of signs so slippery that they cannot be seized. It is precisely this stress on the arbitrariness of the 'signifier' (deriving from the early twentieth-century work of the linguistician Saussure) that has been attractive and irritating outside France. Two points are important here. First, the presentation of a constantly metamorphosing consciousness was, in this context too, welcome to a post-war French intelligentsia that had good reason to doubt certainties and yearned to revive irony. Second, and to recap: it sprang from a centuries-old and culturally singular nurturing of *philosophes* who were allowed to give free rein to imaginative gifts; that nurturing had become integral to France's image of itself.

Let us end this chapter with a paradigmatic extract from the anthropologist Lévi-Strauss (1908–2009). Lévi-Strauss helped create what came to be known as Structuralism. A professor of social anthropology at the prestigious Collège de France from 1959, he had however trained as a philosopher. He came under fire from traditional anthropologists for the supposedly poor evidence of his fieldwork; but his theories do not depend on empirical research to the degree that theirs do, and he claims that understanding consists in the reduction of one type of reality to another – the 'true' reality is never the most obvious. He lauds the kind of intellectual activity that depends on *bricolage*, that is, the putting together of hitherto unlinked 'odds and ends'. The structures beneath variety are what is important; they are based on the 'universal' structures of the human mind. Lévi-Strauss's theories are anti-historicist and anti-individualistic, undermining the human subject's self-image as creator of order; they were attacked for different reasons by other eminent thinkers such as Sartre and Derrida. And Lévi-Strauss would not find favour with feminists: in 1980 he would vote against the admission of Marguerite Yourcenar as the first female member of the Académie Française on the grounds that an institution which had excluded women for three centuries should not precipitately alter its ways. But Lévi-Strauss's theories have proved valuable to numerous writers in a variety of disciplines; and they were seized upon by literary critics (a development of which Lévi-Strauss himself disapproved). His stress on the co-existence of a 'bits-and-pieces' reality with an underlying strong patterning that displaces the individual seemed to 'fit' with post-war developments like the Theatre of the Absurd and the New Novel. In particular, it enabled literary criticism to move away from the assumption that texts could be 'explained' by authors' biographies – an assumption that had been dying out in anglophone literary criticism from the 1920s on, but that still had a stranglehold on French academe. There was thus a striking confluence in France between, on the one hand, a wide-ranging thinker (whose education was not only philosophical but legal, and whose ideas affected psychoanalysis as well as ethnology), and, on the other, new movements in literature and aesthetics. And this confluence was facilitated by Lévi-Strauss's own literary gifts. He can write, with equal ease, wittily or elegiacally, and always with complexity, as our excerpt will show. In his 1955 autobiographical essay *Sad Tropics* (the French title is alliterative: *Tristes Tropiques*), Lévi-Strauss talks about the West's fantasies that 'savages' are cannibals who will pop 'us' in their cooking-pot; in reality it is we who have eaten them. He addresses the natives of the Amazon forest:

Pauvre gibier pris aux pièges de la civilisation mécanique, sauvages de la forêt amazonienne, tendres et impuissantes victimes, je peux me résigner à comprendre le destin qui vous anéantit, mais non point être dupe de cette sorcellerie plus chétive que la vôtre, qui brandit devant un public avide des albums en kodachrome remplaçant vos masques détruits. Croit-il par leur intermédiaire réussir à s'approprier vos charmes? Non satisfait encore, ni même conscient de vous abolir, il lui faut rassasier fièvreusement de vos ombres le cannibalisme nostalgique d'une histoire à laquelle vous avez déjà succombé. (31)

(Poor game, caught in the traps of mechanical civilization; savages of the Amazon forest; tender, impotent victims – I can resign myself to understanding the fate that is obliterating you, but I cannot be fooled by this witchcraft that is punier than your own, that brandishes in front of a greedy public colour photo-albums to replace your masks, now destroyed. Does this public think that, through them, it can appropriate your charms? Not yet satisfied with your destruction, nor even aware that it is destroying you, it must feverishly satiate, from your ghosts, a cannibalism nostalgic for a history to which you have already succumbed.)

The passage is full of poetic cadences, lamenting yet playful metaphors that switch slyly between cultures, and double meanings. 'Charms' means both spells and attractions; 'impotent' means both powerless and sexually impotent, thereby reminding us of another Western myth – that 'natives' are endowed with special virility; and 'tender', finally, conveys both a moral quality and a culinary one – it is we Europeans who are savouring the tender flesh of the Amazon natives. In these three dense sentences we see the measure of what French post-war thinkers dared to do with the language. Combined with their humanity and charisma, their emphasis on slippery representations would be irresistible to other Western cultures.

8

After May 1968

De Gaulle was succeeded by two centre-right Presidents (Pompidou in 1969 and Giscard d'Estaing in 1974), and other centre-right politicians have held the Presidency since 1995 (Chirac from 1995 to 2007, and since 2007 Sarkozy). Yet there were fourteen years during which the Socialist Party held the Presidency, in the person of Mitterrand (1981–95) – almost as long as Napoleon was First Consul then Emperor. During these fourteen years, it is true, the vagaries of the electoral system, with its checks and balances, produced some prime ministers from the centre-right, but Socialist Party ones were in power for the greater part of Mitterrand's Presidency (1984–8, 1991–5); more recently the Socialist Jospin has cohabited as prime minister with the conservative Chirac (1997–2002).

On one view, then, May 68 had little marked effect on the overall direction of French politics, and may even have provoked some to return to the far right. For it was after 1968 that Le Pen and his racist Front National rose to prominence, gaining noteworthy electoral victories from 1983 on – especially in 2002 when in the first round of Presidential elections Le Pen obtained enough votes to qualify for the second round, an unprecedented success for a politician of such extremist views. Horrified liberals ensured that he was decisively beaten in the second round, and defeats in the 2007 elections left the Front National in debt. At the time of writing (2009–10), the party has had to sell its headquarters to a Chinese university in order to raise much-needed cash and its bank accounts have been frozen in disputes with creditors. It seems inconceivable that a politician as right-wing as, say, the Italian Berlusconi could hold power for long in France. However, France does occupy a somewhat more parlous position in this respect than other Northern European countries. To take the most obvious comparison, that with the other major ex-colonial power Britain: Britain has spawned such atrocious crimes as arson attacks on Asian households, and other racist murders, and the British National Party and United Kingdom Independence Party do have a presence; but they have not so far wielded anything approaching the electoral influence of Le Pen, and Britain has no equivalent of a real-life 'Marianne' like Brigitte Bardot mixing with and supporting the extreme right. Nor is there an anglophone Houellebecq (b. 1958), the talented sleaze-and-shock novelist whose *Platform* (2001) led to a prosecution for inciting racial hatred.

Yet, despite its patchy impact on French voters, May 68 has had significant reverberations. The sometimes quirky self-expression paraded by the students who began it all was more far-reaching than could have seemed likely at the time. It encouraged the growth of 'identity politics' that led to numerous legal and social reforms for women and to rights for gays, these latter enshrined in a 1999 law that allowed civil unions (known as PACS: 'Pacte civil de solidarité'). These reforms put France well ahead of many Western democracies, including the UK (whereas it had lagged behind with other liberal measures such as the abolition of the death penalty, 1981). French identity politics would inspire other Western cultures; and May 68 remains a symbolic break in the history of post-war France, a point from which many social and intellectual configurations of the last four decades originate. These include an increase in the influence of the universities and a now general acceptance of the claim that all writing is political, articulating an ideological position whether or not the writer is aware of this.

Concomitantly the sense has grown that historical truths may be as painful as a repressed trauma, and that these truths must be brought out into consciousness and grasped. One of these has been the cruelty of France's colonial practices. Another has been the still-hidden wrongdoing of the Occupation. The acknowledgement of this latter, although piecemeal and reluctant, has indelibly marked late twentieth-century French culture. It started with Ophüls's film of 1971, *Le Chagrin et la pitié* (*Sorrow and Pity*), a four-hour sequence of newsreels and interviews that show the life of the city Clermont-Ferrand under the Occupation. Ophüls had started work on this just before 1968; it was designed in part to shake France out of a complacent Gaullist view of its history, and betokens the shift in awareness that ushered in the May events. The sequence was banned from French television when released and was shown only in private cinemas (thus indicating afresh the link between censorship and psychological repression). Its techniques, echoing those of other post-war forms, adopted multiple points of view and often prioritized image over spoken word. These techniques would become typical of both the films and the fiction that during this period tried retrospectively to explore the contradictions of post-1940 France. Colin Davis puts it thus: 'the "return to history" that can be observed in the 1970s and 1980s has significantly involved, not a rejection of modernist narrative experimentation, but an acceptance of its relevance for a view of history as untotalized, containing numerous alternative or competing narratives that cannot easily be resolved' (Davis and Fallaize, *French Fiction in the Mitterrand Years*, 2000, 64). Older traditions, too, inform these presentations. The elegiac title *Le Chagrin et la pitié* (which reads like a line of verse) endows its two abstract nouns with a dignity characteristic of much great French literature. They suggest a world in which mourning and compassion walk the stage without being directly visualizable. (The title of the more recent *Caché*, a French-language film made in 2005 by the Austrian Haneke, demonstrates similar political and artistic ambiguities: part of the mystery succinctly indicated in the one-word title *Hidden* arises, it transpires, from the Algerian War.)

Le Chagrin et la pitié marked, then, the onset of a slow admission. It was not until 1983 that collaboration was acknowledged in French school textbooks; not until 1985 that the director Lanzmann brought out *Shoah*, a nine-and-a-half-hour documentary on the Holocaust; not until 1991 that the Vichy police chief Bousquet was re-tried for directing the round-up of Jews for concentration camps (he had been acquitted in 1949); and not until 1995 that the French state officially recognized the deportation of the Jews. Literature contributed to this burgeoning awareness with, for example, the painful novel *Quel beau dimanche* (*What a Fine Sunday*, 1981) by Semprun (b. 1923), a Spanish concentration-camp survivor who writes in French and has spent most of his life in France; Wiesel (b. 1928), another concentration-camp survivor and non-French national who has written in French, was awarded the Nobel Peace Prize in 1986. The recent interest shown by scholars of French literature in 'hauntology' derives in part from the perception that much remains to 'haunt' us – memory lurks, with 'uncanny' reminders that it needs to be recovered. (Broadly, 'haunting' here means 'spectral' memory or an impression of a ghostly hovering between presence and absence.) This interest also enters into the work of such French cultural historians as Nora on 'sites of memory'; Antoine Prost's recent analyses of war memorials are a case in point, revealing that it is frequently not the glory of the fatherland that is being publicized in towns and villages throughout the land, but the agony of loss, silently laid before the spectator (*Republican Identities in War and Peace*, 2002).

Thus, the 'post-war epoch' is not, in France, confined to the twenty-five years after the Liberation, but has had a long afterlife – is perhaps better able to be seized as the generation immediately involved in the Occupation grows old and dies. And it is also probable that publishers (and academics) perceived a market here. They sensed a changing public, one freshly receptive to the very idea of commemoration; they picked up not only a wish to acknowledge the Holocaust but also a new kind of curiosity about its now more distant horrors, and they have acted on this. For, in common with other European publishing houses, French ones have, in the last forty years, been on the qui vive, facing competition not only from cinema and television but recently from the internet too. The book trade has had to prove adaptable in a country in which, already in the early seventies, only one French person in four was reading more than one book a month (*Le Figaro* poll of 1972), and in which it is estimated that perhaps 40 per cent of the population are neither buyers nor readers of books. (Even if the paperback revolution transformed book-buying in France, as in other Western countries, it is thought not to have changed reading habits, largely serving already existing readers.)

The logistics of publishing and distribution patterns have also changed, and this too will have a long-term impact on the book trade. By 1990 only one-third of French readers were buying their books in bookshops; other outlets – as elsewhere in the West – have become increasingly important, such as newsagents, book clubs, large stores and especially internet companies such as Amazon and chapitre.com. (However, the self-consciously literary name of the French outlet is telling – 'chapter': such a trade-name is much less likely in an anglophone context.) Publishing houses have merged; already in 1970 only seventeen publishers governed half the turnover of books in France, but by the 1990s three giants were dominating the field – Hachette (the largest), Presses de la Cité and Larousse-Nathan. These firms, controlling 80 per cent of turnover, were themselves controlled by international companies for which French books were a secondary financial activity. For the other challenge to the French book trade is the growth of English as an international language. France does have an export market to francophone countries, but its imports are more significant, and its book trade handles ever more translations: fiction and nonfiction; into and out of English. Internationalization therefore holds the key to the survival of France's book trade, and, still more imperatively than for anglophone publishers, alertness to the tastes of its home-grown audience.

Since these tastes are often still those of a book-buying and intellectually versatile elite, the trend has not all been in the direction of popularization. French academic publishers bring out scholarly and 'difficult' books in paperback and at a much lower sale-price than their British and

American counterparts, which have in many cases given up the idea of selling to any buyers other than libraries, and price their books (almost inevitably hardback) accordingly. Cultural prestige does retain some commercial value in France. But there are other more lucrative markets to be milked, for example that of romance addicts. If 'romance' has been a key literary genre since the Middle Ages, it is only in the twentieth century that publishers have begun to employ the term as a marketing category. The French equivalent to Mills and Boon is Harlequin, originally a Canadian/American publisher and now a major multinational. Having already taken over Mills and Boon in 1971, it opened a French subsidiary in 1978 which has been spectacularly successful. In a recent study, *Romance and Readership in Twentieth-Century France* (2006), Diana Holmes analyses Harlequin's commercial skill, describing how it has promoted its activities in such a way as to make French female readers feel part of a Harlequin 'community'. Holmes also shows how adaptable the genre of romance has been in modern France. During the interwar years and the 1950s, the 'moral romance' dominated the popular market, with writers such as Delly making a living, sometimes a fortune, from romantic stories underpinned by a conservative and largely Catholic ideology. ('Delly' was the joint pen-name of a sister-and-brother team, Marie and Frédéric Petitjean de la Rosière, 1875–1947 and 1876–1949.) However, the moral romance did not have to conform unbendingly to this agenda, and novels published (clandestinely) under the Occupation could figure love between characters working for the Resistance. Then, after 1968, romance adjusted to the new feminism of the 1970s. Now female desire could, indeed had to, be asserted, as well as the right to love freely. But this too functioned according to the economy, converging with major late-twentieth-century material developments. The emphasis on individual freedom followed the liberatory trend of May 1968 and simultaneously fitted with a consumer society that required an adaptable workforce and purchasers willing and able to buy a variety of goods. The culture of the 1990s and early 2000s has thus been shaped in part by a globalized, and commercialized, liking for change and diversity; and this liking extends to the content of the romance novel – itself a consumable. The love story has, for example, had to fit with the increasing acceptability of divorce and the dissolution and re-forming of couples and families if one or other adult moves in with a different partner.

In recent years, too, the romance has tended ever more insistently to make love inseparable from money and possessions. Arguably it always did, but the focus has shifted as French women themselves have become better off, no longer requiring husbands' permission to open bank accounts, and increasingly working outside the home. France has one of the highest rates of female employment in Europe (in 2005, 81 per cent of women between 25 and 49 were in work: Jon Henley, 'France plans to pay cash for more babies', *Guardian*, 22 September 2005). The French government, alarmed by the falling birth-rate and recognizing that modern women are disinclined to give up work permanently in order to raise families, has since the 1970s been bestowing on mothers not only state benefits but also remarkably generous maternity-leave provisions that are the envy of women in other European countries. This then is the post-1968 market for romance, reshaped by a mix of feminism and shrewd pro-natalist legislation which, while it maintains women's new status in the workforce, is essentially designed to promote the nation of France; canny publishers have in turn used this in their own interests. And the so-called 'new-wave' feminism had repercussions in other spheres too.

'Wave' rightly suggests that post-1968 feminism did not arrive unknown. We have seen that feminist ideas had been part of French culture for centuries, as witness, for example, the debate conducted by Pizan in *La Cité des dames* and the impact of the *précieuses* on seventeenth-century court culture. French feminism had been a political movement to be reckoned with since the early nineteenth century: its adoption by the socialist Saint-Simonians was a significant step, even if its progress was more irregular than in some other Western countries. Nineteenth-century French women authors, many of them fiery in their claims for equality, had been among those read by the young Simone de Beauvoir, and had shaped her outlook. And then, in 1949, there was the *The Second Sex* itself; gradually this had gained acceptance, and the events of May 1968 helped to publicize its insights. The development of these insights went in a direction of which Beauvoir herself did not always approve. Broadly speaking, oppressed groups can try to seize and redeem their situation in two diverging ways. They can claim natural equality with their oppressors, basing their arguments on 'universalism': that is to say, we are human and all humans deserve the same rights and opportunities. Or the oppressed can stress their difference from the oppressors, but claim that these different characteristics – the key to their identity – are no less to be valued than any others. These two positions are not entirely incompatible, since it is possible to adopt the stance that there may be 'differences' but that these are not a reason for discrimination. Taken in isolation, however, each position raises difficulties. The problem with universalism is that it (apparently) plays down the individual experience and already-acquired culture of oppressed people – a culture that may in itself be rich. The problem with 'difference' is that it can be 'essentialist'. That is, it is suspect because it is inclined to suggest that (say) *all* women view the world in a 'female' way because their sexual organs are more 'inner' than men's, or that *all* Africans are in tune with the rhythms of the earth. Furthermore, historically 'difference' has been markedly less successful than 'universalism' in actually securing justice and legal rights for the oppressed. It has almost always been universalist arguments that have achieved changes in the law: 'blacks can sit anywhere they like in the bus because they are American citizens just like whites', not 'because their unique identity and culture are as valuable as anyone else's'. 'Universalism' had already brought about such reforms in the condition of French women as new marriage and contraception laws (1965, 1967), and it would remain a driving force in the practical politics of post-1968 France. The seventies saw the legalization of abortion in certain conditions (1975) and of divorce by mutual consent (1974); in the eighties a law was passed to ensure professional equality between the sexes (1983), and in the nineties Edith Cresson became France's first female prime minister (1991).

The divided approach, universalism versus difference, has long historical roots in France. The 'difference' argument was often deployed by writers who judged the moment was not right to press for full equality. For Pizan to do so would have been impossible, so she 'rescues' women by cordoning them off in their own 'city', stressing their specific virtues and unique contribution to a male-dominated society. Some nineteenth-century feminists also took a two-stage view, arguing for advances in women's status as mothers and husbands' helpmeets as a prelude to more sweeping changes.

Beauvoir herself, while emphasizing that most girls, in the world as it now is, necessarily have a different experience of growing up from most boys, is firm in her existentialist affirmation that this does not have to be so: 'You are not born a woman: you become one'. After 1968, however, perhaps ironically, the very perspectives that Beauvoir's great work introduced allowed women writers the luxury of exploring particularly 'female' forms of 'being' – even allowed them to claim certain types of writing as quintessentially 'female', whether by women or men. Virginia Woolf had hinted at this stylistic separatism in *A Room of One's Own* (1929), but in its migration across the Channel it acquired the prominence that linguistic matters often do in France. *Ecriture féminine* was now promoted enthusiastically by some writers, most notably the novelist, playwright and intellectual Hélène Cixous (b. 1937) and the practising psychoanalyst Luce

Irigaray (b. 1932). Contributory were Lacan's and Barthes's writings, with their explorations of *jouissance* (orgasmic enjoyment) and pleasure: women could and did have their own forms of *jouissance*, and this showed in their literary style. Other feminists were more circumspect, concerned that the logical conclusion of all this was to suggest that much previous women's writing was falsely 'male' and had thus in effect sold out to patriarchy. For instance, writing that did not proceed in the manner of, say, James Joyce's *Ulysses*, or that displayed lucidly constructed argument, was sometimes condemned as exemplifying 'false consciousness'.

Some major women poets, dramatists and novelists of the last twenty or thirty years skilfully exploit both 'difference' and 'universalism'. They do weave plots and verse round female protagonists' attachment to family and to heterosexual love, and they do write of a specifically gendered experience of orgasm, but their works also dramatize the injustice of discrimination and the threat yet temptation of the 'gaze' that objectifies women. Thus *Truismes*, an entertaining but sinister novel of 1996 by Marie Darrieussecq (b. 1969), shows an attractive young woman turning into a sow ('truie' in French). Men's reactions to her in either incarnation are virtually interchangeable. Others who juggle with the same duality are the novelist Annie Ernaux (b. 1940), the film-maker Agnès Varda (b. 1928) and the internationally renowned writer Marguerite Duras (1914–96). It is plausible that both the post-1970 legal reforms and the re-assertion of women's 'uniqueness' encouraged many creative women and allowed them to flourish – among them academics who, like post-war male French thinkers, have had a strong impact on anglophone intellectual circles, for instance the French–Bulgarian psychoanalyst and professor of linguistics Julia Kristeva (b. 1940). Women writers also in effect created the 'identity politics' (the promotion of 'difference' under another name) that enabled gays to come forward and publicly proclaim Gide's lesson. They affirmed their right to be free of fear and discrimination and, as we have seen, to enter into civil partnerships. Heart-rendingly, they were now able, too, to write about the tragedy of AIDS that in the West affected them in particular.

A key figure here is Guibert (1955–91), a writer whose work moves across generic boundaries from the documentary essay to the experimental photo-novel, but which always has an autobiographical aspect. Autobiography has long played an important role in French culture; with Guibert, it enters a new sphere. As we have seen, from early on the 'I' had been explored in a variety of works: as well as Montaigne's essays and Rousseau's *Confessions*, these included Machaut's *Le Voir Dit*, Stendhal's *Vie de*

Henry Brulard (1835 – Henry Brulard was Stendhal himself), and Gide's *Si le grain ne meurt* (*If It Die*, 1926). By the time Gide was writing, the border-line between 'genuine' autobiography and first-person fiction had become increasingly blurred. (This is recognized by critics, who have taken to calling all first-person accounts, and third-person biography, 'life-writing'.) *If It Die* was particularly innovative in the attention it drew not only to gaps in memory but also more widely to the dubious nature of the auto-biographical enterprise; its first part even concludes with the assertion that the novel may approach the truth more nearly than memoirs. This has far-reaching implications: if one cannot be sure of one's own past, a history which one should know better than any other, how can one believe histori-cal accounts, derived from still more unreliable third-party onlookers? Perhaps France, which accorded such status to writers, was fertile ground for the growth of ironic, experimental, sometimes outrageous autobiogra-phy. The genre has flourished in the twentieth century, feeding obliquely into identity politics. Duras's fiction has autobiographical elements that she often signals as such, and, after Gide's, noteworthy autobiographies (usually deliberately focused on only fragments of the life) have numbered works by the poet Leiris (one significantly titled *Biffures, Crossings-out*, 1948); Beauvoir's *Memoirs of a Dutiful Daughter* (1958); Sartre's *Words* (1966); Barthes's *Roland Barthes by Roland Barthes* (1975); Ernaux's *The Square* (1981); and Sarraute's *Childhood* (1983). In this culture, interest in the endless permutations of the self is not likely to wane.

Guibert thus has illustrous forebears; his work nevertheless confronts freshly difficult issues, related in part to the complex role of the intellec-tual. Guibert died of an AIDS-related illness and the effects of a suicide attempt. Only a year before his death he had published an account of his HIV-positive eight years: *A l'ami qui ne m'a pas sauvé la vie, To the Friend Who Did Not Save My Life*. Although France in the early 1990s had the highest number of AIDS-related deaths in Europe, there was at that stage relatively little public discussion of the illness, 'not least', says Elizabeth Fallaize, 'because of the association with homosexuality and the central place which heterosexual sex occupies in French culture' (Davis and Fallaize, 104). Guibert's work thus makes a brave stand. Also polemical are his satirical insights into the commercial and professional factors sur-rounding AIDS: the disease, in Guibert's account, provides openings for medical specialists to work not only with patients but also with interna-tional drugs companies, thus offering career opportunities and the addi-tional possibility of making fortunes. Here life-writing and biting social analysis merge.

But *To the Friend* raises other questions about the relationship between autobiography, whether lightly 'fictionalized' or not, and the feeding of something akin to voyeurism. Readers' interest may be prying as well as sympathetic, partaking of that obsession with 'celebrity' which many commentators feel has grown in recent years. Some gays felt that Guibert was exhibitionistic, that he had too readily embraced fame and that he had betrayed such friends as Foucault by providing details of his condition (Foucault had died of AIDS in 1984). Other writers of the same decade approach the subject in a less publicity-garnering manner, for example Pancrazi, who writes about AIDS in the novel *Les Quartiers d'hiver* (*Winter Quarters*, 1990). However, Guibert's ambitions were far-reaching, and besides were, to a degree, legitimized in advance by the national culture. He has, for instance, been seen as exploring and deflating the image of the solitary Romantic, an image which at first dictates the narrator's self-presentation. And, among many possible comparisons, his work can be likened to that of the *philosophes* who sought to grip the imagination, educate their readership and precipitate discussion.

Creating a similarly tight bond between the literary and the political are those works by white authors which, in these post-1968 decades, explore France's relationship with its ex-colonies. (My final chapter will discuss the often fraught experience of first- and second-generation immigrants of this period.) The novelist Michel Tournier (b. 1923) is an arresting case, providing bridges of various kinds in both form and content. Tournier's prize-winning works reached a peak of popularity in the 1980s; they are emblematic of the transition from the New Novel to narratives that reinstate a sense of history, albeit a peculiarly late-twentieth-century one. His writing is crafty and self-reflexive, clearly indebted to those immediate predecessors (and in some cases contemporaries) the New Novelists, but also breaking off into lucid, provocative speculation. His work is satisfying for an elite readership and challenging for intellectuals (it was rapidly taken up by PhD students once he became established). Yet Tournier is also concerned to tell a story, and revives such older forms as myths and fairytales if only to subvert them. Often his retelling turns those stories to the political as well as the fantastical, and this political strain raises disturbing questions about race and colonization as well as about – say – Europe's Nazi past. (His horrific *Erl-King* of 1970 explores this latter.) Thus *Vendredi ou les Limbes du Pacifique* (*Friday or the Limbo of the Pacific*, 1967) recasts the Crusoe story from a decidedly post-Empire perspective; *La Goutte d'or* (*The Drop of Gold*, 1985) follows the adventures of a young North African immigrant worker on a quest in France to recover his own image, stolen as he believes by a white photographer. And in his intellectual autobiography *Le Vent paraclet* (*The Paraclete Wind*, 1977), Tournier tells a joke that links the dilemmas of the post-New Novel writer with those of would-be imperialists. After Independence, an Indian (or Pakistani or Sri Lankan) goes to a pukka London tailor and orders a perfect British suit. The tailor complies; finally, the Indian, in his suit, gazes at himself in the mirror with delight, then collapses in tears onto a chair, groaning 'Yes, but we've lost the Empire!' (189–90). Thus, says Tournier, we may long to kit ourselves out in the clothes of earlier fiction, and may to some extent succeed in doing so (writing stories that look 'traditional'); but it is no use – we can aspire only to travesty: the old structures have gone. Here the post-imperial becomes the postmodern, that unhierarchical espousal of a multiplicity of forms, including the mockingly 'realist'.

There is in this joke something slightly uncomfortable, a presentation of the Indian as pretentious for wishing (vainly) to aspire to the status of his colonizer; and one reason for the waning of Tournier's popularity since the late 1980s may reside in other discomfiting focuses of his: in his presentation of children (it can veer towards paedophilia), of women-objects, of the bedazzled (primitive?) young North African of *The Drop of Gold*. However, his significance lies in the strong steer he gave to post-1968 French fiction. He moved the well-wrought novel away from its dependence on *mise en abyme* to narrative that could be aesthetically pleasing but simultaneously gripping, and could include difficult social issues; he was able to do so because he was unmistakably endowed with the cachet of 'the intellectual'. And the cultural elite has continued to appreciate the figure of 'the intellectual', with, inevitably, some time-lags. It was during the post-1968 decades that Lacan rose to fame, even though his key works had been written earlier: this new visibility has been attributed to the linguistic 'dislocation' and energy of the May events, continuing their subterranean work long afterwards and provoking a surge of interest in psychoanalysis. Similarly, the repercussions of Barthes's 1957 *Mythologies* would show in the later exploration of representations, and the very adoption of the term 'postmodernism', by such thinkers as Baudrillard and Lyotard. Barthes himself would publish influential commentaries on literature and society up to his death in 1980. And the porous French interface between literary criticism and other kinds of critique would continue to be seized on abroad as intrinsic to the culture. Thus the thinker Deleuze (1925–95), famous both inside and outside France, wrote on Proust and Kafka as well as on Nietzsche, Kant and Spinoza; he soon moved to psychoanalytic social theory, collaborating with the anti-Freudian analyst Guattari (in, for example, *Anti-Oedipus* of 1972), and more recently explored contemporary painting and cinema. The critic Girard (b. 1923), who has lived and worked in the US for much of his career, has been able to appeal to readers of widely differing ideological persuasions. Girard argues that literary and social structures are based on the twin needs to imitate idols and to create scapegoats; this has chimed with Christians and atheists, with literary critics and general readers – and with novelists: Girard has influenced the writer Pennac, who plays with scenarios of persecution in such novels as *Au bonheur des ogres* (*Ogres' Delight*, 1985). And following on from Tournier, a broad concern to bring together popular fictions and philosophical seriousness has been perceptible in writing of the 1980s and early 1990s. The anthropologist Michel de Certeau (1925–2002), gifted with extraordinary erudition and a talent for interdisciplinarity, has been a paradigm of the intellectual flexibility that characterizes elite writing of this entire period. Certeau inherits an emphasis on 'the everyday' from Surrealism and, going further back, from Balzac and Baudelaire. In 1976, on the strength of his writings about cultural activity and May 1968, he was commissioned by the French Ministry of Culture to produce a report on future prospects for French culture; again, it is difficult to think of an equivalent figure in the English-speaking world.

Finally, as I indicated in the last chapter, the existence of 'cultural studies' in its twenty-first-century incarnation owes a great deal to post-1968 French thought. The easy movement between analysis of representations and that of power structures, the focus on such 'ordinary' objects as postcards, might well have crept gradually across the Western world after the foundation of Hoggart's Centre for Cultural Studies in 1964; but without the contribution and international status of the French intellectual, 'cultural studies' would probably have remained a more modest affair. Here the writings of Bourdieu (1930–2002) have been crucial, and curiously self-fulfilling, with their remorseless focus on the relationship between intellectual prestige and social might – a prestige Bourdieu himself acquired. And Bourdieu owes his spread in the English-speaking world to the mission of such publishers as Polity Press. (Polity has published translations of Bourdieu and, for example, Derrida, and has brought out books on Deleuze, Beauvoir, Cixous and Lyotard.)

This ever-growing strength of the cultural critic may be attributed not just to the after-shock of 1968 and to the feelings it catalysed, but also to political fear and pragmatic governmental manoeuvring. Mass culture was already viewed as a fascinating object of study in the 1960s, but in the 1970s and even more in the 1980s a certain anxiety, in some quarters panic, gathered pace about its supposed encroachment on society. 'Cultural politics' in France came to be considered a tussle for supremacy between Left and Right. The reasons for this were not purely internal, and here we are in familiar territory. De Gaulle and Malraux had already sought to enhance France's international image through the promotion of its culture, and from 1981 the Mitterrand government would spend hugely on cultural programmes in a still more marked attempt to position France as the world leader of the culturally non-aligned countries (that is, those outside the immediate orbit of the United States and the Soviet Union). But there were some changes of emphasis. Mitterrand tried to brand his broadly left-wing regime as the true inheritor of that Third Republic in which culture and education functioned as a form of social integration. Whilst de Gaulle, Pompidou and Giscard d'Estaing had held their inauguration ceremonies in the Champs-Elysées and at the Tomb of the Unknown Soldier under the Arc de Triomphe, that of Mitterrand took place in the Latin Quarter and at the Panthéon, sites which respectively highlighted the importance of education and drew attention to the socialist and Resistance heroes Jaurès and Moulin. Similarly, under Mitterrand the bicentenary celebration of the 1789 Revolution staged an extravaganza called *La Marseillaise* that commemorated the Third Republic's adoption of the song as an anthem to the republican unity of France.

The inspiration for this staging of culture as a form of political activity emerged from the grass roots too: during the 1970s, theatre companies had taken over public places, or buildings designed for other purposes, and used them for performances – most famously Ariane Mnouchkine's Théâtre du Soleil, which she created as a workers' collective and which in 1970 had staged her *1789*: not so much a play as a carnivalesque interpretation of the French Revolution. Such 'liberations' of public space were viewed as transformations of consciousness following on from the occupation of buildings during the 1968 events. But one striking aspect of the post-1970 urban and cultural re-appropriation was that it bore a familiar quasi-monarchical stamp. Three Presidents had direct involvement in the 'grands chantiers', the 'great work-sites': Pompidou, who created the Centre named after him; Giscard d'Estaing, who began the Musée d'Orsay and the renovation of the La Villette site (its park-design competition of the early 1980s has been called the most important of the twentieth century); and Mitterrand, who commissioned the Pyramid of the Louvre, the Opéra de la Bastille and the massive expansion and relocation of the Bibliothèque Nationale. Indeed, the development of Paris alone in the last forty years could occupy a volume, from these national and Presidential monuments to the 'sell-out' symbolized in the creation of Euro-Disney just outside Paris. However, the very existence of Euro-Disney is also a sign that French officialdom has been canny enough to conceive of the nation's culture as multifarious, and that it has been receptive to the arguments of French intellectuals. For example, governments have increasingly thought of cultural activity as not necessarily Parisian. The Minister of Culture Jack Lang secured financial support not just for the 'great work-sites' but also for newly respectabilized art-forms such as the circus, 'chanson', and *bande dessinée*; his initiatives allowed many provincial cities to restore or renovate their architectural 'heritage', and the regions were able, under Mitterrand and after, to subsidize performing arts. Former colonies have been helped too.

Some of France's recent moves to shield its cultural status have been controversial. Arguably, French culture should be protected from the risk of impoverishment; nevertheless, when France refuses to recognize the rights of its minority languages to exist, its image, here at least, starts to look somewhat dinosaur-like. As we have seen, strenuous efforts to impose French within France's own borders go back for centuries; and although in 1999 France signed the Council of Europe's Charter for Regional or Minority Languages, it neither ratified this nor ensured it would be put into effect, unlike, for example, Austria, Denmark, Germany, Spain and Switzerland. At the time of writing, however, there are moves to revise the French constitution so that regional languages may be recognized. Similarly, Académie-generated attempts to prevent anglicisms entering the language, enshrined in the Bas-Auriol Law of 1975 and the subsequent 1994 Toubon Law designed to shore it up, were doomed to failure. In the early twentieth century, Proust had already waxed ironic about objections to foreign-language imports; and the Académie Française is still a butt of humour within France for this and other stances. (Its actions do however generate more interest and publicity than those of the British Academy – as with, for example, such 'firsts' as its belated election of a woman in 1980: see above, p. 157.) The ambivalence about anglicisms was interwoven with ambivalence towards the United States. In the wake of the Vietnam War, the US was viewed in France as selfish and greedy, at both official and unofficial levels; this view still, however, co-existed with a deep-rooted attraction to American 'glamour'. So far France has been able to turn even this attraction to its advantage, not only through the creation of Euro-Disney but also by way of some commingling of French and American cinema interests and the appetite for American fiction that French publishers have continued to feed through translations.

Equivocation or flexibility – however we regard it – has contributed to other important areas of post-1968 French culture. Duras and Robbe-Grillet had moved easily into cinema (with *Hiroshima mon amour*, 1959, and *Last Year in Marienbad*, 1961), and the overlap between film and literature has continued remarkably fruitful. The concept of the director as author, 'auteur', still enables directors and cinema critics to conceive of film as an elite cultural activity. Two trends are significant here. First, the plain and unembarrassed debt that good French cinema displays to literature. While many recent French films do display the soupy sentimentality that is thought to attract audiences, others like Francis Veber's *Le Dîner de cons* (1998) retain the wit and neat plotting that come from France's theatre traditions as much as from earlier cinema. *Le Dîner de cons* was originally a play: what is significant is how little adaptation was deemed necessary for the cinematic version. Second, 'heritage cinema'. Government backing for films preserving the image of an 'essential' France has in the last few decades brought many classics of French literature to the screen, as well as a luscious adaptation of the Pagnol sequence *Jean de Florette* and *Manon des sources*, directed by Berri (1986; in Britain these were the most successful foreign-language films ever shown). Time-honoured concerns of the intelligentsia are thus kept alive in a popular medium. Berri's two-film sequence, for example, adheres to the old theme of tension between city-dwellers and a rural community at best backward and superstitious, at worst cunningly murderous; it takes atheistic side-swipes at Church ceremony and religious belief; it revives an ancient type of plot, the quasi-Oedipal drama of a final agonizing 'recognition'; and it also echoes the post-1970 emphasis on a painful, inaccessible past.

Another French medium that has a close relationship with elite literature is song. Again it is difficult to draw clear chronological dividing-lines; this relationship has a pre-history. To take only the twentieth century: in a recording of the 1960s, singer Serge Reggiani had started his rendition of Vian's lyric 'Le déserteur' – the credo of a conscript in reaction to his call-up – with a complete reading of Rimbaud's 'Le dormeur du val'. (See above, p. 106.) Other Western cultures have produced politicized singer-songwriters since 1960 (Bob Dylan is an obvious example); nevertheless, French song is unique in the confidence with which it both draws on well-known poetry and presents itself as a vehicle for protest and satire. Arguably, state protection has, in recent years at least, freed singers from the need to be uncontroversial: the Carignon Law of 1994 required

French radio to devote a minimum 40 per cent of music time to French-language songs. But the cast of mind is long-standing too. Old and new causes combine to make French popular song more 'literary' and political than its Anglo-American counterpart. Thus, in 1992 the singer Charles Trenet brought out 'Le cor', whose words and music were written by himself. The first line was taken from Vigny's much-anthologized poem 'Le cor' (from *Poèmes antiques et modernes*, 1826): 'J'aime le son du cor, le soir au fond des bois', a line that has itself been used by numerous other writers since Vigny penned it. ('I love the horn's sound, at evening-time deep in the woods'.) The rest of Trenet's song refers back to this line, cites the sounding of the horn in the *Chanson de Roland* (also in the original Vigny), refers sarcastically to the Emperor of France and other authority-figures, and plays outrageously with the Vigny line itself, for example: 'J'aime le sort du con le soir au fond de moi', 'I love the fate of the idiot [or cunt] in the evenings deep inside myself': all this set to a syncopated, jokey tune.

Radio and television also interact with the cultural elite: Sarraute wrote radio plays from the 1960s on, first collected in the 1970s, and the literary-magazine programme *Apostrophes*, which ran from 1975 to 1990 under the award-winning presenter Pivot, was hugely popular. It was followed by *Bouillon de culture*, a more eclectic mix of literature with film and music; writers, however, still dominated the programme. This being said, and with the exception of the Carignon Law, France's television and radio are perhaps less markedly 'French' than its other forms of expression. Television programmes are borrowed from abroad and 'easy' tastes are catered for (with, for instance, the French equivalent of *Big Brother*, *Loft Story*). Equivalents to *Apostrophes* do exist in other countries, and the BBC, for example, has been more pioneering in these contexts. France's cultural trail-blazers have on the whole chosen other forums.

The internet, and syllabus reforms in schools and universities, may dilute further some of France's historic promotion of its own literary culture. (There are danger signs: see below, p. 221.) Nevertheless, they seem unlikely to dislodge it radically, at least by comparison with other Western countries. It is not simply that 'French literature' is a shared frame of reference, as I suggested in the Introduction; another proof of France's deep-rooted attachment to its cultural past is the tenacity in post-1968 writing of major literary traditions, some going back half a millennium or more. The highlighting of language that has been bound up with France's self-definition as a nation remains visible in its novels. Darrieussecq's punning title *Truismes* refers us to a linguistic phenomenon, the truism.

Ernaux's *Passion simple* (1991) is another half-pun with a grammatical basis: the 'passé simple' is a tense (the past historic). (In the 1960s, one sequence of Sarraute's *Golden Fruit* had gone so far as to animate the imperfect subjunctive, that tense regarded quizzically by native speakers and learners of French alike; it became the bulky train of ornamented clothes deployed with grace by a stately lady – the train representing the 'enormous' grammatical ending of this tense: 30.) The novelist Echenoz (b. 1947) plays with anglicisms in such works as *Lac* (1989) – *Lake* and the English *Lack*. (So does Paul Smaïl with his pseudonym – 'Smile': see below for this fake 'North African' writer, p. 199.)

The belief in 'literature' itself is still strong – in the power of writing, especially ambiguous writing, to change mental habits. For this reason, and again springing from pride in the culture, earlier writers are valued, quoted – and parodied: appropriation at any level is valued as a mark of intellectual suppleness. (Racine figures in Ernaux, for instance.) Also creating this suppleness is the irony that remains a powerful tool for French writers, and that is now fully present in the rhetorical armoury of French women writers (it was often lacking in their nineteenth-century forebears). But irony does not preclude the positioning of the self within history, a positioning that will surely persist in the nation that produced the Enlightenment and numerous distinguished historians. Nineteenth-century France may have been slower than some other countries to recognize the rights of women and slaves; nevertheless, the humanitarian outlook is powerful and has since the eighteenth century been bound up with an exploration of the specificity of political systems. France's literati are too keenly aware of the impact on individuals of prejudice and exploitation to allow truly ahistorical interpretations to prevail.

The still-high status of the intellectual sometimes encourages authors to write in a way that may strike Anglo-American readers as rather heavy: the well-known novelist Modiano is not free from a tendency to portentous generalizations, as in his 1991 novel *Fleurs de ruine* (*Ruin Flowers*), where the narrator discovers a character has given a false name: 'Voulait-il me donner une leçon en me montrant que la réalité était plus fuyante que je ne le pensais?' ('Did he want to teach me a lesson and show me reality was more fugitive than I thought?', 83.) But authors like the prize-winning and eclectic Bon (b. 1953), who depicts the 'ordinary' in such novels as *Sortie d'usine* (*Factory Exit*, 1982) and *Impatience* (1998), create taut and stringent works adhering to the best French practice of comic, touching and politically pointed writing. And if we are looking for an iconic modern literary figure, it might well be the poet and essayist Yves Bonnefoy

(b. 1923). In his early youth Bonnefoy was a student of mathematics and philosophy. He is now regarded as the leading post-war French poet, with works spanning the last half-century and more. (His first famous publication was *Du mouvement et de l'immobilité de Douve*, 1953; his most recent is *La Longue Chaîne de l'ancre*, 2008: *On the Movement and Fixity of Douve; The Long Anchor Chain*.) He explores the role of poetry in our physical, intellectual and emotional relations, and in 'knowledge'. He sees purely conceptual knowledge, and the affirmation of universality, as a kind of stasis or death, and defines poetry as an enactment of mobile experience. Throughout his writing career, he has engaged in this interrogation of the moral and practical 'function' of poetry, not only in verse but also through literary and art criticism, and through teaching: he was elected to a chair at the Collège de France in 1981. Bonnefoy has, furthermore, published major translations into French of Donne, Yeats and particularly of Shakespeare (some dozen plays). Thus this writer of dense and lovely poetry, endowed with a training that included mathematics, has also been a public and university figure, has launched wide-ranging debates about the role of poetry, and has mediated another great literature afresh to his nation and to French-speaking countries elsewhere. With his brilliance in widely differing literary endeavours, his drive to reach out to and 'educate' his public, his humanity and breadth of vision, Bonnefoy is an exemplar of French culture.

9

'Foreignness' Early and Modern

The lines from Lévi-Strauss quoted at the end of Chapter 7 showed a multilayered approach to the 'foreign', evoking an imperialist nostalgia that
had to be imaginatively espoused by the author before being ironized and
rejected. These complex attitudes, and francophone literature itself, have
been most frequently analysed by critics in relation to the post-colonial
epoch, that is, roughly, the period following the Second World War.
('Post-colonial' with a hyphen refers to a historical period; 'postcolonial'
without one refers to assessments of the culture and history of empire. In
this chapter and the next, 'France' means metropolitan France, that is, the
geographical European country; 'francophone literature' means literature
produced outside the borders of France.) The next chapter will focus on
the relations between France and its overseas territories during the most
intense phase of francophone literature, that of the late twentieth century.
It will look at post-1968 works by writers in the former colonies and by
those from immigrant families recently settled in France. The current
chapter sketches out the pre-history.

We should remember that from the earliest stages France's intellectually curious writers have absorbed non-French material and that their
interest in 'the exotic' has not always been exploitative. This is not to be
naive about the conditions that created a literary engagement with the
'foreign'. Anglo-Norman literature already exemplified the fusion of two
cultures, but a fusion that resulted from the deployment of military might:
the Norman Conquest. Similar conflicts, some not yet over, can be seen
in the long-standing attempts to suppress internal 'otherness', as in the
case of Occitan and the various dialects and smaller languages that grew
on native French soil: Breton, for example. (See above, pp. 102, 172.) Over
the centuries, literary cross-fertilization was rarely without an admixture
of unease; at the most extreme, it described the anguish of those whose
culture was being 'used' for literary purposes while in reality this was
being ignored or displaced. And even the most generous adoptions of the
'foreign', those that fully acknowledge other cultures' achievements, have

perhaps harboured a wish to cannibalize on behalf of the nation France – or at least to enhance the writer's own prestige and novelty. Staël is a good example. Swiss herself, she saw that in order to move forward and survive, French culture had to open up to such Northern European art-forms as Romanticism. And she enjoyed being 'original' in her promotion of this Romanticism that itself stressed originality. Napoleon, on the other hand, had a narrow view of the culture: his fury over Staël's praise of Germany was simple-minded by comparison with her own vision. (See above, p. 68.)

Let us start with the most benign of these adoptions. As we have seen, France has benefited from the cultures of ancient Greece and Rome; of Italy (not just Renaissance Italy but a later one, as with Stendhal); and of Spain (*Don Quixote*, the Cid legend, and the picaresque novel). With Tolstoy and Dostoevsky – the latter admired by Gide and Proust – Russian litera-ture began to exert real influence on France, the exchange until then having gone almost exclusively in the other direction. The impact of Celtic and, later, English culture has been uneven but cumulatively important, starting with the Arthurian legends in the Middle Ages (the so-called 'matière de Bretagne'); France eventually seized on British political thought and on Shakespeare's legacy. American culture too, as we have seen, has had an enthusiastic welcome in modern France; this started with the take-up of jazz in 1920s Paris, the warm reception given to the black Ameri-can performer Josephine Baker (1925 on), and a taste for the modern American novel (not only crime-novels: others were read as from the 1930s). Francophone neighbours have been important too. Apart from Staël, Swiss citizens whose contribution to metropolitan France has been immense have been Rousseau and Saussure; illustrious francophone Bel-gians have included Maeterlinck and the poet Verhaeren (1855–1967) (and the Surrealist painter Magritte, 1898–1967).

Also relatively benign is that tradition in French literature that uses 'foreignness' to hold up a mirror to French beliefs and practices. This begins in medieval literature, where clashes between Moors and Chris-tians are not always unequivocally weighted in favour of Christians. There is a degree of cultural overlap in the story of Aucassin and Nicolette (see above, p. 13); this probably derived from the even earlier, and also charm-ing, mid-twelfth-century tale *Floire et Blanchefleur*. Here, a boy of Moorish extraction (Floire) grows up with a girl of Christian extraction (Blanche-fleur); they are educated together, they think alike, they even look alike; they are in love and surmount numerous obstacles to happiness. (Less happy, but still humane, are works in which religious and cultural differences do finally foil love, as in Racine's *Bérénice*, 1670, and Chateaubriand's *Les Aventures du dernier Abencérage*, composed 1809.) And as the centuries go on the traveller or 'foreigner', as we have seen, increasingly casts a quizzical eye on French society, figuring as a naive onlooker who queries customs the French take for granted. (See above, pp. 46–7.) Cyrano de Bergerac's delightful *The Other World, or States and Empires of the Moon* (1657) debates, via a fantastic journey, audacious topics such as philosophical relativism and the existence of God; a lunar utopia is used to bitingly satirical effect. (The work was first published in a heavily expurgated form.) Not all fictional travellers shed an unfavourable light on France: the Persians of Montesquieu's *Persian Letters* show what is liberal as well as what is strange in France. Thus the work is in a sense 'balanced'. But it goes without saying that the purpose of this literature is not to present a cool analysis, and by the time we reach Stendhal's *Charterhouse of Parma* (1839) there is no longer even the vestige of a reasoned attempt to compare two cultures: examples of the so-called 'Italian character' are plucked out of the air in order to attack French vanity, French calculatingness, with heedless internal contradictions (there are plenty of vain and calculating Italians in *La Chartreuse* itself). At its most enlightened, then, metropolitan literature has either problematized the very idea of 'foreignness' or has enlisted it as a means to prick French conceit, perhaps as a reaction to the self-promotion of 'The Nation'. At moments it has, too, attempted to publicize the most obvious abuse of French colonialism: slavery, shamefully not finally abolished until 1848. We saw that Voltaire's Candide wept over it, and that Claire de Duras's black Ourika, rescued from the slave trade at the age of two, nevertheless suffered agonies on realizing that she could never be accepted by white European society. (See above, p. 67.) The twentieth-century Duras, Marguerite, has also written about the manifold tragedies colonialism leaves in its wake; while Marguerite Yourcenar, in her *Mémoires d'Hadrien* (1951), explores in the person of the Roman Emperor Hadrian the pains as well as the pleasures of Empire. (This novel was published just as France was starting to relinquish its own empire.)

But there are many counter-examples of ambivalence or blatant rapacity towards 'the other'. If the Orientalism of much French literature pays homage to the East, if writers' evocations of the West Indies acknowledge native cultures, this is frequently in a self-indulgent, commodifying, voyeuristic mode, scarcely bothering – if at all – to inquire into the inequity that has allowed Europe to plunder other countries and for that matter, in the case of travel writing, has enabled the traveller to make this very journey. (Edward Hughes brings out these attitudes in his *Writing Marginality in Modern French Culture*, 2001.) The paintings of Gauguin (1848–1903) rely on this ambivalence. Are his sculptural Tahitian women, with their opaque, unreadable gaze, challenging the European spectator to endow them with thoughts – possibly rebellious ones despite their Sphinx-like expressions? Or are they simply blank sheets on which white viewers may inscribe their own avidity? The protagonist of Gide's *The Immoralist* (1902) unblushingly equates personal liberation with desire for Arab boys; the outcome makes it clear that Gide himself sees his hero's behaviour as destructive, not emancipatory, yet the text's ambiguity is of a kind that has enabled generations of readers to ignore or underplay the white adult male's sexual tourism. There is, at least, room for interpretation here, but less room in such works as Butor's *Using Time*. Butor was laudably attempting to convey the intermingling of British culture with many others – we drink Indian tea, for example; but it was naive to call his black character Horace *Buck*, with all its racist associations (as in the phrase 'buck negro'). Hergé, the Belgian creator of Tintin, was a right-winger who shows the boy-scoutish hero thwarting wily Orientals and other dastardly unEuropean types: mere ambivalence would be a fine thing.

The history of abolitionism in France is also sobering. Voices other than Voltaire's had been raised against slavery in eighteenth-century France; later, leading nineteenth-century intellectuals such as Constant and the mature Hugo were abolitionists, and French opposition was organized by specifically created societies from 1821 on. The campaigner Schoelcher (1804–93) diffused abolitionist ideas widely in articles and in two books published in the 1840s, and abolition was one of the first measures decreed by the short-lived Second Republic in 1848. However, abolitionism was always weaker in France than in Britain; even now, museums devoted to the history of slavery are more muted in tone than elsewhere; and, as we shall see, no retrospective embarrassment inhibited the Third Republic's zestful expansionism. In short, here is yet another split attitude, now to 'foreigners': sometimes self-deprecating and humanitarian, sometimes blind. These divisions were to some extent exacerbated by the fact that France's grip on its territories was chequered – more so than that of Britain, the only nation whose empire was of a comparable size. France's empire could less easily be taken for granted than that of a complacent Britain which could simply assume that the sun would never set on *its* Empire.

There were also cultural differences that made the French sense of empire less secure. While both nations euphemized their conquests as 'civilizing missions', in Britain this (eventually) took the form of an emphasis on missionary work, with more self-righteousness but at the same time greater tolerance of local languages, whereas in France the mission, in theory, focused on spreading the French language. A similar distinction can be made even now: the French equivalent of the monarch-centred Commonwealth is 'Francophonie' with a capital F, a supposed coalition of French-speaking nations. (It has been dubbed 'Franco-phoney' by the Saint Lucian poet Derek Walcott.)

French colonialism, then, operated during a total of four centuries, and in two chronological phases, in the following areas: the Americas, mainly North America and the West Indies; Africa, both North and sub-Saharan; the Middle East; and Indo-China. The first phase lasted from the sixteenth to the eighteenth centuries, when France acquired territories in the Americas, in the Indian Ocean, and in the Indian subcontinent. François I sent an explorer to Canada as early as 1534, but it was not until the seventeenth century that a serious attempt was made to settle 'La Nouvelle France', as Canada was then called, when Quebec was founded (1608). Meanwhile hundreds of peaceable French Huguenot settlers had emigrated to Florida in the sixteenth century (all killed by the Spanish: this is why a town in Florida is called 'Matanzas', 'slaughterings'). France claimed the Mississippi basin in 1682 and named it Louisiana after Louis XIV. Colonization was slow, with the number of North American settlers never totalling more than 80,000. (North America provides an example of what eventually happens to a dominant culture when it finds itself isolated by a still more dominant one. In Louisiana and francophone Canada, French culture became the 'underdog', in danger of being wiped out or relegated by the anglophone one. In Acadian and Québecois cultures (that is, francophone Canadian), this has led to a sometimes poignant literature whose anger and lamentation are nevertheless different in tone from the more tormented and tragic ones that emerged – and still emerge – from territories bloodily conquered by the French and kept going through slavery.)

More profitable were French activities in the Caribbean. Guadeloupe, Martinique and what we now call Haiti came under French control from 1625 on, and the commodities produced in the Caribbean made up most of the French empire's trade. This trade depended on the labour of African slaves, whose capture and shipment in turn relied on coastal trading posts in Senegal (West Africa). The prosperity of the Ancien Régime was so dependent on slavery and the slave trade that in 1763 France preferred to relinquish most of its American colonies rather than give up the sugar-producing island of Martinique. By 1754 – the high point of the first French empire – France had also acquired such Indian Ocean islands as Réunion and Mauritius, had set up trading posts on the Indian coast, and had established a protectorate over a substantial part of the Indian subcontinent; the population of this empire was about thirty million.

By 1815, however, most of these territories had been ceded to Britain and other nations as the result of French military defeats. France then proceeded to build up a second colonial empire in Africa, Indo-China and Oceania. It started with the conquest of Algeria, initiated in 1830. From the coast of Senegal, France pushed into the interior of West Africa; in 1842 and 1853, it established protectorates and annexations in the Pacific Ocean (Tahiti and New Caledonia); southern Vietnam was annexed in 1859, Cambodia was made a protectorate in 1863. The Third Republic launched a still more aggressive colonial expansion: France now made huge territorial gains in sub-Saharan Africa, finally controlling most of West and Central Africa; it gained protectorates over Tunisia, Morocco, Laos, and central and northern Vietnam. (In 1883, France without provocation shelled the imperial city of Hué in North Vietnam. The Emperor surrendered to the French in order to prevent further slaughter of his innocent people.) Finally, after the First World War the redistribution of colonies held by Germany and the Ottoman Empire resulted in France's gaining mandates over Syria and Lebanon, as well as yet more West African territories. At its height, between 1918 and 1939, this French empire – second only to Britain's – covered more than twelve million square kilometres and had a population of nearly seventy million (about twice that of metropolitan France). Settlers from France numbered one-and-a-half million, most of them coming to the North African territories and particularly Algeria (where they became known as *pieds noirs*, 'black feet', from the colour of the leather boots they wore). Countries where white French people had settled were called 'colonies de peuplement' (populating colonies) whereas the others, nakedly, were known as 'colonies d'exploitation', that is to say colonies for commercial development. This twentieth-century imperial success contributed to the continuing confidence of the right wing in inter-war metropolitan France.

The long-term aim claimed by propagandists was that of *assimilation*, that is, the shaping of the overseas conquests in the mould of French 'civilization'; this gradually changed to an aim of *association*, that is, the retention of separate identities for colonizers and colonized while at the same time all would collaborate for mutual benefit. Whatever the supposed goal, native peoples had no political rights: a law of 1854 ensured that colonies would remain under the rule of a metropolitan administrator, and this law stayed in place even after the creation, a century later, of the four Overseas Departments (Départements d'Outre-Mer, DOM). In the DOMs, then, self-rule was obviated despite representation. Similarly, only a very small proportion of native elites received a French education. (Those elites would, however, play a leading role in the struggle for autonomy.)

Most of these territories gained either independence or a substantial degree of self-determination between 1945 and 1962; France let them go at the cost of relatively little bloodshed, except in Indo-China and Algeria, where there were long and violent conflicts. There were two main factors in France's eventual twentieth-century decolonization. (Strictly speaking, the term 'decolonization' can be applied only to France's 'loss' of its second empire, since the one acquired in the early modern period was handed over to other powers rather than achieving anything we would now recognize as autonomy for the occupied areas.) First, all the European colonial powers were weakened by the Second World War and started to perceive that it was in their own financial and even military interests to shed their overseas territories. This process was however more difficult for France than for others, for at this stage its empire was more bound up with national prestige than was even the case for Britain. Britain had been on the winning side in the war, whereas France had suffered the humiliation of the Occupation. Thus France viewed its empire as one way of reinstating its image as a great power. Additionally, the case of Algeria posed special problems from the metropolitan perspective. One million French *pieds noirs*, many from families that had lived in Algeria for three generations, had to flee back to France. De Gaulle addressed them with the equivocal phrase 'Je vous ai compris', 'I've understood you' (but I'm not going to do what you want). The Algerian issue nearly provoked civil war in France. High-ranking military officers determined to preserve Algeria as a colony formed the OAS (Organisation Armée Secrète) as an anti-Gaullist conspiracy: this included at least two serious assassination attempts on de Gaulle. And many post-war French intellectuals were not entirely free from this perspective; even if they criticized the excesses of Empire, they were reluctant to relinquish it. It was only Sartre's circle that called for the complete independence of the colonies (in, for example, *Les Temps modernes*, the interdisciplinary journal founded by Sartre in 1945 whose editorial board included Beauvoir, Leiris and Merleau-Ponty); Genet also intervened with his 1958 play *Les Nègres*, which portrays the psychology of racial hatred. (The English version, *The Blacks*, ran in the States from 1961 to 1964 and contributed to the Civil Rights movement, in which Genet became active after 1968.)

There was, then, and had always been, some liberal pressure from metropolitan writers that seeped through as minimal encouragement to the colonized. But this could do relatively little in the face of *force majeure*. A more important factor in French decolonization was the growing determination of the colonized themselves. During the early decades of the twentieth century, native elites made increasingly insistent demands, both directly and through the writing of powerful works in French: it was by way of a more general contribution, therefore, that metropolitan literature really 'helped'. This new consciousness had been growing ever since the slave rebellion in Haiti led by the black leader Toussaint Louverture (*c.*1743–1803). Louverture was born a slave but was freed by his owner in 1776. He led an uprising from 1794 to 1802, when he was captured by the French and imprisoned in France, dying there shortly before his country achieved full independence in 1804. His life inspired many literary works (including a novel by the young Hugo, *Bug-Jargal*, published in an early equivocating version in 1818, when he was only sixteen; harder-hitting was the 1850 play by Lamartine, *Toussaint Louverture*). Haiti's independence, following from a rebellion that was the only successful slave revolt in the history of the Americas, was an 'Enlightenment Revolution': its leaders were actively inspired by eighteenth-century and Jacobin ideals of liberty. Self-interest on the part of metropolitan France also played a part: local planters were turning to the British for help, and it was an alliance between slave rebels and French colonial officials against these planters that led to the abolition of slavery in Haiti. Be that as it may, this 'Enlightenment Revolution' was a force in modern political culture; if it tends to be overlooked these days, that is because of the island's unfortunate twentieth-century history as a target for the United States' neo-colonial policies and the consequent installation of the Duvalier regime, which lasted for nearly thirty years (1957–86) and stifled dissent and intellectual activity.

In other colonies, the goal of assimilation was at first accepted by many French-educated natives; however, the continuing gross inequalities between colonizers and colonized led to distrust of the French. The native elites began to challenge the demotion of their cultures implied by assimilation, a challenge that gave rise to the 'négritude' movement among black intellectuals during the 1930s. 'Negritude' is a word coined from 'blackness' and a suffix that augments it, as in 'multitude' or 'magnitude'; it also carried connotations of 'pulchritude' well before the North American 'Black is Beautiful' movement of the 1960s. The stated aim of the negritude movement was to create between blacks the world over an intellectual and moral 'meeting-place' that would allow them to arrive at better self-knowledge and 'make their race illustrious'. A notable part in its development was played by three educated young women from the black middle class of Martinique, the Nardal sisters: Andrée, Jane and Paulette. In the early 1930s they ran a salon at their home in the Paris suburbs that brought together black students and intellectuals from the Caribbean, francophone Africa and the United States. They were largely responsible for the seminal influence of Harlem Renaissance writers on the negritude movement. (The Harlem Renaissance was the name given to a flowering of African-American cultural and intellectual life during the 1920s and 1930s.) The Nardals' salon laid the foundations for the important *Revue du monde noir* (*Black World Review*); Paulette in particular contrasted North American blacks' strong sense of racial identification with that of French Caribbean blacks, hesitant in embracing their blackness.

One of the dangers of negritude was that it was 'essentializing': it ran the risk of playing down social and historical conditions in favour of a promulgation of 'the black soul'. Nevertheless, Marxist ideologies did also inform the thinking of these and other intellectuals – for example the francophone Vietnamese leader who would later be known as Ho Chi Minh – and, after the Second World War, the colonized gained confidence from the presence of the Soviet Union as a player on the world stage prepared to back anti-colonial movements. Finally, the emergence of the United States and the Soviet Union as the key post-war powers weakened the global image of the European colonizing nations. Thus, among colonized peoples the drive for independence emerged from a changing perception of both themselves and of the 'masters' – a perception shaped by their own most brilliant writers.

In the wake of Algerian independence in 1962, France established a policy known as *coopération*, instituting economic and cultural aid programmes with most of the ex-colonies, and concluding defence agreements with a majority of the newly independent sub-Saharan states. These can be seen as neo-colonialist, but they have survived, as has the main cultural legacy of colonialism, *francophonie*/*Francophonie*: not only the continuing use of the French language, but, equally important, its institutionalization. Often French is the only language common to diverse groups within the formerly colonized countries: it is thus on a relatively secure footing.

From this *francophonie*, both before and after independence, there slowly emerged a variety of poems, novels, plays, scholarly studies and polemic in French. Conditions on the ground were not easy. Francophone African publishing is a case in point. This has had achievements but also signal failures. Publishing activities have succeeded in only a few African countries: Senegal, Ivory Coast and, to a lesser extent, Cameroon and Togo. The first full-scale local publishers were Editions CLE in Cameroon, founded in 1963 with the help of Dutch and German Protestant missionaries. (CLE stands for Centre de Littérature Evangélique – the acronym also means 'key'.) Its early list included such authors as the Cameroonian Francis Bebey (1929–2001), well known as a fiction-writer, composer, musician, musicologist and broadcaster. Orphaned at an early age and brought up by his elder brothers and sisters, he earned a scholarship to study at a *lycée* in France and then at the Sorbonne. His first novel, *Le Fils d'Agatha Moudio*, won the Grand Prix Littéraire d'Afrique Noire in the year it was published, 1967. Among other authors published pre-1968 by CLE were the Ivory Coast poet, playwright, chronicler and political activist Bernard Binlin Dadié (b. 1916), who would become Minister of Culture in the government of Ivory Coast from 1977 to 1986. CLE thus did host distinguished figures. But many African publishing ventures were precarious, showing in raw form the connection between prosperity and cultural activity. In the main, publication of francophone writing had to be based in Paris, including that of the outstanding journal *Présence Africaine*. Founded in 1947 through the relentless efforts of the Senegalese Alioune Diop, it published poems, essays and other compositions by black Africans, by white metropolitan authors writing about race and eventually by anglophone blacks. The journal itself has gone from strength to strength. But this general dependence on metropolitan publishers was, and still is, a factor in both the material conditions of literary production and also, as we shall see, in the content of francophone works.

Let us now look more closely at the francophone literature that was gestating from the 1930s on. Seven key authors in the mid-twentieth-century history of francophone writing, in rough order of their major works, are: Aimé Césaire (Martinique, 1913–2008); Léopold Sédar Senghor (Senegal, 1906–2001); Driss Chraïbi (Morocco, 1926–2007); Sembène

Ousmane (Senegal, 1923–2007); Frantz Fanon (Martinique, 1925–61); Cheikh Hamidou Kane (Senegal, b. 1928); and Cheikh Anta Diop (Senegal, 1923–86). Since, strikingly, four of these seven are Senegalese, it is appropriate to start with Senghor. Poet, critic and social theorist, he was the joint founder, with Césaire, of the negritude movement in Paris, where their studies brought them together – with the help too of the Nardal sisters. For decades Senghor was the doyen of African francophone writing. His poetry is admired throughout the world; in 1983, he became the first African member of the Académie Française. Like the nineteenth-century metropolitan writers who saw no division between political activity and their literary calling, Senghor was also a prominent statesman, dominating West African politics both as an inspirational cultural leader and as President of Senegal for twenty years (1960–80). The relationship between Senghor's ethnicity and his public role was significant. He was a Serere, as was his successor Abdou Diouf. The Wolof were the dominant tribe in Senegal, but for that very reason they tended to avoid assimilation. The 'subordinate' Serere jumped at the chance to go to French schools, to study on scholarships in France, and then to assume administrative posts. The dominant groups realized what was happening only when it was too late for them to share power with the colonizer. (The resulting social dislocation was wrenching: many African francophone novels have discussed it, for example Kane's *L'Aventure ambiguë*: see below, p. 196.)

Senghor, then, had been educated at mission schools and the Sorbonne; in his poetry, an orthodox French and classical literary inheritance mingles with African culture. Erudition and traditional versification combine with off-beat rhythms to create a form of free verse resembling that of metropolitan authors and also, it has been said, the grammatical elisions and parallelisms of some African languages. All his writing – verse and prose – offers a defence of African civilization and promotes both its common ground with European culture and the value of cross-fertilization. Senghor's own main collections appeared between 1945 and 1984, their titles sometimes making clear this stance (for example, *Hosties noires*, Black [Communion] Hosts, in 1948 and *Ethiopiques* in 1956). He writes of the black exile's search for identity, of Europe's spiritual and moral 'bankruptcy' and of Africa's potent landscape; and, with some conflation between 'woman' and 'Africa', he evokes the poignancy of separation from the beloved. His prose writings, published under the collective title *Liberté*, are shrewd and practical, turning a critical African perspective on the cultural and political issues raised by decolonization; he adapts such diverse sources as Marx and the Jesuit palaeontologist Teilhard de Chardin (1881–1955) to create a pragmatic ideology for newly self-determining African nations. With his combination of statesmanship and literary gifts, Senghor was a towering figure; he was supported by Sartre, who wrote a famous preface to his 1948 anthology, *Anthologie de la nouvelle poésie nègre et malgache de langue française*. In this preface, 'Black Orpheus', Sartre addresses white readers: blacks are now turning on *you* the gaze with which for so long you, whites, have oppressed blacks; what did you expect, Sartre asks sardonically: that they would intone your praises?

But this preface had already been anticipated by what would become the most influential francophone work of the twentieth century: Aimé Césaire's long poem of 1939, *Cahier d'un retour au pays natal* (*Notebook of a Return to the Native Land*). Césaire, a poet, dramatist, historian and politician, grew up in a black middle-class French-speaking Martinican family and at the age of eighteen went to the Lycée Louis-le-Grand in Paris, thence to the prestigious Ecole Normale Supérieure in 1935. There he collaborated with Senghor and fellow Caribbean students on the journal *L'Etudiant noir* (1935), which had only a single number but was no less path-breaking for that. Césaire published in it an article, 'Nègreries (slave compounds/black quarters): Black youth and assimilation', in which he rejected the doctrine of assimilation and declared the need for the colonized to assert separate identities at all levels: cultural, psychological, 'racial'. He returned to Martinique just before the outbreak of the Second World War, remaining there until 1944 and teaching and influencing a generation of young Martinicans, among them Frantz Fanon and the distinguished Edouard Glissant. (For Glissant, see next chapter.)

Together with his wife, the Martinican poet Suzanne Roussy, and other Martinican writers, Césaire founded the review *Tropiques* in 1941. This, despite attempted censorship by the local arm of the Vichy regime, developed the argument for cultural and psychological self-assertion by the colonized, promulgating Surrealism in particular as a way of breaking through the alienation inflicted by colonialism. After the Liberation, Césaire was approached by the Communist Party of Martinique to stand as its candidate for mayor of the capital Fort-de-France, and as deputy for the constituency of Martinique at elections for a new National Constituent Assembly to be convened in Paris. Césaire, though not then a member of the Communist Party, accepted and was elected to both positions in 1945. He held them for more than four decades, finally standing down as deputy in 1993. His political and literary careers had, like Senghor's, been interwoven during that entire period: he was rapporteur (an official investigator charged with producing a report) in the legislation that turned Martinique, Guadeloupe, French Guiana and Réunion into *départements* of France; as well as political and self-reflexive verse and drama, he also published, in 1950, a famous *Discours sur le colonialisme*, which gained him a world-wide reputation as an enemy of colonialism and a spokesman for the history and future paths of colonized peoples. There was, however, always a contradiction between Césaire's claims for the distinctive identity of blacks, rooted in 'race' and culture, and the class-based universalist analyses of the Communist Party, and this contradiction became increasingly disturbing for him. He resigned from the Party in 1956 and in 1958 formed his own Parti Progressiste Martiniquais, which promoted local self-government within a relationship with France as the best way forward for Martinique. Césaire did not advocate outright independence for Martinique; as a pragmatist, he sought what he saw as the best practical solutions, but his own longstanding embeddedness in metropolitan culture no doubt played a part. (Thus, only two years after the Liberation, the mainstream French publisher Gallimard issued poems that had appeared in *Tropiques* during the war; Picasso – based in France himself – illustrated another collection with thirty-two engravings: *Corps perdu, Lost Body*, 1950.) Césaire eventually became an Establishment figure, at least in the eyes of younger Martinican nationalists, who would view the setting-up of the Regional Council of Martinique – of which Césaire became the first president in 1982 – as merely one further neo-colonialist mechanism. Césaire's belief in the 'African-ness' of West Indian culture, as opposed to its 'créolité', would also come under attack. ('Créolité' is a theory of West Indian identity that stresses not its 'African-ness' but its composite nature, made up of many elements: European, Amerindian and Asian as well as African.) With hindsight, we can see that there were always two tensions at work in Césaire: that with the Communist Party, and a more continuous conflict between the seditious implications of his literary works and his moderate political practice, bound to disappoint radicals.

For sedition informs Césaire's drama and verse: the plays *Et les chiens se taisaient* (*The Dogs were Silent*, 1946) and *Une tempête* (1963) treat of slavery, colonialism and racism, the second being a bold reworking of Shakespeare's *The Tempest* told from Caliban's viewpoint. And in 1960 he published a book of poems called *Ferrements*: this politically punning title evokes both 'ferrements', irons, and 'ferments'. But it is above all on *Cahier d'un retour au pays natal* that Césaire's renown as an author rests. He had begun work on it in 1935, the same year that *L'Etudiant noir* was published. At first rejected by French publishers, it was finally published in August 1939, and crowned by the Surrealist Breton, who after a visit to Martinique in 1941 wrote an essay on Césaire called 'A great black poet'. Breton's essay became the preface to a revised and expanded version of the poem, published (together with a translation into English) in New York in 1947. This launched Césaire's reputation in both colonizing and formerly colonized countries.

The impact of the *Cahier* derives not only from the 'narrative' it tells but also (inseparably) from the power and flexibility of its language, characterized at times by smooth harmonies and cadences, at other moments by dissonance and incongruity. For example, the work's title is a perfect French decasyllable. This is reassuring but misleadingly so, for the work that it introduces now proceeds to mix short prose-poem paragraphs and free verse, both of which, but especially free verse, involve a constant slippage between recognizable versification and games with this versification. The reader thus has to grapple with a blend of satisfaction and dissatisfaction, of familiarity and defamiliarization, in the rhythms and in the very genre.

Similar deliberate incongruities govern the *Cahier*'s narrative procedures. This is a poem with an ever-present first-person narrator – it is his 'notebook' – but he is a supple narrator, both modest and confident. Thus the title is casual – not 'my book' but 'a notebook', suggesting mere jottings; the poem opens casually too, with the words 'Au bout du petit matin . . .', 'At the end of the wee hours . . .'. (Translations by Eshleman and Smith.) Both the phrase and the ellipsis (Césaire's own) convey the indeterminacy of this time of day (on a symbolic borderline between night and dawn, sleep and awakening), and suggest a tailing-off, hesitation on the part of the speaking voice. The flexible narrator can weave together, too, diverse cultural and historical strands. He can evoke, almost in one breath, family Christmases in Martinique, the jazz and dances that a condescending New York appropriates from its black population, and the vicious history of slavery. He can pay homage to the Haitian slave leader Louverture (to whom Césaire would devote a major study in 1960); remind us of the slave ships that brought Africans to these islands; and shockingly slip in the racist clichés through which those Africans' descendants are perceived: 'niggers-are-all-alike . . . / nigger-smell, that's-what-makes-cane-grow / remember-the-old-saying: / beat-a-nigger, and you feed him' (58–9). But by the end, after a lateral, fragmented and metaphorical exploration of the geography, history and present customs of the island, this voice is speaking both for Martinique and for all oppressed blacks. It tells us, for example, that a friendly and fresh source of light is to be found with those who (unlike Europeans) 'have invented neither powder nor compass', 'could harness neither steam nor electricity', but 'without whom the earth would not be the earth'; 'my negritude,' the narrator tells us, 'is neither tower nor cathedral / it takes root in the red flesh of the soil / it takes root in the ardent flesh of the sky'; and the voice cries triumphantly: 'Eia for those who have never invented anything / for those who never explored anything / for those who never conquered anything' (66–8). The whites' achievements, both constructive and destructive, are to be set to one side for a celebration of those they enslaved.

The work culminates with a declamation both of the narrator's status as spokesman for his people and country and of the 'Moi', the creative self: 'The master of laziness? Master of the dance? / It is I! . . . Rally to my side my dances / you bad nigger dances' (82–3). This 'Moi', with its very last words, tells a dove, symbol of peace, to soar up: 'rise sky-licker / and the great black hole where a moon ago I wanted to drown it is there I will now fish the malevolent tongue of the night in its motionless veerition!' This last word is a neologism (in French, 'verrition'). It evokes swirling, a lack of direction that, however, sums up both the sea and island setting of the *Cahier* and more generally its openness. Rigid structures can be fruitfully, and in the end joyously, rejected. Unlike the slave ships that, too unidirectionally, knew where they were going and why, the narrator's veering 'ship' will salvage peace from the heart of darkness.

Yet in all this the poem reveals, and at moments almost shows off, its debt to European and French literary traditions, not least that of the elusive and changeable narrator, here drafted into the service of a self that is – often willingly – caught between cultures. Phrases like 'paradises lost' echo Milton, Romantic writers and Proust. Ready shifts between formal and informal registers follow a late nineteenth-century pattern, and a careful placing of repellent images situates the *Cahier* in a line descending from Baudelaire and Rimbaud. For Césaire, especially in the first part of the *Cahier*, represents his home island as full of pustule-like objects waiting to explode with long pent-up frustration: here is an 'aesthetics of disgust' that comes from the destruction of 'taste' – linked in France at least with an attack on the socially powerful. Another rewriting of mainstream French literature comes with Césaire's play on light and dark; this echoes (distantly) Racine, and (more recently) Hugo's grandiose oppositions. But now the playing becomes a potent political weapon, enlisted to query 'white' and 'black': in the *Cahier* the sun at times – Sartreanly – represents the controlling white gaze, but also symbolizes the black (about half-way through it becomes a 'frizzy Angel'). Thus 'France' and 'blackness' are sometimes separate, sometimes merge in a suggestiveness that is part of the *Cahier*'s achievement.

Altogether more violent was a work published fifteen years later, Driss Chraïbi's *Le Passé simple* (*Simple Past*) of 1954: this title is not simple itself, for (as we saw with Ernaux's pun) it also means 'past historic', the formal French tense of chronicle for which there is no equivalent in English. A grammatical structure and a historical one are being simultaneously targeted. The novel came out during the Moroccan struggle for independence and has been called a 'literary bombshell': it attacked French colonialism, but even more savage was its assault on a patriarchal Moroccan society. This led to accusations of betrayal by his compatriots such that Chraïbi publicly disowned the novel in 1957. The work is that of an 'angry young man', or at least depicts the narrator-hero, Driss Ferdi, as an angry young man. He rejects Moroccan modes of thought at all levels: religious proscriptions, anti-Semitism, sexism, the harsh treatment meted out to schoolchildren by their teachers. (The hero was routinely beaten on the soles of his feet, with the result that he can now walk miles: 'I'm sincerely grateful to my masters for having so successfully levelled out and strengthened the soles of my feet', 40.) Women are openly oppressed: the hero's own mother is 'weak, submissive, passive'; women are for 'fucking', are to be ignored until the next bout of 'pleasure', and the Seigneur (the hero's father) has the right of life and death over the mother (43–4). Invective and arguments punctuate the text: the father tells Driss that a whole generation has become like him: insolent, cynical, praying for their fathers' deaths, priding themselves on being 'nationalist' – this younger generation, according to the father, thinks Atatürk is guiding it from beyond the grave. (Atatürk was the reformist Turkish leader who in the 1920s and 1930s turned Turkey into a secular democracy.) Driss is, however, allowed to leave Morocco to study in France: the Sultan, whose permission is required, tells him: 'Yes, my son, the Fatherland [Morocco] will be waiting for you; our young academics will be our weapons of tomorrow' – to which the father adds: 'Remember, France is the brothel of the world and the closet of that brothel is Paris. We're sending you to Paris – we trust you completely' (270–1). But for the narrator neither the urging to give Morocco the benefit of his education, nor the admonitions to be careful, weigh one jot. On the plane, he thinks: 'Now it's my turn to enjoy myself. Not one bit of my past escapes me, it runs on, it's simple:

I've played, I've won' (272). He has rebelled, he will rebel, Morocco 'in some sense' belongs to him. And the novel ends with the narrator urinating in the plane's toilet and hoping each drop will fall on the heads of those he knows well, who know him well, 'and who disgust me'. The last paragraph reads: 'As for you, Seigneur, I say not "farewell", I say: "We'll see each other soon!"' (273).

This novel of revolt is not solely that. It is laden with references to metropolitan French and European culture that are homage as much as revisionism. Allusions to German and Latin literature and Greek myth underpin the story; chapter epigraphs are from Hugo and Gide; and the final flourish may remind readers of Balzac's *Old Goriot* (1835): at the end the hero Rastignac, from a high point if not from a plane, addresses Paris society 'with these grandiose words': 'It's between us two now!' The very title of Chraïbi's novel springs from that central importance of language in French culture. Chraïbi, then, overlays rebellion with 'French education' in a mode that would prove liberating for subsequent writers.

Less provocatively iconoclastic, but no less disturbing, was the 1960 novel by Sembène Ousmane, *Les Bouts de Bois de Dieu* (*God's Bits of Wood*). This work has figured on the Baccalauréat syllabus in France. It is a fictional recasting of the 1947 railway workers' strike in the French Sudan, tracing the stories of individual characters and communities from the regions involved. It juxtaposes contrasting attitudes to the strike: those of the hard-line militant; the statesman-like older negotiator; the arrogant whites; the self-centred local shopkeeper; the young boys who see the enforced idleness as a chance to be naughty – one ends up shot dead by a fearful white. Women play an active role, from Ad'jibid'ji, the thoughtful little girl through whose eyes we see part of the action – including the initial meeting to call the strike – to the nursing mother who names her baby 'Grève' (Strike) and the women's groups who for the first time dare to speak in public, eventually marching for miles in support of the strike. Like many of his contemporaries, Sembène evokes too the tension between modern ways of thinking and established custom. Here, the key traditions are polygamy and superstition of various kinds – one of these gives the book its title: counting people is thought to shorten their lives, so members of groups are deemed to be 'God's-bits-of-wood'. But there is no strident rejection of these traditions. The title itself is a rich one, suggesting the instrumentality of the whites' view of these people – just bits of wood – and also the fact that they are 'God's', in a collectivity that deserves respect. Sembène's humane vision, then, encompasses his compatriots' benighted beliefs without open accusation; that is reserved for their exploiters. His is a compassionate voice that conveys both humour and pathos – the human comedy as well as tragedy. And part of this complexity is Sembène's presentation, unusual at the time, of the relationship between African languages and French. Sembène shows, as clearly as Césaire and Chraïbi, that the whites have the upper hand, with their inventions and the material benefits they bring, and he ironically has the priests and imams of the novel advise the populace to 'thank God for the French'. But his approach to the language of the colonizers is matter-of-fact: it is there, it has to be used, it must be supplemented where necessary with local languages. When the Governor speaks to the strikers for an hour, he does so in French, a language half of them do not understand: 'Why doesn't he speak in Wolof?' asks one of them; and when, in turn, they are addressed by their own delegate Bakayoko, he does speak in Wolof, asking why the previous speakers used a language incomprehensible to most of their audience. Bakayoko even repeats the last sentences of his speech in two more local languages ('bambara' and 'toucouleur') and finally in French (332–6).

So the choice of language is less anguished than pragmatic, and this goes hand in hand with the Marxist analysis that informs Sembène's novel. For instance, while describing the deplorable disadvantages imposed on women by polygamy, he shows that this custom is seized upon by the French to save money on benefits. They assert that the multiple wives have the status only of concubines and their children that of bastards, but, as Bakayoko points out, when men were conscripted to fight in the war no one asked then if they were legitimate or illegitimate. By focusing on such issues as these, and by presenting the African freedom-fight in class terms, Sembène avoids the sentimentality and the morass of doubt that sometimes ensnares other writers of this period, torn between age-old practices and material progress; he is also able to give the nascent debates about language a tough and down-to-earth edge. These perspectives come from his own life and career, which followed a different trajectory from those of many fellow French-educated Africans. Expelled from school at fourteen, he worked as a builder, joined the army, then later became a mechanic and docker in France, going to evening classes meanwhile. He joined the Communist Party and was active in the trade-union movement before returning to Africa in 1958. Sembène believed that Africa would be liberated not by the elite but by working-class movements, and it was partly this that made him the pioneer of African cinema: here again, the involvement in film sprang from his concept of art as a means of making the poor and exploited aware of their political situation, and as a way of reaching African audiences who not only did not know French but might be unable to read. Sembène criticized African leaders who colluded with Western capitalism, as well as the negritude and 'Francophonie' movements that he saw as reinforcing French cultural hegemony. Fiercely independent-minded, compassionate and high-principled, Sembène was an admirable figure. He too, it goes without saying, owes something to metropolitan culture, but unlike many of his predecessors and successors, he looks directly to Zola (whose *Germinal* clearly influenced some scenes of *Les Bouts*, for instance in contrasts between starving strikers and those who have plenty to eat). He draws too on Malraux and Sartre, deriving from them the collage structure that can depict political crisis dramatically yet panoramically; Malraux's *La Condition humaine* even appears in the novel, invoked at one point by a character as having 'all that's needed' for the present situation – it does not matter that it was written by a Frenchman – even if it is also held to be 'complicated'(144, 148).

Sembène's *Bouts de bois* fuses politics with a Tolstoyan sense of pity; half a century on, it still ranks as one of the greatest works of francophone literature. It asks: 'How can one rise up against injustice without hatred?', for perhaps 'one needs to hate in order the better to fight'; however, the last words of the work, quoted from an old 'complainte' (lament), are: 'But happy is he who fights without hatred' (368, 379).

Frantz Fanon too starts from an uncompromising stance on colonialism. In 1952 he published a seminal work on the psychology of racism and on relations between the races, *Peau noire masques blancs* (*Black Skin, White Masks*). This was influenced by Hegel, Freud, Jung, and Sartre. Nine years later came his best-known work: *Les Damnés de la terre* of 1961, translated into English as *The Wretched of the Earth*. (Sartre wrote the preface to this also, a decade or so after 'Black Orpheus'.) The work had a world-wide influence on the battle against colonialism and racism, and in the United States became a key text for the Black Power movement of the 1960s and 1970s. A brilliant analysis of the social psychology of colonialism, it controversially argues that only violence can liberate the colonized from their alienation. Fanon was of mixed racial origin. He was born into a lower middle-class family in Martinique and studied medicine in France, specializing in psychiatry. Active in politics like other francophone writers of the period, Fanon resigned from his psychiatric post in 1956 to become directly involved with the Algerian insurgency; his 1959 account of the sociology and psychology of the war in Algeria, *Year Five of the Algerian Revolution*, was banned by the French government, and in the same year an assassination attempt was made on him in Rome. The metropolitan colonizer had no illusions as to the threat posed by eloquent black writers.

More hesitant than Sembène's or Fanon's work is Cheikh Hamidou Kane's *L'Aventure ambiguë*, *Ambiguous Adventure*, which came out in 1961, the same year as *The Wretched of the Earth*. This novel explores the hypothesis that a dominant group could accept assimilation: the matriarch, 'la Grande Royale', reluctantly agrees to send (and persuades the powerful men around her to send) the protagonist to a white school and eventually to France, so that he can learn French skills and in particular learn how, like the French, to 'vaincre sans avoir raison', conquer without being in the right. But the hero is so demoralized by culture-shock in Paris that he cannot function in either country, and is killed by a madman who wants him to remain the devout Muslim he once was. Much of the narrative, especially the parts set in Paris, unfurls by way of lengthy conversations between characters; at times it resembles a parable or dialogue as much as a novel, making it not only an 'ambiguous adventure' but an equivocal, ultimately stagnant work. But the sense of stagnation is deliberate, representing dilemmas facing non-metropolitan elites. This novel would set the tone for some important post-1968 francophone writing, and its constant hovering on the verge of the dialogue form has precedents in Enlightenment works by Montesquieu and Diderot.

For many of these francophone authors were, like the *philosophes*, 'intellectuals' in the French meaning: their hunger for knowledge was bound up with a desire to educate and to change the course of history. One of the most distinguished and exciting intellectuals of this period was the philosopher, linguist, Egyptologist, mathematician and scientist Cheikh Anta Diop. His work has revolutionized our view of ancient Egyptian and African culture. Using both linguistic and radio-carbon evidence, he proved that many of the ruling class of ancient Egypt had been black Africans. Given that the achievements of these Egyptians had been long revered by Europeans, this research constituted another 'bombshell' – or a series of them – with repercussions far wider than those of Chraïbi's novel. Resistance from the French and even the Senegalese establishments was vigorous. Diop's first doctoral thesis was rejected by the Sorbonne but was published in 1954 under the title *Black Nations and Culture*. Although his reputation grew with successive publications, he was never allowed to lecture at the University of Dakar, lacking Senghor's support. (Ironically, after Diop died this university was named after him.) Diop's theories undermined the Western belief in African cultural inferiority, a theory that had 'justified' colonial exploitation; his demonstration of the unity underlying African cultures also served as a critique of the splitting-up of Africa by the Western powers. Diop's proposition that black Africa contributed to ancient Egyptian civilization is now generally accepted; it was taken up and expanded by the British scholar Martin Bernal, whose *Black Athena* (1987–2006) is on many US university syllabuses.

Diop's major work, *The Anteriority of Black Civilisations: Myth or Historical Truth*, appeared in 1967, on the cusp of the youth militancy sweeping Europe and the United States. Its tone is as striking as its content. It is a study of wide-ranging scholarship, but is always lucid and readable. It sets out its case calmly, yet its dignity does not exclude the occasional sarcasm and courting of controversy. For example, Diop explains from the start that he is not proposing a theory of negritude, but wants – he says – to elucidate 'a precise point of human history'. He thus coolly suggests that the idea of 'negritude' is a vague one. And his sideswipe at those who plagiarize his theories while criticizing them is all the more devastating for its concise sting in the tail:

> There are certain writers – this is actually amusing – who draw on my works throughout their own without citing them, in the belief that all they have to do to mask this is to criticise me at the same time! In this case, at least, they cannot deny they have located a *black*. (11)

Diop calls for an acceptance of 'cultural plenitude', arguing that it makes a people better able to contribute to the 'general progress of humanity'; and in his conclusion (more heated now) he describes imperialism as an octopus whose tentacles liberate the developing world on one side the better to try to grip it on another; nor does imperialism 'hesitate to live on a cultural lie' ('un mensonge culturel': 276). Diop's exposure of that cultural lie would contribute to the flowering of francophone literature in the post-1968 decades.

Thus these seven writers, and other mid-twentieth-century francophones, moved towards a self-definition that varied from one author and country to another, but always incorporated live political difficulties. Whichever the imperialist power – whether Dutch, British, Portuguese – this politicization of writers from former colonies is no doubt inevitable; but in the case of francophone writers the political involvement often has a special intensity and directness, many of them, as we have seen, being

activists as well as fine writers. That arises from the particular circumstances of France's colonialism and decolonization, yet it is also oddly
recognizable from the history of metropolitan literature. Familiar too is
the overt acknowledgement of that literature. Is it another act of colonialism to suggest what these and later francophone writers 'owe' to metropolitan France? Maybe. But their use of French culture can also be seen as
a colloquy with France, even as a wish to educate it that would not have
been disowned in the age of the *Encyclopédie*. At the least, these writers are
reminding the French of an open-mindedness to 'foreigners' that goes back
to the Middle Ages, even if they are pushing it in urgent new directions.
Finally, the overseas territories have by 1968 learned for themselves the
metropolitan lesson of pride in 'cultural nationhood'. All these motifs will
run through the following four decades, in subtler form but no less potently.

10

Francophone Literature: Recent Developments

We saw in Chapter 8, 'After May 1968', that the French writer Tournier had viewed 'postcolonial' characters and settings as part of a late twentieth-century aesthetic remit. Two more indicators of the new status of 'the francophone' are, first, the success in metropolitan France of the works of 'Paul Smaïl', a mysterious middle-aged white who fooled the public with the pretence that he was the immigrant author of such works as *Ali le magnifique* (2001); second, the post-1968 renown of the also white Marguerite Duras, who grew up in Indo-China and for whom, like Tournier, formal experimentation in these years is intertwined with a vision of disintegrating Empire. Future cultural historians of French writing may look back on these last four decades as ones in which the fresh inspiration came from overseas – from a thriving body of literature that rivalled or surpassed anything the metropolitan country was producing.

Indeed, the French literary establishment has increasingly recognized non-white writers, not only electing Senghor to the Académie Française in 1983 but in recent years awarding mainstream French literary prizes to other overseas writers. (The prestigious Goncourt Prize was, for example, won two years running by francophone novelists: in 1992, by the Martinican Patrick Chamoiseau for *Texaco*; in 1993, by the Lebanese Amin Maalouf for *Le Rocher de Tanios*. (And in 2008 the prize went to the francophone Afghan Atiq Rahimi for *Syngue Sabour, Stone of Patience*.) There has been a comparable development in Britain, which in the last few decades has both promoted and honoured writers from the former colonies. But in France, the recognition is all the more striking since it co-exists with the rise of the Front National. This rise itself has sharpened the work of left-wing white and non-white writers and film-makers inside and outside France. But that cannot be the whole story: the fertility of post-1968 francophone literature does not arise solely from current schisms in France. This literature, taking the best from its own predecessors and from metropolitan writing, has pushed French culture forward with a succession of rich and original texts.

Market forces have played a part. Wavering metropolitan support for local initiatives has meant that the publishing situation in most franco-phone countries is scarcely better than it ever was. In 1972, a decade after the founding of Editions CLE, there did come a significant move: the launching of the Nouvelles Editions Africaines consortium. This was a joint undertaking of the governments of Senegal, Ivory Coast and Togo, along with French publishing interests. Its aims were to encourage African authorship, to promote reading, and to produce schoolbooks that reflected African experience. The NEA, a model of enlightened govern-ment attitudes, soon occupied a crucial role in all areas of African pub-lishing, with a list that included works by most of the key African academics and authors; it also produced excellent children's books. The other publisher of note in francophone West Africa is the Centre d'Edition et de Diffusion Africaines (CEDA) in Abidjan (Ivory Coast); in Togo a number of small publishing houses have been set up, including Editions HaHo ('for all'), started in 1984 and publishing in African languages as well as in French; while Ibis Rouge, founded in French Guiana in 1995, produces a range of Caribbean and other francophone works. But other moves have not always had the desired long-term impact, and – particu-larly since the recession of the 1990s – indigenous publishing has declined: government funding for textbooks and libraries has fallen, and home-grown activities in many parts of francophone Africa are now scarcely in evidence. Big multinational and French publishers dominate, crowding out small autonomous African ones. (If publishing thrives in such North African countries as Morocco and Algeria, it is because many works are in Arabic.) African literary reviews set up from the 1960s on again present a mixed picture of success. Little magazines have been born, then to die, in, for example, Brazzaville (capital of the Republic of the Congo) and Madagascar. To be sure, this is the fate to which little magazines are often destined, and some periodicals have been longer-lived, among them the Ivory Coast *Revue de littérature et d'esthétique négro-africaines*, founded in 1983. The Senegalese *Ethiopiques. Revue socialiste de culture négro-afric-aine*, published from 1974 on, has provided a forum for left-wing and aesthetic debates; Senegal also for several years (from 1968) published *L'Afrique littéraire et artistique*, covering cinema as well as literature, drama, art and music; and the Institut Culturel Africain publishes the bilingual Cameroonian periodical *Abbia. Revue culturelle camerounaise/ Cameroon Cultural Review* and *ICA Information*, an again bilingual quarterly that provides information on cultural activities in member states. Finally, one significant event was the production in the 1970s of an analytic index to the 1947–72 issues of *Présence Africaine*. This index was compiled by Femi Ojo-Ade, a Nigerian educated in Nigeria, Senegal, France, Spain and Canada, where he obtained a doctorate in francophone 'Negro-African' literature. The preface to the index, written by the Caribbean literary encyclopedia editor Maurice Lubin, stresses that since its founding the journal has been the 'sincere, profound reflection of cultural life in the black world', and that its remit has widened to take in not just similarities between blacks but also 'variations in the Black heritage' (x–xi). The index, then, signalled a coming-of-age and drew attention to a sense of community yet difference.

But it is sobering that the two key Africa-centred periodicals *Jeune Afrique* and *Présence Africaine* are both published in Paris; Paris is also the base of the publisher L'Harmattan, dedicated to francophone literature or discursive works focused on francophone issues. And it is clear that most authors from the former colonies have to write in French to be published at all. They also tend to cleave to French as a way of affirming their position in their own country, not simply because this is still the language of the social elite but also because, as has already been suggested, French often occupies a position comparable to that of English in India: the only language common to different regions. (Paradoxically, then, it is a means of preserving local languages by preventing any single one from becoming dominant; but this 'advantage' does not conduce to a strong sense of cultural identity.) More important for our purposes: if these writers are to be taken on by a mainstream French publisher, they must make their techniques 'recognizable' to the public that will be buying their books – a public almost certainly middle-class, educated in the French system, and doubtless comprising many readers with a taste for the avant-garde.

This being said, post-1968 francophone imaginative literature is buoyant in part because it acknowledges the reality of its own situation – usually laterally and wryly. The buoyancy comes too from increasingly skilful techniques that allow these writers to acknowledge a mutual plight while evoking local distinctiveness. Emphasizing such local individuality is one way of approaching post-1968 francophone literature (we should really say 'literatures'). Another way is to draw out the commonality, which has the advantage of highlighting the widest developments and showing international influences. In this chapter I adopt the latter approach, bringing out francophones' shared politicization of the French language and their interaction with metropolitan literature – almost always an admiring interaction, whatever the variations. I discuss sixteen authors from five different areas (there are numerous outstanding writers among whom to choose, but at the present time these are probably the best known): from Canada, Anne Hébert (1916–2000), Antonine Maillet (b. 1929), Michel Tremblay (b. 1942) and Michèle Lalonde (b. 1937); from North Africa (or the Maghreb, an Arabic term for this region now widely used in French), Assia Djebar (Algeria, b. 1936) and Tahar Ben Jelloun (Morocco, b. 1944); from sub-Saharan Africa, Ahmadou Kourouma (Ivory Coast, 1927–2003), Aminata Sow Fall (Senegal, b. 1941), Boubacar Boris Diop (Senegal, b. 1946), Sony Labou Tansi (Congo, 1947–95) and Werewere Liking (Cameroon, b. 1950); from Vietnam, Linda Lê (b. 1963); from the Caribbean, Edouard Glissant (Martinique, b. 1928), Maryse Condé (Guadeloupe, b. 1937), Patrick Chamoiseau (Martinique, b. 1953) and the post-1968 Césaire. I end with the writing that, within metropolitan France itself, has sprung from immigrant culture.

Post-1968 francophone literature has grown ever more sophisticated about the verbal medium in which it is operating. In Césaire's hands the French language had become elastic enough to usher in the narrator's discovery of a 'Martinican' voice and to incorporate an African cry of triumph, *Eia*. Now, however, the very use of French is foregrounded and the inventiveness can be exuberant, as in Tremblay's play *Les Belles-Sœurs* (*The Sisters-in-Law*), written in 1965 and first performed in August 1968 – just after the May events, then. The heroine has won a million trading-stamps and enlists family and neighbours to help her stick them in booklets. As the women perform the task, chatting to each other, bleakly comical life-histories and tensions emerge; some of the women start to filch the stamps; at the end, they throw the booklets at each other, and as they sing 'O Canada' a shower of stamps falls slowly from the ceiling. This drama is an Absurdist one: the spectator will think of Beckett, Adamov and Ionesco. But the language is more politically charged than in those three. The play jokes with grammar in a manner that could scandalize the Académie and draws attention to the status of Canadian French by incorporating local (lower-class) pronunciation and usage. One lucky woman has been to Europe, where there are, according to her, only posh people ('grand monde'). In Paris, indeed, everyone speaks well (she says '*perle* bien'); 'it's real French all over the place, not like here': 'c'est du vrai français partout . . . C'est pas comme icitte . . .' (42; author's ellipses). The dialogue is also peppered with such American-English words as 'fun' – the characters bemoan their lack of it, and this oft-recurring word finally makes a linguistic and social point in one: 'fun' is missing from the women's lives both because of their class and gender and because the Canadian community is in thrall to a Catholicism that emphasizes sin.

Michèle Lalonde too combines linguistic and social concerns in her witty *Défense et illustration de la langue québécoise* of 1973. Acknowledgement of the language and culture of France is announced by her very title, taken from the sixteenth-century Du Bellay's promotion of the vernacular, *Défense et illustration de la langue française*. (See above, p. 19.) And throughout her long essay, Lalonde affectionately pastiches sixteenth-century French (the title and much of the text rapidly appears in sixteenth-century spelling, thus: 'La Deffence et illustration de la langue quebequoyse'). But the pastiche is in itself a weapon in Lalonde's argument, reminding her reader that other 'vernaculars' need promotion now; that the true originality of Quebec French is that it is *not* an elite language; that it is 'neither as solid as people would like it to be nor as badly constructed as people think'; and that 'the norm of the metropolis' must not be allowed to drain away the 'verve' of 'joual' (21, 26–7). ('Joual' is the form of popular French spoken in Quebec province, particularly in Montreal.) Speakers must, says Lalonde, still be discriminatory, but must be aware that there are political reasons for being proud of this 'bastard' means of expression – for example, an identification with the proletarian majority.

This lively work promulgates, then, a new status for local versions of French via Du Bellay's landmark polemic. A self-assertion that simultaneously draws on metropolitan culture also shapes Antonine Maillet's *Pélagie-la-Charrette* of 1979. *Pélagie* narrates the late eighteenth-century return 'home' of Acadians (that is, French Canadians of New Brunswick, Nova Scotia and Prince Edward Island). From 1713 on, the British had exiled and brutally scattered Acadians, some as far afield as Louisiana; but now the heroine Pélagie, in her cart ('charrette'), leads a group on an epic journey back to the homeland. The odyssey is by turns dramatic, humorous and tragic; Pélagie is a Canadian Mother Courage. Maillet creates the same impression as Tremblay and Lalonde that here is a community of ordinary people whose version of French can and does acquire dignity, and whose history is no less History for being an oral one. Cunningly, the characters' demotic makes this very point, for it typically uses the 'we' verb-ending with a 'je' subject (the equivalent of 'I are': 'Où est-ce que j'allons les crècher?', 'je devions boire': 32). The 'I' in a 'nous' form entertainingly suggests that an individual has transmuted, will transmute, into a society – which is indeed the case in this story. Muted allusions to metropolitan literature reinforce this sense of sharing. For example, Chrétien de Troyes's *Le Chevalier de la charrette* had also used the 'cart' as an implicit invitation to ponder different kinds of status (see above, p. 14); and one of the old Acadian families is called Landry, a nod to George Sand's Landry, the main male character in her *Petite Fadette*. (Francophone literature owes a debt to this nineteenth-century promoter of 'the regional'. Widely read, if only as a 'children's author', she made it permissible not only to write about the sorrows and joys of far-flung communities but also to give the flavour of their speech – true, in discreetly Bowdlerized form: nevertheless, this was bold.)

Recent Caribbean authors, too, lovingly manipulate the language and culture of metropolitan France – not without an element of defiance, for now the culture is that of the oppressor. The prolific cross-genre writer Maryse Condé gives us the history of this. She herself heard Creole (the native Caribbean language or patois) only by accident, when her mother was helping at the birth of a servant's child: she did not even know her mother spoke it. Condé points out in her account of Caribbean oral narratives that for educated nineteenth-century blacks the only means of self-differentiation from 'the mass of their brothers' was neither land nor wealth, 'but the possession of the master's culture. The mastery of his Word' (52). This path-breaking work is *'Bossale' Civilisation: Reflections on the Oral Literature of Guadeloupe and Martinique* (1978): the 'bossale' was the African brought by the slave-trade to the plantations of Martinique and Guadeloupe. These educated blacks, says Condé, denied or ridiculed their own culture; and, she claims, for the whole of the late nineteenth century (that is, after the abolition of slavery and the institution of schooling), the black 'will not dare open his mouth' unless it is to 'recite by heart the lessons he has been taught' (52).

But this doubting use of language would change, at first slowly but, in the Caribbean and elsewhere, given impetus first by Césaire's *Cahier*, and then by the novelist, playwright and essayist Glissant, writing from the 1960s on. Glissant defends solidarity among the black Caribbean 'diaspora', but metropolitan self-awareness is not far away: he calls his 1981 collection of radical essays *Le Discours antillais* (Discourse of the Antilles), and his epigraphs cite not only Martinican sayings and Fanon but also de Gaulle and Rousseau. The Rousseau epigraph, taken from *Essay on the Origin of Languages*, reads: 'But the most energetic language is that in which the sign has said everything before a word is uttered'. Here is that foregrounding of language that marks mainstream French culture; and, in a fine long poem published four years later, *Pays rêvé, pays réel: Poème* (Dreamed Country, Real Country: Poem, 1985), Glissant draws attention to the medium, almost to the mechanics, of reading:

Nous épelions du vent la harde de nos cris
Vous qui savez lire l'entour des mots où nous errons ('Pays', 11)

(We *spelled out* from the wind the flock of our cries / You who *can read* the surrounding of the *words* where we wander)

The *p* alliteration of the very title suggests an intimate connection between poetry in French and the native land: dreams about it, its reality. And, like Césaire, Glissant uses the imagery of the sea that was beloved by turn-of-the-century metropolitan artists, musicians and writers, but is now laden with fraught memories of the slave-trade voyages. (Celia Britton, in a discussion of Caribbean writers' use of *The Tempest*, remarks on the symbolism of the father who has drowned but is now changed 'Into something rich and strange'. The slaves thrown overboard to drown, the 'fore-fathers', stand for Caribbean trauma and the 'Caribbean unconscious', but are also 'the necessary foundation for a freer, more mobile identity' – have become part of a new culture: *Race and the Unconscious*, 2002, 100–4.)

Glissant writes in the closing section, also called 'Pays':

Nous avons pris main dans l'alphabet roué
Aux brumes de ces mots voilé le cri, éclaboussé
Le long cri des oiseaux précipités dans cette mer
Et nous avons aux mers plus d'écriture qu'il paraît
Yoles blessées où les lézardes s'évertuèrent . . .
L'œuvre que nous halons est un songe de mer (95–7)

(We have taken a hold in the sly alphabet / In the mists of these words have veiled the cry, splashed / The long cry of birds thrown into this sea / And we have more writing in this sea than it seems / Wounded skiffs in which the cracks strove . . . / The work that we haul in is a sea-dream)

Again consciousness of the medium fuses with a terrible history, as it continues to do in Césaire. His linguistic deftness is no less evident in his late verse than it had been forty years earlier: in his 1982 poem *Moi, laminaire . . .*, 'laminaire' is seaweed (laminaria or oarweed), but the word will also remind the French reader of 'liminaire', 'liminal' or 'on the threshold', 'prefatory': the sea is merged with a forward-looking marginality in a wordplay highlighted by the ellipsis (Césaire's own). And a kind of moral wordplay appears in the very first lines, in a punning association of 'maux' and 'mots' ('ills' and 'words'), where the very word for 'word' is associated with the problem of evil. The deftness sustains the whole work, as do cross-overs with metropolitan culture. (Echoes of Mallarmé's *Un coup de dés* are obvious, for example.)

But perhaps the most stylistically subversive Caribbean interaction with mainstream French comes in Chamoiseau's prize-winning novel *Texaco* of 1992. The 400-page work is a humane yet parodic narrative told largely by the character Marie-Sophie Laborieux, who lives in a shanty-town called Texaco because it is located beside petrol reservoir tanks. An urban planner, jokingly referred to as 'Christ', comes to Texaco; Marie-Sophie tells him the story of Texaco, going back to her father Esternome's tales of growing up on a slave plantation. The novel takes us through two world wars and up to the late twentieth century; rather like Maillet's Pélagie, Marie-Sophie is herself responsible for the founding of Texaco.

The work is announced via the simultaneous linguistic and political challenge that will permeate it. The epigraph to the first section, 'Annunciation', quotes from an 'epistle' written by a (fictional) literate Haitian editor, Ti-Cirique, who uses deliberate archaisms to declare that he could have written about deep matters such as the nature of man, of death, of love and of God in a French more French than that of the French ('un français plus français que celui des Français'). He addresses a 'lamentable' interlocutor (the author/narrator/second editor), telling him that he does not wish to write as 'you' do, 'in the negro quarters of your Creoleness [Créolité] or in the dilapidated asbestos cement of Texaco'. You, he says, lack Humanism – and especially greatness. To this, his interlocutor replies: 'Dear master, literature in a living place is something to be taken alive' (19). The status of 'respectable' French language and literature must give way to a new presence, to utterances that must be seized on the spot. And indeed, Marie-Sophie's history, with its admixture of Creole, is that of a people with only oral traditions; but the narrator, Nabokov-like, breaks in periodically with footnotes and with fragments of text presented in scholarly manner, supposedly from Marie-Sophie's notebooks, kept in an archive in the Schoelcher Library. A 'Western' desire to preserve and, perhaps, to fossilize the past is thus contrasted with, yet contributes to, the lithe mobility of the culture of Texaco.

Chamoiseau, like all francophone writers, wants to be widely understood; local words are usually followed by a mainstream French synonym, as in the following reflection on so-called 'strong men' (that is, dispensers of remedies and magic): 'History calls them quimboiseurs, séanciers or sorcerers' (62). And he is, from one point of view, advertising the robustness and adaptability of French. But the insertions, neologisms and verbal twists and turns are also saying: 'you, conqueror, *will* do what I require'; or, at the very least, they urge a clean start at all levels of expression and perception. As the narrator of Werewere Liking's 1983 poem declares: 'The idea of a new language appeals to me . . . a new language / for the Race of jasper and coral'. For in Liking's *Elle sera de jaspe et de corail*, the 'Elle' of the title is a race that is neither black nor white but all the precious and wondrous colours under the sun. (Translation by Marjolijn de Jager, 78–9.)

This special blend of linguistic self-consciousness and fresh perception, this 'politico-stylistic' creativity, is at its most obvious in Assia Djebar's novel of 1985, *L'Amour, la fantasia* (*Love, Fantasia*). Djebar was the first Algerian woman to study at the Ecole Normale Supérieure (the one for women at Sèvres). Part of Djebar's purpose is to portray the restrictions within which Arab women traditionally operate, and the liberation that a French education represents for any such woman; but her presentation of the abuses of French colonialism is uncompromising. Thus *L'Amour, la fantasia* interweaves scenes from the nineteenth-century French conquest of Algeria with the life of an Algerian girl (the narrator) growing up in the mid-twentieth century; tragic tableaux of French barbarity are spliced with fine-spun, often droll, scenes enacting home-grown prejudices. What is striking is the 'literariness' of the work. The role of writing, the style of writing, are considered even in the accounts of conquest from which Djebar quotes, for these were after all relayed by French writers, including the reputable Fromentin (1820–76) (235, 313). More widely, the drama of 'the French language' is brought alive through a wide range of metaphors and allegories: French, a language 'given' to the narrator by her father, is like a procuress ('entremetteuse'), or a 'husband' in a forced marriage, or a stepmother; French is the 'sign' of the enemy; her female compatriots are either 'veiled', if she does not speak of them in French, or are implicitly 'stripped': 'Strange little sister whom, from now on, I inscribe in a foreign language, or whom I veil' (12, 188, 201, 297–9). French changes the narrator's very physicality: 'so I studied French, and my body, during that education, westernized itself in its own way' (181); sitting cross-legged, for example, now becomes uncomfortable. We finally understand that the narrator's relationship with French must necessarily be an oblique, 'arabesquing' one (the fantasia is an Arab dance). Yet, clearly, it is also the medium that has made her articulate. For *L'Amour, la fantasia* has the same qualities, and sometimes the same faults, as Butor's *Using Time*: the sheer density of its alliterations can overwhelm, sometimes seeming overdone or awkward. But that too is, perhaps, the point. Certainly it is possible to adopt a political perspective on the artificiality that could not be read into Butor. Djebar's fine novel is elegiac at many complex levels.

Another fruitful complexity in recent francophone novels is their use of 'style indirect libre', free indirect style. Sembène, as we saw, owed a debt to Zola's use of the strike as a fitting subject. But Zola also bequeathed to successors a particular type of free indirect style. In his hands it had bestowed dignity on the vulgar phrasing – whether spoken or thought – of his working-class characters. (See above, p. 108.) Zola thereby enacted a cultural tension; compassion; and a newly daring demonstration that 'low' language could become aesthetically pleasing. And many post-1968 francophone novelists use free indirect style, whether leaning towards Zola or Flaubert; apart from anything else, it is an ideal instrument to suggest the contradictions of characters' consciousness while creating an irony that – it is implied – may often be the only adequate response to the situation of the francophone.

One striking case is Kourouma's *Les Soleils des Indépendances* (1968), published at the very beginning of our period. The title, *The Suns of Independence*, is itself ironic; independence for Ivory Coast turns out to be far from a new dawn for the hero, Fama, the 'fallen' prince of the royal line of the Dumbuya. Fama respects the traditions of the elders in spite of the recent political upheavals: he organizes funerals according to the old rites, prays to Allah. But in a land where violence and wretchedness predominate, his hopes have turned sour.

> He, Fama, born to gold, food in plenty, honour and women! Bred to prefer one gold to another, to choose between many dishes, to bed his favourite of a hundred wives! What was he now? A scavenger . . . A hyena in a hurry. (Translation by Adrian Adams, 5; author's ellipsis)

Bitterness is, then, expressed, yet a distance is established from the often benighted Fama. Here he is, for example, wondering why his wife Salimata is still sterile: 'What curse dogged her? She always behaved as a Muslim woman should, performed the proper ablutions, fasted the full thirty days, gave alms and prayed five times daily ['four' in the original]; Fama could testify to that' (16).

As we might expect, the free indirect ironizes not only the protagonist but also the white ex-colonizers, whose business interests still prosper under the 'sun' of independence; so here the free indirect suggests that the protagonist 'sees true':

> . . . the sun, already harried by drifting clouds in the west, had ceased to shine on the African quarter to concentrate on the white buildings of the white men's town. Damnation! Hell! The African is in hell! The buildings, bridges and roads over there, all built by African hands, were lived in by

Europeans and belonged to them. Independence couldn't do a thing about it! Everywhere, under every sun, on every soil, Africans hold the beast's feet, while the Whites carve it up and wolf down the meat and fat. Was it not Hell to toil in the shadows for others? like the giant ant-eater to dig burrows for others? (11).

And ironized too through free indirect is the new black President: Fama finds himself in prison along with others who have been detained on suspicion only; they could be freed, but will not be: 'Only the president can release them, and a president of the suns of Independence never has the time' (111).

Near the end of the novel, a friend advises Fama to move with the times: 'The suns have turned over with the colonial period and independence; let these new suns keep you warm! . . . Be adaptable! Accept the world as it is!' (126). But Fama does not; he dies and, symbolically, the novel ends as it began, with a funeral whose rites will go on and on. The last words are: 'the fortieth-day funeral rites, and . . .' (136; author's ellipsis). This open ending is Beckettian, but would lack its modernist punch if not for the constant preceding use of free indirect, which has forced an 'open-endedness' on the reader throughout.

Anne Hébert's 1970 *Kamouraska*, published two years after Kourouma's *Soleils*, also switches into free indirect at key moments. This nightmarish tale is set in a repressive nineteenth-century Canada: the heroine plots her husband's murder with her lover. The narrator shifts between 'she', 'I' and even 'you', but free indirect creates a particular intensity when, for example, the heroine contrasts her wish to escape a man's control with the restraint she must now exercise towards her second husband in order to be the perfect spouse: 'Accept being checked by him, put up with this insult. Consent to this disgusting surveillance, after an entire life as a model wife' (22). We are not meant to 'swallow' this version of events – the heroine has hardly been a paragon: though never convicted, she is naturally an object of suspicion and will now be watched both by this second husband and the community. But there is a truth here too, and one which emerges as the novel goes on: pressures from family and (Catholic) Church had indeed initially forced the heroine to play the 'model wife' and to suffer the brutalities of her first husband, the upper-class 'seigneur' of Kamouraska (with all the Ancien Régime echoes of that word 'seigneur'). The free indirect, allowing for sympathy as well as detachment, can convey a social critique mingled with sophistry.

Free indirect also permeates Maillet's *Pélagie la Charrette*. The narrator will address the reader half as herself, half as Pélagie: no speech indicators introduce such interjections as 'Quelle affaire!' or 'Parlez-moi de ça!' ('What a business!'; 'Tell me about it!', 61); often paragraphs begin and end not with quotation-marks or dashes but with the more indefinite ellipsis, to indicate (à la Sarraute) the blurred borderline between thought, speech and narrative. It is not only Pélagie's responses that are conveyed in free indirect: one character smiles at the snobbish distortions of history promulgated by another: 'Old or new stock, that didn't mean much in a land where everyone had emerged together from Touraine and Poitou; . . . where everyone, except deserters who'd fled into the woods, had been sent off to the south or into the Islands' (89–90). A compassionate irony thus encompasses both the reality of unpleasant historical facts and the characters' wish that life was not thus.

Finally, the remarkable 1997 novel by the Vietnamese immigrant Linda Lê, *Les Trois Parques* (*The Three Fates*), frequently moves into an extended free indirect style as the narrative switches between the thoughts of characters. This novel – whose structure flows on as fluidly as its style, without chapters and in long paragraphs – tells the story of three young women, two sisters and a cousin, who emigrate from Vietnam to Geneva. One is physically mutilated by war; one attempts desperately to recreate her home culture in an unhappy marriage of convenience; the youngest allows herself to be seduced by the worst and shallowest delusions of Western culture. Lê uses not only free indirect but also a first-person, modernist, unreliable narrator like Céline's; there is nevertheless a fusion, and a clear line of descent from the free indirect adopted by other francophones. Here are two examples: 'In her flight from Saigon, grandmother had put in her bag the two statuettes, the jade pot and the Buddha-shaped emerald beside a crucifix. *Two forms of protection were better than one* . . .' (68). And: 'for the sweet girl – he'd put his hand in the fire for this – had an Ophelia complex, mad about her father . . . Nor had it escaped him that the generous, attentive one was afflicted with a Cordelia complex . . . Cordelia, the generous, attentive one – would she refuse him a place at the Christmas-time celebrations?' (172). And it is as if Lê's intermingling perspectives give her licence to play wildly with that hallowed medium, the metropolitan language. Thus, again in free indirect: 'Car, en atten*d*ant le *d*emi-*d*ieu qui *d*evait lui *d*é*d*ier son *d*ard, la *d*onzelle s'était *d*émenée comme un beau *d*iable, avait *d*ompté un *d*a*d*a après l'autre . . .' (75). I have signalled all the *d* alliterations; a rough translation would be: 'For, awaiting the demi-god who would dedicate his dart to her, that fast woman had flung herself about like a fine devil, had tamed one cock-horse after another. . .', and so on. Like many of these post-1968 authors, Lê is a virtuoso manipulator of French – ludic, inventive: the free indirect becomes part of that.

Many critics have grouped francophone writers according to two broad concepts. First, they are seen as attempting to preserve memories of an older language, literature, culture – or any combination of these – in exile, or at least when far from the mother country. Second, they are seen as evincing a post-traumatic reaction to slavery, racial prejudice, banishment, persecution, or memories and knowledge of such atrocities perpetrated on their ancestors. Free indirect style is one particularly apt way to juggle remembrance and present, trauma and healing, and keep them in indefinite suspense.

However, hovering between perspectives is not the only technique adopted by francophone writers, nor is irony their only register. Their works are full of zesty comedy, satire and black humour (this latter a more immediate attempt than irony to exorcize trauma). *Les Trois Parques* itself, as the last quotation indicated, is farcical as well as painful. (Important papers get lost in recipe books, and the like.) Vulnerability can be narrated with an exaggerated sarcasm, political points can be made via slapstick. Critics writing about francophone literature sometimes overlook its liking for the preposterous, for the hyperbolic. Does their own survivors' or conquerors' guilt make them approach it too piously? We have already seen the humour in such writers as Tremblay, Maillet and Chamoiseau. Sub-Saharan African authors, for their part, write satirical works that draw on sometimes physically absurd, sometimes amusingly rueful, stories from African oral traditions. (Maryse Condé analyses the permutations these traditions have undergone in a Caribbean context in her *Civilisation du bossale*.) But the broad humour and satire also hark back to certain overtly comic scenarios in Voltaire's tales, Stendhal's novels, Jarry's puppet plays and many other metropolitan works. And the plots themselves sometimes echo those of earlier French authors.

Aminata Sow Fall, for example, creates an entertainingly uncomfortable parable in her 1979 novel *La Grève des bàttu ou Les Déchets humains* (*Strike by the Bàttu, or Human Debris*). This novel won the Grand Prix Littéraire d'Afrique Noire, was shortlisted for the Goncourt Prize, and was made into a film. In the early 1970s, Senghor, on the advice of the World Bank, had launched a campaign to attract tourism to Senegal; one result was legal and police action against the beggars of Dakar (the 'bàttu' of the title: its literal meaning is a calabash, a gourd, held out for alms). In the novel, the beggars have, then, been sent out of town to avoid shocking the tourists. But one day, crushed by successive humiliations, they decide to strike.

They will no longer beg! Alms-giving is one of the five duties, or 'Pillars of Islam', incumbent on every Muslim; so the moral and social life of the country is turned upside down now that there no longer exists a target for beneficence – a beneficence that should in principle bring the beggars' prayerful thanks and blessings down on the donors' heads, thus in turn bringing them success.

Sow Fall's work arises, then, from a local situation, but at the same time it interacts with metropolitan literary predecessors. First, Zola's promotion of humble lives and trades is still perceptible, lying behind *La Grève des bàttu*. Second, the novel's implicit criticisms of the limits of Senghor's political vision, and its satire of his political circle, lead into a wider medita-tion on the authenticity or inauthenticity of humanism; in this it is remi-niscent of Camus's probing of secular hypocrisy in *La Chute*. Third, the characters frequently use the language of the Enlightenment and of the French Revolution. The beggars comment: 'just because we're beggars, they think we're not human beings like them!'; for these Rousseauists, 'the contract that binds each individual to society can be summed up as: to give and to receive' – what they 'give' is their good wishes. And the arriviste politician Mour, longing to become Vice-President of the country and finally concluding that, to this end, he needs to hand out alms to the men-dicants, portentously decides that 'We must restore their citizens' status . . .' (43, 45, 160; author's ellipsis).

Boubacar Boris Diop is still more biting than Sow Fall. His contribution to modern Senegalese culture has been profound: a novelist, dramatist and journalist, he is also the co-founder of the Sengalese weekly *Sud-hebdo*. His 1981 novel *Le Temps de Tamango* describes the historical events of the late 1960s in Senegal from a futuristic twenty-first-century standpoint: the post-colonial state has been replaced by a Communist one. Diop sets against each other the incompetence of the current administration; the ideals – and pitfalls – of revolutionary movements; and the role of intellectuals. No group is spared in this satire, which is simultaneously grim, funny and formally experimental. It is peopled by caricatures: those of the Minister of Culture; the union- and demonstration-hating President; and the French military official François Navarro, ordered to take a position in 'Black Africa', for he is 'the man for the situation: a pitiless grip, a jewel of the white race: not too bright and totally antipathetic' (21). He will be allowed to jump a number of ranks to become General, but only, he is told, when he has had 'real contact with a primitive country' (24). 'Negroes' are seen as 'monkeys'. So it goes on, all overlaid by yet another kind of humour when a further narrator steps forward to let us know that the story was set down in 2050 but the notes for it not actually gathered until July 2063. As in *Texaco*, the narrator pretends at times to be a chronicler and ludicrously precise 'scholar' (Western educational systems are being parodied here too); in the end, historical 'realities' themselves cannot be trusted, for they may, it seems, be myths put about by the twenty-first-century Communist government.

The work carries an outspoken preface by the Cameroonian polemicist and satirist Mongo Beti, who claims it will annoy those who want to deny creative Africans the right to aesthetic experimentation, bold research and depth of thought; 'the African reader will, no doubt, be of a very different opinion'. Why – he asks – was decolonization such a failure in those parts of Africa ruled by the French? Why are we *francophones* (the sarcastic italics and inverted commas are his) subjected to a colonialism that doesn't even try to hide its designs and methods? How can we free ourselves definitively like our brother African peoples? Diop has, he says, given us an 'Ubuesque world' that provides the key to the multidimensional drama of so-called francophone Africa. This angry preface is less subtle than the work itself. To be sure, Diop is arousing indignation on behalf of those whom the French colonized. But he is also appealing to the aesthetic sophistication of French-speaking literati wherever they may be, and that includes metropolitan France: the mention of Ubu shows that Beti recognizes this too. The name 'Tamango' is taken from a short story by the nineteenth-century Mérimée about the slave trade: Tamango is a tyrannical African chief who at first collaborates with the white traders, then rebels against them (*Tamango*, 1829). And the cavalier interventions of the narrator and super-narrator create a comedy resembling the deliberate tricks of the New Novel. Thus, having read of how one militant becomes the servant of Navarro in order to avenge the assassination of another, we find: 'But let's not anticipate. Let's pretend to believe that real events are stupid enough to proceed like this, one following another, according to our derisory wishes. For the moment, the bell's being rung' (85).

Yet more fantastical are the prize-winning satirical dramas of the Congolese novelist and dramatist Sony Labou Tansi – also interwoven with metropolitan culture. He made regular presentations at the Limoges Festival International des Francophonies and collaborated with well-known French theatre directors. A collection of his plays was published in the mid-1990s (1995–8); these include *Qu'ils le disent, qu'elles le beuglent* (*Let Them [males] Say It, Let Them [females] Bellow It*) and *Qui a mangé Madame d'Avoine Bergotha?* (*Who Ate Madame d'Avoine Bergotha?*). The three main characters of the somewhat mysterious *Qu'ils le disent*, a woman, her husband and her brother, have sold their house and are on a boat. They debate whether to go home, for 'This boat drives you mad'. Seeing a smaller boat in trouble, they again debate whether to rescue its occupants, the husband wanting to stick to the 'contract', the woman responding that they'd wanted to be 'no longer the slaves of insignificant matters and petty emotions . . . we chose to live according to the laws of greatness.' 'Exactly!' replies her husband: 'we aren't responsible for their disaster . . . those you want to save chose . . . (*Renewed cries for help*) to die stupidly' (17; second ellipsis author's). Soon – it is claimed – there are three or four thousand shipwrecked people in the water, clinging to buoys. The wife and husband strip and make love; 'Dr Ghost' and the 'Ace of Clubs' tell the audience they have played a trick on them all: they have, 'centimetre by centimetre, led them to hate each other' (26–7). They wanted to take over, get rich, compete with the 'president-king of the Belgian Congo'; they see themselves as rich Europeans. But the husband discovers it's all a joke, a drama that has played itself out ('La comédie est jouée', 28). The play ends with a terrible storm that leaves bodies and flotsam everywhere; from the bottom of the ocean, the voice of 'Saint Zakaya' growls out a vision of death and chaos, concluding: 'The storm still has a few fibs to put in place' (31). This apocalyptic drama would be unrelievedly grim if not for the black humour of the main characters' vanity and their absurd discussions. Evoking Africa-specific disasters, it is also speaking to an audience reared on Symbolist and Absurdist theatre. Darkly humorous too is *Who Ate Madame d'Avoine Bergotha?*, first performed in 1989 at Limoges. This stages the fictional island dictator Walante, simultaneously cowardly and grotesque in his delusions and arbitrary despotism. Walante has banished all males from the island except himself and his nominated 'national inseminators'; he is 'His Eminence Monsieur the Supreme Inseminator'. Eventually, his commander-in-chief reports that 'the people' are discontented: 'That's ungrateful of them!' responds Walante. The two of them agree that this discontent constitutes treachery, and Walante orders the traitors to be shot dead 'without distinctions as to race or sex!' The commander tells him that the treachery emanates from his, Walante's, own nephew. 'So what?' replies Walante: 'I'm not like the Negroes [les Nègres] who function on the basis of emotion and feeling. *I* am governed by reason; shoot my nephew!' (63). Colluding English envoys appear on the scene: these ex-colonizers are as repellent as the colonies' new leaders. Finally, in a surprise ending, it turns out that Walante is already in 'Hell'. Certainly this play is targeting known African dictators, but here, unmistakably, are shades of the risible yet threatening tyrant of Stendhal's *Charterhouse of Parma*, of Ubu again – and of Gide's burlesque *Vatican Cellars* (1914), for one of Walante's misdeeds is the sequestration of the Pope (supposedly kidnapped in the Gide work also).

Part of the savage farce of the play is created by the 'de-masculinizing' of the tyrant. For he has fallen in love with a beautiful lady who is none other than a man of the island disguised as a woman to escape persecution; it is only during the wedding that Walante discovers 'Madame d'Avoine Bergotha' is male. This 'biter bit' situation (known to the audience from the beginning) opens up a number of gender-related jokes. And *Madame d'Avoine Bergotha* is not the only post-1968 francophone work to exploit this vein of humour. A doubly arresting feature of francophone literature of the last four decades has been its play with gender and the irruption on the literary scene of women writers. These developments did not spring from nowhere: we have already seen powerful matriarchs and politically aware women in the pre-1968 works of, for example, Cheikh Hamidou Kane and Sembène Ousmane. But arguably a post-colonial hope for authentic national liberation has combined with the post-1968 identity politics of metropolitan France to free the imaginations of both male and female writers and to cut through different kinds of stereotype.

Thus, of my list of sixteen writers half are women (not chosen for that reason but because of their renown): from Canada, Hébert, Lalonde, Maillet; from the Caribbean, Condé; from Vietnam, Lê; from the Maghreb, Djebar; from sub-Saharan Africa, Sow Fall and Liking. And, almost as often as heroes, these works have heroines, such as Maillet's Pélagie and Chamoiseau's Marie-Sophie; these two are not only the consciousnesses through which the narrative unfolds but are also 'founders of the nation'. The first epigraph to *Texaco* cites 'all those women condemned to perpetual childbirths', 'those women who, struggling for subsistence as equals with men, made what is called a fatherland and whom the calendars reduce to a few resounding dates, to certain boasted-about presences who have turned into street-names'. Djebar's female narrator, too, speaks for her nation. In *Les Belles-Sœurs*, Tremblay represents his working class not through men but through a group of pathetic yet sassy women; Lê's trio of heroines are Fates who (however ironically) hold human destiny in their hands. And much of this literature is 'gender-bending'. Liking invents the term 'misovire' (modelled on 'misogyne') to designate, as she somewhat defensively explains, not a disliker of men but 'a woman who cannot find an admirable man'. Sony Labou Tansi invents the corresponding 'vaginocrate'. These neologisms are straws in the wind: something profound is happening. Not

universally – Sow Fall writes less as a feminist than as a 'citizen', and Diana
Holmes points out that many immigrant and francophone women writers
in and beyond metropolitan France are less concerned with 'love' and
sexuality than with the difficulties of biculturalism and the quest to belong.
But for others, redefinitions of gender are central to the narrative. In Djebar's *L'Amour, la fantasia* the protagonist's shedding of stereotypical female
behaviour, and the French language with which her male parent endows
her, contribute – as she herself is aware – to a lessening of her 'feminine'
attributes. And the most famous novel by the Moroccan Tahar Ben Jelloun,
his 1985 *L'Enfant de sable* (*The Sand-Child*), revolves around an outrageous
gender-'swap'. The protagonist's father has had seven daughters – too
many; he would prefer them dead! He and his wife are expecting an eighth
child; whichever sex it is, he will claim it is a boy, to be called Ahmed. As
he explains to his wife, the child will then be brought up as a boy, and will
govern and protect her after his death. The eighth daughter duly arrives,
but the father announces the birth of a boy in the national paper, ending
the announcement with 'Vive Ahmed! Vive le Maroc!' ('Long live Ahmed!
Long live Morocco!') Such difficulties as circumcision are (apparently)
dealt with, and although, later, periods and developing breasts receive a
mention, the narrator airily explains that round about adolescence, the
story gets rather lost: it is an obscure time! The father meanwhile seems
genuinely to believe the child is a boy. 'He' learns to fight, and mistreats
his sisters, who in turn are afraid of him. 'Normal! He's being prepared for
the succession.' Here, the narrator comments that if Ahmed really existed,
he must by now be in a lunatic asylum; maybe this is all made up in order
to play with our time and patience (42–3). In other words: you, reader, are
free to believe it or not.

Ahmed becomes a monster. 'Efficace, moderne, cynique, il était un
excellent négociateur . . . il était craint.' ('Efficient, modern, cynical, he
was an excellent transactor of business . . . he was feared', 51–2.) We might
gloss this as: he was the opposite of 'feminine': hard-headed, caring nothing
for tradition, sentiment or pity. He wants to marry; he chooses his ill
cousin Fatima, with whom the pretence of his maleness can be maintained.
When the father dies, Ahmed calls together his sisters, telling them he is
now their guardian; they must obey and respect him. 'If,' he says, 'woman
in our society [chez nous] is inferior to man, it's not because God wished
it or the Prophet decided it, but because she accepts this destiny. So submit
and live in silence!' (65–6).

Yet Ahmed becomes increasingly uncertain; he listens to his ill wife
when she talks to him about the links society creates between 'infirmity'

and 'femaleness', and after her death he loses control of the business and shuts himself away. In his diary and correspondence he appears, wearily, to want to give up the very idea of gender: 'To be a woman is a natural disability that everyone adapts to. To be a man is an illusion, it's a state of violence that everything justifies, licenses. Simply *being* is a challenge. I'm tired' (94). Both the masculine and feminine forms of the adjective 'tired' are used here: 'Je suis las et lasse.' In the last few pages the narrator hears the story and is given the diary of 'Bey Ahmed': 'Now this story is in you . . . You can't escape it any more'. And the narrator tells his readers that if any of them want to know the sequel, they should ask the full moon (208–9). (There is indeed a sequel, published two years later: *La Nuit sacrée*, which won the Goncourt Prize.)

This bold, poignant mind-experiment would not have been possible before Beauvoir: at times it almost seems written to illustrate the dictum 'On ne naît pas femme: on le devient'. (And there are shades of both Beauvoir's and Sartre's existentialism in the weariness that overcomes Ahmed when s/he ponders the challenge of 'being'.) But it would equally have been impossible before the 1970s, the decade in which metropolitan France saw new-wave feminism, pressure for gay rights, and the beginnings of postmodernism.

Ben Jelloun has a French doctorate in psychiatric social work: his thesis was based on case histories of North African immigrant workers whom he had counselled, mostly for the sexual dysfunction they sometimes suffered once in France. This already indicates the psychological and social difficulties encountered by these immigrants. Their children and by now, in some cases, their grandchildren, immersed in the complexities of their families' marginality, have made a powerful contribution to post-1968 French culture. The 'Beur' generations, like Jews since the nineteenth century, have grown up in a society that both rejects and accepts them: they have witnessed support for the Front National and the movement against it, for in metropolitan France minorities have been championed in both film and literature since the 1970s.

The term 'Beur' gained widespread currency during the 1980s; it denotes children born to North African Arab parents who have emigrated to France. It is a modified inversion of the word 'Arabe'. Perhaps this verbal playfulness is some kind of tribute to the receiving culture, one of whose argots, 'verlan', consists of inverting the order of letters in a given word. (Verbal sophistication also went into that apparently simple anti-racist slogan chosen by the organization SOS Racisme, founded in 1984: 'Touche pas à mon *pote*', 'Hands off my mate'. Good slogans in any language tend to the alliterative, but this one is especially neat, with the two *t*s enclosing the two *p*s.)

Beur culture has been created by film directors as well as novelists or autobiographers – who are sometimes one and the same: for example, Mehdi Charef (b. 1952) published in 1983 *Le Thé au harem d'Archi Ahmed*, a fictionalized account of his adolescence in a working-class suburb, and two years later turned this into the feature film *Le Thé au harem d'Archimède* (*Tea in Archimedes' Harem*). Farida Belghoul (b. 1958), like Charef of Algerian descent, also made films and was involved in Beur politics before publishing her first novel *Georgette!* in 1986; this narrates the conflicts of a seven-year-old girl torn between her French schoolteacher and her illiterate Algerian father. Unsurprisingly, most Beur authors – men as well as the women cited by Holmes – display a preoccupation with personal and cultural identity not dissimilar to that felt by non-metropolitan francophones, but in this case arising from tensions between Arab-Islamic traditions on the one hand and secular French influences on the other. Such tensions show in their style too: they incorporate into their narratives the slang and colloquialisms both of their family communities and of young middle-class (mostly Parisian) people. This serves a political as well as a literary purpose, emphasizing their rootedness in metropolitan French society. Similarly – and like their overseas contemporaries – they acknowledge canonical writers and draw on their literary techniques; through this too Beurs affirm that they are not 'alien' – that they are indeed part of elite as well as mainstream culture. The works of Beur authors are remarkably good-tempered in the light of the provocations, threats and actual violence inflicted on their communities by the French right wing; they often treat deprivations and prejudice with mockery rather than anger.

One notable integration has been that of the popular African-American musical forms hip-hop and rap. In France, rap has acquired literary and intellectual characteristics that would be improbable in the anglophone world. As Chapter 8 suggested, French popular song has throughout its history had specially close links with the political and literary; in no period has this been more striking than our own, when French song is competing globally with anglophone and should on the face of it be abandoning its most 'difficult' characteristics. But, as we saw, the Carignon Law guarantees the proportion of French songs that must be played on the radio, and this cultural protectionism has allowed rappers like MC Solaar to flourish. Claude M'Barali (his real name) rose to prominence in the 1990s. Of Chadian origin, he was born in Dakar, Senegal, and raised in the Paris suburb of Villeneuve-Saint-Georges. *Le Monde* described his lyrics as a 'new urban poetry'; he was, as Peter Hawkins puts it, 'welcomed by the French establishment as the acceptable face of suburban alienation, to such an extent as to embarrass the rapper himself, who comments ironically on it in several of his texts: "Tournicoti tournicota / Claude MC prend le mic et l'élite au bic aime ça [Tournicoti tournicota / Claude MC takes the mike and the pen-pushing elite like it]"' (Hawkins, *Chanson: The French Singer-Songwriter from Aristide Bruant to the Present Day*, 2000, 204). MC Solaar alludes to a wide range of literary and philosophical writers, from Rimbaud, Perec and Umberto Eco to Plato, Descartes and Rousseau. In Baudelairean manner, the rapper casts himself as a street performer (acrobat and tight-rope walker), a wanderer, a *flâneur*; like many in the French comic literary tradition, he parodies himself. His alliteration and assonance are ostentatious, his wordplay sometimes dizzying: 'Dieu sait qu'elle sait quelles séquelles' ('God knows, she knows what the consequences are'). And he even describes himself as a structuralist linguistician!: 'I pose, compose, recompose, decompose new prose like a structural linguist'.

The role that will be played by francophone authors in the future 'cultural history' of French literature looks set to be a major one. Their energy, so far, has had a double source: it has come from painful political situations and also from their creative engagement with a metropolitan literature that has not been solely self-serving. It is because it has so often reached outwards that overseas writers have been able to find inspiration in it. Montaigne and the *philosophes* opened the way to the work that is part 'literature', part argument, setting important precedents for much francophone writing. George Sand would have recognized francophone authors' use of local superstition and their promotion of regional landscapes, as in Hébert's *Kamouraska* and Ben Jelloun's *L'Enfant de sable*; and these same authors create self-conscious allegories with their landscapes that would not be out of place in Beckett and Robbe-Grillet, as the Canadian snow and the Moroccan sand become blank shifting surfaces on which any story and any identity can be temporarily written. Finally, not only Hugo and Zola but also Villon, Stendhal, Flaubert and Rimbaud are still presences in francophone writers' promotion of the 'humble', from low-caste labour to the living conditions of the oppressed. The language and literature of both metropolitan France and its former colonies are invigorated by adaptation and mutual acknowledgement as well as by collision.

Conclusion

In the course of this book I have singled out features of French literature of special importance for cultural studies. First is the generally exalted position of literature in France, arising from the strong investment of a would-be centralizing state in its language and in its elite culture. Arguably the two richest European literatures are Britain's and France's. But there are differences between them, and here is where one of the differences lies. France is prouder of its literature, and it is at least plausible to propose that over the centuries the valuing of excellent writing by French courts, then by the French state, has contributed to the obvious self-awareness and confident sophistication of French writing. The assurance has played a part in the willingness of French writers to experiment; the sophistication has often led to delight in quasi-mathematical patterns; and the state's efforts at centralization have been in the long term responsible for the unusual visibility of the capital as a cultural model in literature, as in other arts.

Second is the mixing in French literature of appeals to an intellectual and artistic elite with 'popular' material and down-to-earth approaches. This blend has been worked out in varying proportions according to the period; definitions of 'elite' have changed; but, with the exception of seventeenth-century classical literature, the intermingling has been a constant. The elegant and the bawdy, the 'highbrow' and 'lowbrow' co-exist; an exquisite conformity to the rules still lets dissent through in sometimes startling ways.

Third is the respected role of the thinker, from medieval academics and Montaigne to the *philosophes* and Sartre, which has allowed French intellectuals, and many imaginative writers, to marry philosophy to public instruction, philosophy to fiction, philosophy to metaphor, with relative ease. It is remarkable that French thinkers' ideas, which ought to seem culture-specific and to some extent are (having been shaped by unique national events such as the Wars of Religion and the French Revolution), have affected the entire Western world.

Leading on from this, the fourth feature that students and scholars might focus on more than hitherto is the very fact of the international influence wielded by French culture. Most recently, for example, the New Novelists' sleights-of-hand are still visible in the work of the Spanish film-maker Pedro Almodóvar and the English novelists A. S. Byatt and Ian McEwan. Public denigrations of the French by British tabloids and American Republicans have been in vain, at least as far as the liberal classes are concerned. A snapshot of *Guardian* articles in June 2008 reveals the following: a cover story about Faïsa Guène, a Beur writer billed as 'the Bridget Jones of the Paris banlieues'; an article on holiday reading in France that starts 'The problem is that there is no such thing as France. There are infinite Frances – because there are infinite places, and infinite times. So the happy summer reader needs to choose both a place and a time'; and a piece by the former editor Peter Preston about Truffaut's film *Jules et Jim*, headlined 'Jules and Jim – and me', in which Preston says that 'the world had taken its great, exhilarating spin a decade earlier [than 1968] when Truffaut made Les Quatre Cents Coups. Nothing would ever seem quite the same again' (*Guardian*, respectively 5, 14, 2 June 2008). The love-affair of anglophone liberals with France is not going to end soon.

Yet the study of French literature itself is endangered. In the UK, Modern Languages is no longer a compulsory school subject; the number of final-year pupils taking French is dropping year by year, as are applications for university degrees in French. Along the West Coast of the United States, the Chinese Government is pouring tens of millions of dollars into subsidizing the teaching of Mandarin; to make room for these new courses, school principals are eliminating French, German and Latin, and redefining themselves in commercial rather than cultural terms as belonging to 'Pacific Rim States'. The US College Board Exam in Advanced Placement French Literature will be cancelled nationwide in 2010. Even in France, public universities are being forced to subordinate their French Studies syllabuses to a choice of three approved vocational tracks with demonstrable employment opportunities. In Lille III, for example, one of the three new courses permitted is 'The Tourism of Northern Europe'.

But French literature is important to Western civilization. Cultural studies can perhaps restate this. A cultural history of French literature is not the death-knell of the 'great author' but a way of looking outside the literary monuments, then to come back to them. A balancing-act is needed: we should revise the canon and look at its history in new ways, but retain a sense of which cultural manifestations are complex and challenging. French literature is one of the most stellar the world has produced: intensely pleasurable, diverse, self-affirming; ironic, inquisitive, humane; endlessly alive to the different forms that can be taken by aesthetic beauty.

Bibliography

Place of publication is Paris unless otherwise stated

PRIMARY TEXTS QUOTED

Apollinaire, Guillaume, *Alcools* (Gallimard, 1944)
—— *Calligrammes* (Gallimard, 1966)
Aucassin et Nicolette (Flammarion, 1984)
Balzac, Honoré de, *La Cousine Bette* (Librairie Générale Française, 1963)
—— *Grandeur et décadence de César Birotteau* (Librairie Générale Française, 1972)
—— *Illusions perdues* (Gallimard, 1972)
Baudelaire, Charles, *Les Fleurs du Mal* (Gallimard/Librairie Générale Française, 1965); trans. Shapiro, Norman, *Selected Poems from 'Les Fleurs du mal'* (Chicago/London: University of Chicago Press, 1998)
—— *Le Spleen de Paris* (Garnier, 1962)
Beauvoir, Simone de, *Le Deuxième Sexe* (Gallimard, 1976), 2 vols.
Ben Jelloun, Tahar, *L'Enfant de sable* (Seuil, 1985)
Camus, Albert, *La Peste* (Gallimard, 1947)
Césaire, Aimé, *Cahier d'un retour au pays natal*, in *The Collected Poetry*, with translations by Eshleman, Clayton, and Smith, Annette (Berkeley/Los Angeles: University of California Press, 1983)
—— *Moi, laminaire . . .: Poèmes* (Seuil, 1982)
Chamoiseau, Patrick, *Texaco* (Gallimard, 1992)
La Chanson de Roland (Librairie Générale Française, 1990)
Chateaubriand, François-René de, *René*, in *Atala, René, Le Dernier Abencérage* (Garnier, 1962)
Chraïbi, Driss, *Le Passé simple* (Gallimard, 1993)
Condé, Maryse, *La Civilisation du bossale: Réflexions sur la littérature orale de la Guadeloupe et de la Martinique* (L'Harmattan, 1978)
Constant, Benjamin, *Adolphe* (Garnier, 1968)
Corneille, Pierre, *Œuvres complètes* (Seuil, 1963)
Diderot, Denis, *Jacques le fataliste* (Librairie Générale Française, 1972)
Diop, Boubacar Boris, *Le Temps de Tamango, suivi de Thiaroye terre rouge* (L'Harmattan, 1981)

Diop, Cheikh Anta, *Antériorité des civilisations nègres: mythe ou vérité historique?* (Présence Africaine, 1993)

Djebar, Assia, *L'Amour, la fantasia* (Albin Michel, 1995)

Dumas, Alexandre, *Les Trois Mousquetaires* (Garnier, 1959); trans. Pevear, Richard, *The Three Musketeers* (London: Penguin, 2007)

La Farce de Maître Pierre Pathelin (Flammarion, 1986)

Flaubert, Gustave, *Correspondance* (Conard, 1926–33), 9 vols.

—— *Madame Bovary* (Bordas / Garnier, 1990)

Gaulle, Charles de, *Mémoires* (Gallimard, 2000)

Gautier, Théophile de, *Mademoiselle de Maupin* (Garnier-Flammarion, 1966)

Giraudoux, Jean, *Amphitryon 38* (Grasset, 1929)

—— *Pleins pouvoirs* (Gallimard, 1939)

Glissant, Edouard, *Le Discours antillais* (Seuil, 1981)

—— *Pays rêvé, pays réel: poème* (Seuil, 1985)

Hébert, Anne, *Kamouraska* (Seuil, 1970)

Hugo, Victor, *Les Contemplations* (Gallimard, 1973)

—— *Notre-Dame de Paris – 1482* (Garnier, 1959)

—— *Théâtre complet* (Gallimard, 1963, 1964), 2 vols.

Huysmans, Joris-Karl, *A rebours* (Fasquelle, 1968)

Ionesco, Eugène, *La Cantatrice chauve*, in *Three Plays* (London: Heinemann, 1965)

Jarry, Alfred, *Ubu Roi*, in *Tout Ubu* (Librairie Générale Française, 1962)

Kane, Cheikh Hamidou, *L'Aventure ambiguë* (Julliard, 2003); trans. Woods, Katherine, *Ambiguous Adventure* (Oxford: Heinemann, 1963)

Kourouma, Ahmadou, *Les Soleils des indépendances* (Seuil, 1976); trans. Adams, Adrian, *The Suns of Independence* (London: Heinemann, 1981)

La Bruyère, Jean de, *Les Caractères ou les mœurs de ce siècle* (Garnier, 1962)

Laclos, Choderlos de, *Les Liaisons dangereuses* (Flammarion, 1964)

La Fontaine, Jean de, *Fables* (Garnier, 1962)

Lalonde, Michèle, *Défense et illustration de la langue québécoise, suivi de Prose et poèmes* (Seghers / Laffont, 1979)

La Rochefoucauld, François de, *Maximes* (Garnier, 1967)

Lê, Linda, *Les Trois Parques* (n.p.: Christian Bourgeois, 1997)

Lévi-Strauss, Claude, *Tristes Tropiques* (Plon, 1955)

Liking, Werewere, *Elle sera de jaspe et de corail: Journal d'une misovire* (L'Harmattan, 1983); trans. Jager, Marjolijn de, *It Shall be of Jasper and Coral* and *Love-Across-a-Hundred-Lives* (Charlottesville / London: University Press of Virginia, 2000)

Maillet, Antonine, *Pélagie-la-Charrette* (Grasset / Fasquelle, 1979)

Mallarmé, Stéphane, *Œuvres complètes* (Gallimard, 1998, 2003), 2 vols.; poetry trans. Bosley, Keith, *The Poems* (Harmondsworth: Penguin, 1977)

Maupassant, Guy de, *Boule de suif et autres contes de la guerre* (Walton-on-Thames: Nelson, 1984)

MC Solaar: see discography in Hawkins, Peter, *Chanson: The French Singer-Songwriter from Aristide Bruant to the Present Day* (Aldershot: Ashgate, 2000)

Meun, Jean de (et Lorris, Guillaume de), *Le Roman de la rose* (Champion, 1965–70), 3 vols.; trans. Horgan, Frances, *The Romance of the Rose* (Oxford: Oxford University Press, 1994)

Molière, *Œuvres complètes* (Gallimard, 1971), 2 vols.

Montaigne, Michel de, *Œuvres complètes* (Gallimard, 1962); trans. Screech, M. A., *Michel de Montaigne: The Complete Essays* (London: Penguin, 1991)

Nerval, Gérard de, *Les Chimères* (Geneva/Paris: Droz/Minard, 1966)

—— *Sylvie*, in *Les Filles du feu*, suivi de *Aurélia* (Gallimard, 1961)

Pascal, Blaise, *Pensées* (Seuil, 1962)

Présence Africaine, 1947–

Proust, Marcel, *A la recherche du temps perdu* (Gallimard, 1987–89), 4 vols.

Rabelais, François, *Gargantua* (Seuil, 1986)

—— *Pantagruel* (Gallimard, 1964)

Racine, Jean, *Œuvres complètes*, vol. I: *Théâtre; Poésies* (Gallimard, 1950)

Rimbaud, Arthur, *Œuvres* (Garnier, 1960)

Sand, George, *Correspondance*, ed. Lubin, Georges (Garnier, 1964–91), 25 vols.

Sarraute, Nathalie, *Les Fruits d'or* (Gallimard, 1963)

—— *Le Planétarium* (Gallimard, 1959)

Sartre, Jean-Paul, *Huis clos* (Gallimard, 1947)

—— 'Orphée noir': see under Senghor

Sembène, Ousmane, *Les Bouts de bois de Dieu: Banty Mam Yall* (n.p.: Le Livre Contemporain, 1960)

Senghor, Léopold Sédar, *Anthologie de la nouvelle poésie nègre et malgache de langue française*, précédée de 'Orphée noir' par Sartre, Jean-Paul (Presses Universitaires de France, 1969)

—— *Poèmes* (Seuil, 1984)

Sony Labou Tansi, *Théâtre I* (Carnières-Morlanwelz: Lansman, 1995)

Sow Fall, Aminata, *La Grève des bàttu ou Les Déchets humains* (Monaco: Le Serpent à plumes, 2004)

Stendhal, *Racine et Shakespeare: Etudes sur le romantisme* (Garnier-Flammarion, 1970)

—— *Romans et nouvelles* (Gallimard, 1952), 2 vols.

Tremblay, Michel, *Théâtre I* (Quetigny-Dijon: Leméac, 1991)

Trenet, Charles, 'Le cor', in *Mon cœur s'envole*, CD (Rozon, Warner Music, 1992)

Tournier, Michel, *Le Vent paraclet* (Gallimard, 1977)

Valéry, Paul, *Œuvres* (Gallimard, 1957, 1960), 2 vols.

Verlaine, Paul, *Jadis et naguère* (L. Vanier, 1891)

Vigny, Alfred de, *Chatterton* (Edinburgh: Constable, 1967)

—— *Poésies complètes* (Calmann Lévy, 1882)

Villon, François, *Poésies* (Flammarion, 1992)

Voltaire, *Candide*, in *Romans et contes* (Garnier, 1960)

Zola, Emile, *Le Roman expérimental* (Garnier-Flammarion, 1971)

OTHER WORKS QUOTED OR DRAWN ON (SELECT LIST)

Adams, Henry, *Mont-Saint-Michel and Chartres* (n.p.: Massachusetts Historical Society, 1919)

Alter, Robert, *Partial Magic: The Novel as a Self-Conscious Genre* (Berkeley: University of California Press, 1975)

Atack, Margaret, *May 68 in French Fiction and Film* (Oxford: Oxford University Press, 1999)

Auerbach, Erich, trans. Trask, Willard, *Mimesis* (Princeton: Princeton University Press, 1971)

Ayres-Bennett, Wendy, *A History of the French Language through Texts* (London/ New York: Routledge, 1996)

Baldwin, Elaine, et al. (eds), *Introducing Cultural Studies* (Hemel Hempstead: Prentice Hall Europe, 1999)

Bann, Stephen, *Parallel Lines: Printmakers, Painters and Photographers in Nineteenth-Century France* (New Haven/London: Yale University Press, 2001)

Barthes, Roland, *Critique et vérité* (Seuil, 1966)

—— *Le Degré zéro de l'écriture* (Seuil, 1972)

—— *Essais critiques* (Seuil, 1964)

—— *Mythologies* (Seuil, 1957)

—— *Le Plaisir du texte* (Seuil, 1973)

—— *Roland Barthes par Roland Barthes* (Seuil, 1975)

—— *S/Z* (Seuil, 1970)

Becker, Carl L., *The Heavenly City of the Eighteenth-Century Philosophers* (New Haven: Yale University Storrs Lectures, 1931)

Benhaïm, André, 'Proust's Singhalese song (a strange little story)', in Benhaïm, André (ed.), *The Strange M. Proust* (London: Legenda/MHRA, 2009), 57–70

—— *Panim: Visages de Proust* (Villeneuve d'Ascq: Presses Universitaires du Septentrion, 2006)

Bénichou, Paul, *Les Mages romantiques* (Gallimard, 1988)

—— *Morales du Grand Siècle* (Gallimard, 1948)

Benjamin, Walter, trans. Eiland, Howard and McLaughlin, Kevin, *The Arcades Project* (Boston: Harvard University Press, 1999)

—— trans. Underwood, J., *The Work of Art in the Age of Mechanical Reproduction* (London: Penguin, 2008)

Bersani, Leo, *Balzac to Beckett: Center and Circumference in French Fiction* (New York: Oxford University Press, 1970)

Bishop, Michael, *Contemporary French Women Poets* (Amsterdam: Rodopi, 1995)

Booth, Wayne C., *The Rhetoric of Fiction* (Chicago: University of Chicago Press, 1961)

Bourdieu, Pierre, [various essays] ed. Johnson, Randal, *The Field of Cultural Production* (Cambridge: Polity, 1993)

—— *La Distinction: critique social du jugement* (Minuit, 1979)

—— *Homo Academicus* (Minuit, 1984); trans. Collier, Peter (Cambridge: Polity, 1996)

—— *Règles de l'art: genèse et structure du champ littéraire* (Seuil, 1992)

Bouwer, Karen, 'Lyric and gender', unpublished PhD dissertation, Michigan State University

Bowie, Malcolm, *Lacan* (London: HarperCollins,1991)

—— *Mallarmé and the Art of Being Difficult* (Cambridge: Cambridge University Press, 1978)

—— *Proust Among the Stars* (London: HarperCollins, 1998). See also under Kay

Bowman, Frank P., *Le Christ romantique. 1789: Le sans-culotte de Nazareth* (Geneva: Droz, 1973)

Braudel, Fernand, trans. Reynolds, Siân, *The Identity of France* (London: Collins, 1988, 1990), 2 vols.

Britton, Celia, *Race and the Unconscious: Freudianism in French Caribbean Thought* (Oxford: Legenda, 2002)

Brooks, Peter, *The Melodramatic Imagination: Balzac, Henry James, Melodrama, and the Mode of Excess* (New Haven/London: Yale University Press, 1995)

—— *Reading for the Plot: Design and Intention in Narrative* (Oxford: Clarendon, 1984)

Burke, Peter, *History and Social Theory* (Cambridge: Polity, 2000)

—— *A Social History of Knowledge: From Gutenberg to Diderot* (Cambridge: Polity, 2000)

—— *Varieties of Cultural History* (Cambridge: Polity, 1997)

Caillois, Roger, *Au cœur du fantastique* (Gallimard, 1965)

—— *L'Homme et le sacré* (Gallimard, 1961)

—— *Le Mythe et l'homme* (Gallimard, 1972)

Carroll, Raymonde, *Cultural Misunderstandings: The French–American Experience* (Chicago/London: University of Chicago Press, 1988)

Cassirer, Ernst, trans. Koelln, Fritz C. A., and Pettegrove, James P., *The Philosophy of the Enlightenment* (Princeton: Princeton University Press, 2009)

Catani, Damian, *The Poet in Society: Art, Consumerism, and Politics in Mallarmé* (New York: Peter Lang, 2003)

Cave, Terence, *The Cornucopian Text: Problems of Writing in the French Renaissance* (Oxford: Clarendon, 1979). See also under Kay

Certeau, Michel de, *La Culture au pluriel* (Seuil, 1974)

—— *L'Invention du quotidien: I, Arts de faire* (Gallimard, 1990); *II, Habiter, cuisiner* (with Giard, Luce, and Mayol, Pierre) (Gallimard, 1990)

Chambers, Ross, *Room for Maneuver: Reading (the) Oppositional (in) Narrative* (Chicago: University of Chicago Press, 1991)

Charlton, Donald, *Secular Religions in France, 1815–1870* (London/New York: Oxford University Press, 1963)

Chartier, Roger, trans. Cochrane, Lydia, *Cultural History: Between Practices and Representations* (Cambridge: Polity, 1993)

Clark, Timothy, *The Painting of Modern Life: Paris in the Art of Manet and his Followers* (London: Thames and Hudson, 1985)

Coward, David, *A History of French Literature: From 'Chanson de geste' to Cinema* (Oxford: Blackwell, 2004)

Curtius, Ernst Robert, trans. Trask, Willard, *European Literature and the Latin Middle Ages* (New York: Harper and Row, 1963)

Dällenbach, Lucien, *Le Récit spéculaire: essai sur la mise en abyme* (Seuil, 1977)

Darnton, Robert, *The Forbidden Best-Sellers of Pre-Revolutionary France* (London: HarperCollins,1996)

—— *The Great Cat Massacre and Other Episodes in French Cultural History* (New York: Vintage Books, 1985)

Datta, Venita, *Birth of a National Icon: The Literary Avant-Garde and the Origins of the Intellectual in France* (Albany: State University of New York Press, 1999)

Davis, Colin, *Ethical Issues in Twentieth-Century French Fiction: Killing the Other* (Basingstoke: Macmillan, 2000)

—— *Michel Tournier: Philosophy and Fiction* (Oxford: Clarendon, 1988)

—— and Fallaize, Elizabeth, *French Fiction in the Mitterrand Years: Memory, Narrative, Desire* (Oxford: Oxford University Press, 2000)

Davis, Natalie Zemon, *Society and Culture in Early Modern France* (Cambridge: Polity, 1998)

Deleuze, Gilles, *Logique du sens* (Minuit, 1969)

—— *Proust et les signes* (Presses Universitaires de France, 1976)

—— and Guattari, Félix, *L'Anti-Œdipe: capitalisme et schizophrénie* (Minuit, 1999)

De Man, Paul, *Allegories of Reading: Figural Language in Rousseau, Nietzsche, Rilke and Proust* (New Haven/London: Yale University Press, 1979)

—— *Wartime Journalism, 1939–1943* (Lincoln, Nebraska: University of Nebraska Press, 1988)

Derrida, Jacques, *De la grammatologie* (Minuit, 1967)

—— *La Dissémination* (Seuil, 1993)

Diamond, Jared, *Guns, Germs, and Steel: The Fates of Human Societies* (London: Jonathan Cape, 1997)

Fallaize, Elizabeth, *French Women's Writing: Recent Fiction* (Basingstoke: Macmillan, 1993)

—— *The Novels of Simone de Beauvoir* (London: Routledge, 1990). See also under Davis, Colin

Fawtier, Robert, trans. Butler, Lionel, and Adam, R. J., *The Capetian Kings of France* (London: Macmillan, 1960)

Feuillerat, Albert, *Comment Marcel Proust a composé son roman* (New Haven: Yale University Press, 1934)

Finch, Alison, *Proust's Additions: The Making of 'A la recherche du temps perdu'* (Cambridge: Cambridge University Press, 1977), 2 vols. [under name Winton]

—— *Women's Writing in Nineteenth-Century France* (Cambridge: Cambridge University Press, 2000)

Forbes, Jill, and Kelly, Michael (eds), *French Cultural Studies: An Introduction* (Oxford: Oxford University Press, 1995)

Forsdick, Charles, and Murphy, David (eds), *Francophone Colonial Studies: A Critical Introduction* (London: Arnold, 2003)

Foucault, Michel, *Folie et déraison: histoire de la folie à l'âge classique* (Plon, 1961)

—— *Les Mots et les choses: une archéologie des sciences humaines* (Gallimard, 1993)

—— *Surveiller et punir: naissance de la prison* (Gallimard, 1975)

France, Peter (ed.), *The New Oxford Companion to Literature in French* (Oxford: Clarendon, 1995)

Frank, Grace, *The Medieval French Drama* (Oxford: Clarendon, 1954)

Gaunt, Simon, *Retelling the Tale: An Introduction to Medieval French Literature* (London: Duckworth, 2001)

George, Albert J., *The Development of French Romanticism: The Impact of the Industrial Revolution on Literature* (Syracuse: Syracuse University Press, 1955)

Gibson, Ralph, *A Social History of French Catholicism 1789–1914* (London: Routledge, 1989)

Giddens, Anthony, et al. (eds), *The Polity Reader in Cultural Theory* (Cambridge: Polity, 1994)

Gildea, Robert, *Marianne in Chains: In Search of the German Occupation of France 1940–45* (London: Pan/Macmillan, 2003)

—— *The Past in French History* (New Haven/London: Yale University Press, 1994)

Girard, René, *Mensonge romantique et vérité romanesque* (Grasset, 1961)

—— *La Violence et le sacré* (Grasset, 1972)

Girardet, Raoul, *L'Idée coloniale en France de 1871 à 1962* (Table Ronde, 1972)

Godin, Henri, *La France, pays de mission?* (Union Générale d'Editions, 1962)

Goldmann, Lucien, *Le Dieu caché: Etude sur la vision tragique dans les 'Pensées' de Pascal et dans le théâtre de Racine* (Gallimard, 1959)

Gordon, Rae Beth, *Ornament, Fantasy, and Desire in Nineteenth-Century French Literature* (Princeton: Princeton University Press, 1992)

—— *Why the French Love Jerry Lewis: From Cabaret to Early Cinema* (Stanford: Stanford University Press, 2001)

Gossman, Lionel, *Between History and Literature* (Cambridge, MA/London: Harvard University Press, 1990)

Gunn, Alan M. F., *The Mirror of Love: A Reinterpretation of 'The Romance of the Rose'* (Lubbock: Texas Tech Press, 1952)

Hall, Stuart, 'The question of cultural identity', in Giddens, Anthony, et al. (eds), *The Polity Reader in Cultural Theory* (Cambridge: Polity, 1994), 119–25

Harrow, Susan, *The Material, the Real, and the Fractured Self: Subjectivity and Representation from Rimbaud to Réda* (Toronto: University of Toronto Press, 2004)

Haskins, Charles Homer, *The Renaissance of the Twelfth Century* (Cambridge MA: Harvard University Press, 1971)

Hawkins, Peter, *Chanson: The French Singer-Songwriter from Aristide Bruant to the Present Day* (Aldershot: Ashgate, 2000)

Hazard, Paul, *La Crise de la conscience européenne (1680–1715)* (Boivin, 1935)

Hemmings, F. W. J., *The Theatre Industry in Nineteenth-Century France* (Cambridge: Cambridge University Press, 1993)

—— *Theatre and State in France, 1760–1905* (Cambridge: Cambridge University Press, 1994)

Henley, Jon, 'France plans to pay cash for more babies', *Guardian*, 22 September 2005

Herzfeld, Michael, *The Poetics of Manhood: Contest and Identity in a Cretan Mountain Village* (Princeton: Princeton University Press, 1985)

Hoggart, Richard, *The Uses of Literacy* (London: Penguin, 1984)

Hollier, Denis (ed.), *A New History of French Literature* (Cambridge, MA / London: Harvard University Press, 1994)

Holmes, Diana, *Romance and Readership in Twentieth-Century France: Love Stories* (Oxford: Oxford University Press, 2006)

Hughes, Edward J., *Marcel Proust: A Study in the Quality of Awareness* (Cambridge: Cambridge University Press, 1983)

—— *Writing Marginality in Modern French Literature: From Loti to Genet* (Cambridge: Cambridge University Press, 2001)

Huntington, Samuel, *The Clash of Civilizations and the Remaking of World Order* (London / Sydney: Simon and Schuster, 1997)

Huppert, George, *Les Bourgeois Gentilshommes: An Essay on the Definition of Elites in Renaissance France* (Chicago: University of Chicago Press, 1977)

Inglis, Fred, *Cultural Studies* (Oxford: Blackwell, 1993)

James, Henry, 'Emile Zola', in *Literary Criticism*, vol. 2 (New York: Library of America, 1984), 871–99

Jameson, Fredric, *The Cultural Turn: Selected Writings on the Postmodern 1983–1998* (London: Verso, 1998)

—— *The Political Unconscious: Narrative as a Socially Symbolic Act* (London: Routledge, 2002)

Johnson, Barbara, *Défigurations du langage poétique: la seconde révolution baudelairienne* (Flammarion, 1979)

Kay, Sarah, Cave, Terence, and Bowie, Malcolm, *A Short History of French Literature* (Oxford: Oxford University Press, 2003)

Kertzer, David I., and Barbagli, Marzio (eds), *The History of the European Family* (New Haven / London: Yale University Press, 2001–3), 3 vols.

Kidd, William, and Reynolds, Siân (eds), *Contemporary French Cultural Studies* (London: Arnold, 2000)

Knight, Diana, *Balzac and the Model of Painting: Artist Stories in 'La Comédie humaine'* (London: Legenda, 2007)

—— *Flaubert's Characters: The Language of Illusion* (Cambridge: Cambridge University Press, 1985)

Lacan, Jacques, *Ecrits* (Seuil, 1966)

Lapp, John C., *Aspects of Racinian Tragedy* (Toronto: University of Toronto Press, 1964)

Lough, John, *Writer and Public in France: From the Middle Ages to the Present Day* (Oxford: Clarendon, 1978)

Lovejoy, Arthur O., *The Great Chain of Being: A Study of the History of an Idea* (Cambridge MA: Harvard University Press, 1970)

Lucey, Michael, *Never Say I: Sexuality and the First Person in Colette, Gide, and Proust* (Durham NC/London: Duke University Press, 2006)

Lukács, Georg, 'Narrate or describe?', in *Writer and Critic and Other Essays* (London: Merlin, 1970), 110–48

Maclean, Marie, *The Name of the Mother: Writing Illegitimacy* (London: Routledge, 1994)

Martin, Richard P., *The Language of Heroes: Speech and Performance in the 'Iliad'* (Ithaca and London: Cornell University Press, 1989)

Mitscherlich, Alexander, *Society without the Father: A Contribution to Social Psychology* (London: Tavistock Publications, 1969)

Moore, Will G., *Molière: A New Criticism* (Oxford: Clarendon, 1949)

Moriarty, Michael, *Taste and Ideology in Seventeenth-Century France* (Cambridge: Cambridge University Press, 1988)

Moses, Claire Goldberg, *French Feminism in the Nineteenth Century* (Albany: State University of New York Press, 1984)

The New Oxford Companion to Literature in French: see under France, Peter

Nicholson, Marjorie Hope, *Mountain Gloom and Mountain Glory: The Development of the Aesthetics of the Infinite* (Ithaca: Cornell University Press, 1959)

Nora, Pierre (ed.), *Les Lieux de mémoire: La République, La Nation, Les France* (Gallimard, 1997), 3 vols.

O'Brien, Conor Cruise, *Camus* (London: Fontana/Collins, 1970)

Ory, Pascal, *L'Histoire culturelle* (Presses Universitaires de France, 2007)

Pernoud, Laurence, *J'attends un enfant* (Horay, 2009)

Picard, Jeanine, *Pierre-Jakez Hélias, Le Cheval d'orgueil: mémoires d'un Breton du pays bigoudien* (Glasgow: University of Glasgow French and German Publications, 1999)

Porter, Laurence M., *The Crisis of French Symbolism* (Ithaca/London: Cornell University Press, 1990)

Prendergast, Christopher, *For the People by the People? Eugène Sue's 'Les Mystères de Paris': A Hypothesis in the Sociology of Literature* (Oxford: Legenda, 2003)

—— *The Order of Mimesis: Balzac, Stendhal, Nerval, Flaubert* (Cambridge: Cambridge University Press, 1986)

—— *Paris and the Nineteenth Century* (Oxford: Blackwell, 1992)

Prost, Antoine, trans. Winter, Jay, and McPhail, Helen, *Republican Identities in War and Peace: Representations of France in the Nineteenth and Twentieth Centuries* (Oxford: Berg, 2002)

Rojek, Christopher, *Cultural Studies* (Cambridge: Polity, 2007)

Rousset, Jean, *La Littérature de l'âge baroque en France: Circé et le paon* (Corti, 1968)

Ruthven, K.K., *Faking Literature* (Cambridge: Cambridge University Press, 2001)

Saka, Pierre, and Saka, Jean-Pierre (eds), *L'Histoire de France en chansons* (Larousse, 2002)

Schama, Simon, *Citizens: A Chronicle of the French Revolution* (London: Penguin, 1996)

Sheringham, Michael, *Everyday Life: Theories and Practices from Surrealism to the Present* (Oxford: Oxford University Press, 2006)

—— *French Autobiography: Devices and Desires: Rousseau to Perec* (Oxford: Clarendon, 1993)

Steiner, George, *The Death of Tragedy* (London: Faber, 1995)

Taylor, Charles, *Modern Social Imaginaries* (Durham, NC/London: Duke University Press, 2004)

Tompkins, Jane, 'Sentimental power: *Uncle Tom's Cabin* and the politics of literary history', in *Sensational Designs: The Cultural Work of American Fiction, 1790–1860* (New York: Oxford University Press, 1985), 122–46

Unwin, Timothy, *Flaubert et Baudelaire: affinités spirituelles et esthétiques* (Nizet, 1982)

—— *Textes réfléchissants: réalisme et réflexivité au dix-neuvième siècle* (Oxford: Peter Lang, 2000)

Waller, Margaret, *The Male Malady: Fictions of Impotence in the French Romantic Novel* (New Brunswick: Rutgers University Press, 1993)

Warner, Marina, *Alone of All Her Sex: The Myth and Cult of the Virgin Mary* (London: Vintage, 2000)

Webber, Andrew, and Wilson, Emma, *Cities in Transition: The Moving Image and the Modern Metropolis* (London: Wallflower, 2007)

Weber, Eugen, *Peasants into Frenchmen: the Modernization of Rural France, 1870–1914* (London: Chatto and Windus, 1979)

White, Hayden, *The Content of the Form: Narrative Discourse and Historical Representation* (Baltimore/London: Johns Hopkins University Press, 1992)

—— *Metahistory: The Historical Imagination in Nineteenth-Century Europe* (Baltimore/London: Johns Hopkins University Press, 1993)

Williams, Raymond, *Culture and Society, 1780–1950* (New York: Columbia University Press, 1958)

—— *The Long Revolution* (London: Chatto and Windus, 1961)

—— *Marxism and Literature* (Oxford: Oxford University Press, 1995)

—— *Modern Tragedy* (London: Chatto and Windus, 1966)

Wilson, Emma, *Sexuality and the Reading Encounter: Identity and Desire in Proust, Duras, Tournier, and Cixous* (Oxford: Clarendon, 1996). See also under Webber

Winspur, Stephen, *La Poésie du lieu: Segalen, Thoreau, Guillevic, Ponge* (Amsterdam: Rodopi, 2006)

Wright, Gordon, *France in Modern Times: From the Enlightenment to the Present* (New York/London: Norton, 1995)

Wylie, Laurence W., *Village in the Vaucluse* (Cambridge MA: Harvard University Press, 1974)

Zeldin, Theodore, *A History of French Passions 1848–1945* (Oxford: Clarendon, 1993, 2000), 2 vols.

Index

Abélard, Pierre 7
Absurd, Theatre of the: see Theatre of the Absurd
Académie Française 29, 39, 58, 157, 172, 187, 199, 202
Action Française 104, 120, 126
Adamov, Arthur 202
Adams, Adrian 208
advertisements 76, 89, 116, 145
Aesop 12
Afghanistan 199
Africa, languages 187, 194
Africa, North 12, 139, 141, 143, 168–9, 181, 182, 196–7, 200, 202, 207, 215, 217–18; see also under individual authors and countries
Africa, sub-Saharan 181, 182, 185, 187, 188, 189, 190, 193–5, 196–7, 200, 201, 202, 204, 208–9, 212–13, 214, 215; see also under individual authors and countries
AIDS 166–8
Alembert, Jean d' 43
Algeria 139, 141, 144, 161, 182, 183, 185, 195–6, 200, 202, 207, 218
Almodóvar, Pedro 221
Alsace and Lorraine: see Versailles, Treaty of
Alter, Robert 148
America: Constitution 45; Declaration of Independence 1; Revolution 1; see also Americas; United States
Americas 181, 182; see also under individual countries; United States

Ancien Régime 26–52, 55, 57, 66, 181, 209
Anglo-Norman culture 12, 177
anglophone countries 84, 145, 155–6, 157, 162–3, 166, 170, 190, 201, 218; see also Britain; United States
anti-Semitism: see Judaism and Jews in France
Apollinaire, Guillaume (pseud. of Wilhelm de Kostrowitsky) 80, 101, 120, 128–9, 148, 152
Apostrophes 174
Arabic culture and language 2, 12; see also Africa, North; Islam; 'Orient'
Aragon, Louis 134, 136
Argentina 137
Aristotle 29
arithmetic: see mathematics
Artaud, Antonin 131, 152, 153–4
Arthurian narrative 14, 178; see also Chrétien de Troyes; romance
art nouveau 110
Ashbery, John 1
Atatürk, Mustafa Kemal 192
atheism 11, 35, 45, 49, 51, 63–4, 87, 103, 104, 108, 123, 129, 130, 131, 143, 153, 170, 173, 179
Auber, Daniel-François-Esprit 70
Aubigné, Agrippa d' 24
Aucassin et Nicolette 13, 59, 178
Auerbach, Erich 71
Augier, Emile 96, 97
Austen, Jane 46, 66
Austria 2, 53, 72, 172

autobiography: *see* first-person narrative and autobiography
Avignon 6

Baker, Josephine 178
ballet 12, 33–4, 131
Ballets Russes 131
Balzac, Honoré [de] 3, 55, 76–7, 80, 81–3, 87, 93, 99, 106, 107, 122, 133, 134, 148, 153, 170, 193
bande dessinée 79, 131–2, 172
Barante, Guillaume-Prosper de 69
Bardot, Brigitte 101, 160
Barney, Natalie 112
Barrès, Maurice 104, 118, 150, 155, 166, 167, 169
Barthes, Roland 150, 155, 166, 167, 169
Bas-Auriol Law 172
Basques 8
Baty, Gaston 152
Baudelaire, Charles 16, 43, 80, 91–5, 99, 116, 117, 122, 123, 124, 134, 170, 191, 219
Baudrillard, Jean 169
Bayle, Pierre 45
BBC 174
Beardsley, Aubrey 4
Beaumarchais, Pierre-Augustin de 1, 43, 51–2, 55
Beauvoir, Simone de 1, 66, 140, 144–5, 164, 165, 167, 170, 184, 217
Bebey, Francis 186
Becket, Thomas 6
Beckett, Samuel 1, 138, 140, 142, 145, 152–3, 202, 209, 219
Beethoven, Ludwig van 136
Belghoul, Farida 218
Belgium and Belgian culture 70, 110, 132, 178; *see also under individual artists and authors*
Benda, Julien 133, 134
Bénichou, Paul 32
Benjamin, Walter 94

Ben Jelloun, Tahar 202, 216–17, 219
Bentham, Jeremy 32; *see also* Panopticon
Bergson, Henri 117, 133
Berlin, Academy of 2
Berlioz, Hector 97
Berlusconi, Silvio 159
Bernal, Martin 197
Bernanos, Georges 132
Bernardin de Saint-Pierre, Jacques-Henri 46
Berri, Claude 173
Beti, Mongo (pseud. of Alexandre Biyidi) 213
Beur writers, film-makers 217–18, 221; *see also* immigration to France
Bibliothèque Bleue 44, 46
Bibliothèque Nationale 121, 171
bisexuality: *see* gender boundaries
Bizet, Georges 97
Blanchot, Maurice 155
Bloomsbury circle 1; *see also* Virginia Woolf
blue-stockings 50
Blum, Léon 120, 131
Boccaccio, Giovanni 15, 25
Bodel, Jehan 14
Boileau, Pierre 2
Bois de Boulogne 92, 123
Bon, François 175
Bonnefoy, Yves 175–6
book trade 4–5, 17–18, 44, 48–9, 55, 60, 76–7, 79–80, 83, 90–1, 109, 111, 112, 117, 131, 136, 145, 151, 156, 162–4, 170, 172–3, 186, 189, 200–1
Booth, Wayne C. 132–3
Bosley, Keith 114
Bossuet, Jacques-Bénigne 37, 68
Bouillon de culture 174
Bourbon (dynasty) 54, 58
Bourdieu, Pierre 126, 128, 170
bourgeoisie 26, 32, 36, 52, 65, 74, 75, 77, 81, 82, 90, 94, 96–7, 102, 106, 109, 111, 118, 122, 127

Bousquet, René 161
Brasillach, Robert 138
Braudel, Fernand 6–7
Brazil 22
Brecht, Bertolt 16, 108–9, 143, 203
'Bretagne, matière de' 178
Breton, André 120, 134, 135, 190
Breton language 177
bricolage 157
Britain 2, 10, 12, 21, 41, 44–5, 46, 52,
    53, 56, 58, 59, 61, 66, 69, 80, 81, 85,
    88, 107, 109, 111, 120, 121, 140,
    146–7, 150, 152, 155–6, 159–60, 165,
    169, 170, 172, 173, 174, 175, 178,
    180, 181, 182, 183, 184, 197, 199,
    203, 214, 220, 221
British National Party 159
Britton, Celia 205
Buñuel, Luis 131
Butor, Michel 146–7, 148, 150, 180,
    207
Byatt, A.S. 221

Cabinet des fées, Le 44
cabinets de lecture 77
Calvino, Italo 154
Cambodia 52, 182
Cameroon 186, 200, 202, 213
Camus, Albert 135, 140, 141, 143–4,
    145, 149, 212
Canada 181, 201, 202–4, 209–10, 215,
    219; *see also under individual authors*
canon, literary 54, 55, 99, 221
Capet, Hughes, and Capetian kings 6,
    7, 53
capital punishment 33, 54, 84, 85, 138,
    160
Caran d'Ache (pseud. of Emmanuel
    Poiré) 104
Caribbean 139, 179, 181, 185, 188,
    189, 200, 201, 202, 204, 205, 206,
    211, 215; *see also under individual
    authors,* départements *and countries*

Carignon Law 173–4, 218
cathedrals: Chartres 11, Rouen 108
Catherine the Great 45
Catholicism 6, 7, 12, 18, 20, 21, 33,
    36, 40, 47, 48, 58, 61, 71, 74, 78, 87,
    96, 102–3, 104, 111, 132, 135, 136,
    137, 163, 173, 203, 209; *see also*
    Papacy
Catholic novel 132
Cave, Terence 20, 21
Céline, Louis-Ferdinand (pseud. of
    Louis-Ferdinand Destouches)
    132–3, 210
Celtic culture 178; *see also* Arthurian
    narrative
censorship 21, 48, 55, 75, 95–6, 98,
    160, 188; *see also* Catholicism;
    Sorbonne
Certeau, Michel de 170
Cervantes, Miguel de 3, 20, 49, 178
Césaire, Aimé 186, 187, 188–92, 194,
    202, 204, 205
Chad 218
Chamoiseau, Patrick 199, 202, 206,
    211, 213, 215
Chandler, Raymond 151
'chanson': *see* song
chanson de geste 10, 14, 24
Chanson de Roland, La 8–10, 27, 68,
    128, 174
Charcot, Jean-Martin 62
Charef, Mehdi 218
Charlemagne 7, 8, 9, 17
Charles IX 23, 83
Charles X 53–4, 58, 84
Charrière, Isabelle de 50, 58
Chateaubriand, François-René de 58,
    59, 60–3, 89, 108, 179
Chaumette, Pierre-Gaspard 66
Chekhov, Anton 152, 154
Chénier, André 55
child, status of 85; *see also*
    paedophilia

China, Chinese culture and language
    125, 133, 159, 221
Chirac, Jacques 159
Chopin, Frédéric 126
Chraïbi, Driss 186, 192–3, 194, 196
Chrétien de Troyes 11, 14, 203–4
cinema 2, 119, 131, 135, 143, 148, 151,
    156, 160–1, 162, 166, 170, 172–3,
    194–5, 199, 200, 211, 218, 221
Civil Code 54, 66
Cixous, Hélène 165, 170
Classical culture, Greek and Roman
    6, 12, 19, 22–3, 28, 57, 62, 70, 79, 87,
    92–3, 108, 129, 130, 135, 173, 178,
    179, 193; *see also* Latin
Claudel, Paul 99, 104, 120, 132
Clermont-Ferrand 160
Cocteau, Jean 131, 132
Code Noir 33
Colbert, Jean-Baptiste 30, 32
Colet, Louise 91
Colette, Sidonie-Gabrielle 112, 131
Collège de France 157, 176
colonialism 3, 9, 19–20, 33, 54, 92–3,
    123–4, 139, 144, 158–9, 160, 162,
    164–5, 168–9, 172, 177–219; *see also*
    slavery
commedia dell'arte 152
commemoration 161–2, 211
Commune de Paris 92, 99, 100, 104,
    109
Communism, Communist Party 120,
    134, 136, 140, 141, 194, 212–13; (of
    Martinique) 188, 189; *see also* Marx
Comte, Auguste 107
concentration camps 120, 137, 144, 161
Condé, Maryse 202, 204, 211, 215
Condorcet, Jean-Antoine-Nicolas de 69
Congo, Belgian Congo, Republic of
    the Congo 200, 202, 214
Constant, Benjamin 54, 58–60, 62, 71,
    180
Constantinople (Istanbul) 20

Copeau, Jacques 152
Corneille, Pierre 26–9, 30, 31, 39, 41,
    60
Cottin, Sophie 66–7
Council of Europe 172
Courtois d'Arras 14
courts 7, 10, 19, 20, 32–3, 34, 37, 39,
    41, 42, 43, 220
couture 12, 43, 122, 148
'créolité' 189, 204, 206
Cresson, Edith 165
Croix-de-feu Party 120
cruelty and violence, late nineteenth-
    century 105–6, 109–13, 115
Crusades 7, 8–9
Cubism 108, 115, 125, 126
cuisine 2, 12, 43, 122
cultural history, cultural studies 67–8,
    81, 122, 144, 150, 155–6, 161, 170–1,
    199, 219, 220–1
Cyrano de Bergerac 179

Dadié, Bernard Binlin 186
Daladier, Edouard 130
Dalí, Salvador 131
Danton, Georges-Jacques 56
Darrieussecq, Marie 166, 174
Daumier, Honoré 74, 131
Davis, Colin 160–1
Debussy, Claude 110, 126
Decadence 110–11, 113, 116, 126
Degas, Edgar 126
Degeyter, Pierre 100
Delacroix, Eugène 101
Delaunay, Robert 101
Deleuze, Gilles 169–70
Delly (pseud. of Marie and Frédéric
    Petitjean de la Rosière) 163
Deneuve, Catherine 101
Denmark 172
Départements d'Outre-Mer (DOMs)
    183
Derrida, Jacques 1, 140, 156, 157, 170

Descartes, René 43, 219
detective-story and thriller 79, 150–51, 178
Diamond, Jared 3
Dickens, Charles 85, 111
Diderot, Denis 45, 47, 48, 49, 51, 64, 73, 97, 148, 196
'difference': *see* 'universalism'/ 'difference'
Diop, Alioune 186
Diop, Boubacar Boris 202, 212–13
Diop, Cheikh Anta 187, 196–7
Diouf, Abdou 187
Directoire 53, 82
Djebar, Assia (pseud. of Fatima-Zohra Imalayène) 202, 207, 215–16
Dolet, Etienne 18
Donizetti, Gaetano 136
Donne, John 176
Dostoevsky, Fyodor 178
drama and theatre 14–16, 25, 29–31, 39–40, 41, 43, 48, 52, 55, 56–7, 64–5, 74, 77–8, 80, 84, 95–8, 109–10, 130–31, 142–3, 144, 151–4, 156, 166, 171, 172, 173, 200, 213–15; *see also under individual playwrights*; melodrama; Theatre of the Absurd; spectacle
Dreyfus Affair 7, 103–4, 117, 120
Du Bellay, Joachim 19, 203
Dumas, Alexandre ('Dumas *fils*') 97
Dumas, Alexandre ('Dumas *père*') 77–9, 97, 113
Duras, Claire de 67, 179
Duras, Marguerite (pseud. of Marguerite Donnadieu) 145, 166, 167, 173, 179, 199
Durkheim, Emile 117
Duvalier, François and Jean-Claude 184
Dylan, Bob 173

Echenoz, Jean 175
Eco, Umberto 219

écriture féminine 165–6
Edict of Nantes 33
education, educational aims 20, 54, 56, 66, 74, 75–6, 79, 96, 101–3, 111, 112, 116, 117, 118, 120, 124, 126, 142, 161, 168, 171, 174, 183, 186, 187, 188, 192, 193, 196, 198, 201, 204, 207, 213, 218, 221; *see also Encyclopédie*; literacy; universities
Egypt 53, 66, 196–7
Eiffel Tower 101, 129
Eisenstein, Sergei 2
Eliot, George (pseud. of Mary Ann Evans) 3, 88
Eliot, T.S. 94, 120
Elizabeth I (of England) 25
Eluard, Paul (pseud. of Eugène Grindel) 120, 134
Empire, Second 75, 76, 96, 106
Encyclopédie 48–9, 198
enlightened self-interest 44
Enlightenment, French 1, 22, 43–52, 104, 142, 180, 184, 196, 212
Enlightenment, Scottish 45
Ernaux, Annie 166, 167, 175, 192
Eschleman, Clayton 190
Estoire de Griseldis 15
Euro-Disney 172
exceptionalism, French 3, 139
existentialism 145; *see also* Beauvoir; Malraux; Sartre

fabliaux 14, 25
fairground performance 56, 57, 116
fairy-tales 2, 43–4, 168
Fallaize, Elizabeth 167
Fanon, Frantz 187, 188, 195–6, 204
Farce de Maître Pierre Pathelin, La 15–16, 21
Fénelon, François de Salignac de la Mothe- 43
Fermat, Pierre de 43
Ferry, Jules, and 'Ferry Laws' 102

Feuillerat, Albert 121–2
Feydeau, Georges 109
fin'amour 11
Finch, Alison 65, 121
first-person narrative and
    autobiography 62, 166–8, 190–1; *see
    also under individual authors*
First World War: *see* War, First World
Fischart, Johann 21
flâneur, the 80, 91, 219
Flaubert, Gustave 75, 81, 89–91, 93,
    95, 99, 103, 108, 126, 127, 148, 208,
    219
Floire et Blanchefleur 178
Florida 181
Forain, Jean-Louis 104
Foucault, Michel 1, 32, 107, 140, 156,
    168
Fouquet, Nicolas 33
François I 19–20, 24, 181
'Francophonie' 181, 185–6, 195, 213;
    see also French language
Franco-Prussian War: *see* War,
    Franco-Prussian
Frederick II (of Prussia) 45
free indirect style 108, 208–11
freethinkers: *see* atheism
French Guiana 100, 189, 200
French language, role and status of
    1–2, 3, 7, 17–19, 64, 76, 78–9, 87,
    102, 162, 172, 174–5, 177, 181, 192,
    193, 194, 201–11, 219, 220, 221;
    see also 'Francophonie'
Freud, Sigmund 62, 134, 195
Froissart, Jean 10, 17, 68
Fromentin, Eugène 207
Fronde, the 27, 32, 38
Front National 159, 199, 217
Furetière, Antoine 64
Futurism 125

Gaboriau, Emile 151
Galland, Antoine 44

Gallicanism 6, 126
Gallimard (publishers) 189
Galsworthy, John 107
Gance, Abel 131
Garbo, Greta 97
gardens 43
Gauguin, Paul 88, 180
Gaulle, Charles de 92, 120, 137, 139,
    140, 149, 159, 160, 171, 183, 204
Gautier, Théophile 80, 81, 111
gay rights, gay writing and characters
    95, 112, 118, 121, 124, 125, 134, 145,
    160, 166–8, 217; *see also* gender
    boundaries
Gay, Sophie 67, 89
gender boundaries 13, 112, 118,
    125–6, 215–16; *see also* women;
    Simone de Beauvoir
Genet, Jean 152, 153, 184
Genlis, Stéphanie-Félicité de 66, 67,
    75
Germany, language, culture and
    politics of 2, 3, 8, 9, 21, 44, 45, 46,
    52, 58, 68, 99–100, 101, 103, 119,
    120, 130, 136, 138, 152, 172, 178,
    182, 186, 193, 221; *see also* Berlin,
    Academy of; First World War;
    Franco-Prussian War; Occupation;
    Second World War
Gide, André 99, 112, 120, 125, 133–4,
    147, 148, 166, 167, 178, 180, 193, 215
Gildea, Robert 136
Girard, René 123, 143, 170
Girardin, Delphine de 97
Girardin, Emile de 76, 77, 97
Giraudoux, Jean 120, 128, 130, 132
Giscard d'Estaing, Valéry 159, 171
Glissant, Edouard 188, 202, 204–5
Gluck, Christoph Willibald 70
Godard, Jean-Luc 151
Goethe, Johann Wolfgang von 49, 62,
    136
Gothic literature 56, 61

Gouges, Olympe de (pseud. of Marie Gouze) 66
Gournay, Marie Le Jars 31
Graffigny, Françoise de 47, 50
Grandes Chroniques de France, Les 17, 68
'grands chantiers' 171–2
'Grand Siècle' 26–43, 68, 99
Grégoire, Henri 102
Greuze, Jean-Baptiste 46
Guadeloupe 181, 189, 202, 204
Guardian, The 164, 221
Guattari, Félix 170
Guène, Faïsa 221
Guibert, Hervé 166–8
guilds and professional societies 15, 88, 98
Guillard, Nicolas-François 70
Guimard, Hector 110
Guizot, François-Pierre-Guillaume 69, 74

Hachette (publishers) 162
hagiography 8, 11, 14, 17, 27
Haiti 181, 184, 190, 206
Halévy, Ludovic 97
Hall, Stuart 81, 156
Haneke, Michael 161
Harlem Renaissance 185
Harlequin (publishers) 163
Harmattan, L' (publishers) 201
hauntology 161
Haussmann, Haussmannization 91–2, 96, 123
Hawkins, Peter 219
Hazard, Paul 43
Hébert, Anne 202, 209, 215, 219
Hegel, Georg Wilhelm Friedrich 49, 195
Heidegger, Martin 150
Henley, Jon 164
Henry II (of England) 12
Hergé (Georges Remi) 132, 180

Herzfeld, Michael 7–8
hip-hop 218
'history', historiography 10, 17, 18, 24, 58, 64, 67–73, 78, 81, 86, 91, 107, 122, 160–1, 167, 168, 175, 203, 210, 213; *see also chanson de geste*
Hitchcock, Alfred 2
Hitler, Adolf 120, 130, 136
Ho Chi Minh 185
Hoggart, Richard 81, 155–6, 170
Holland 8, 47, 48, 50, 95, 143, 186, 197
Holmes, Diana 163, 216, 218
Holocaust, the 120, 137, 161, 162
Holy Roman Emperor 19
Horgan, Frances 12
Houellebecq, Michel 160
Hughes, Edward 180
Hugo, Victor 1, 55, 63–5, 68, 76, 84–6, 90, 96, 106, 108, 109, 117, 127, 180, 184, 191, 193, 219
Huguenots: *see* Protestantism
Hume, David 45
Husserl, Edmund 150
Huysmans, Joris-Karl 110–11, 115, 156

identity politics 160, 167, 215
Ile-de-France 6
Iliad, The 28
Illuminism 86
immigration to France 177, 202, 217–18
Impressionism 2, 108, 115, 125; *see also* Monet
incest 39–41, 62
income, writer's: *see* writer, income of
India 169, 180, 181, 182, 201
Indo-China 139, 181, 182, 183, 199; *see also under individual countries*
industry and technology 74, 76, 82, 96, 101, 119, 122, 128; *see also* book trade

ingénu, ingénue 46–7
intellectual, the 109, 117–18, 129, 133, 134, 149, 156–8, 165, 167, 168, 169, 170, 172, 175–6, 183, 196, 212–13, 220; *see also* universities
'Internationale, The' 100
internet 162, 174
Ionesco, Eugène 138, 152, 153–4, 202
Irigaray, Luce 165–6
Islam 6, 8, 9, 13, 20, 178–9, 194, 196, 208, 212, 218
Italy, art, culture and language of 2, 10, 19, 20, 23, 24, 30, 53, 58, 70, 72, 81, 146, 150, 152, 159, 178, 179
Ivory Coast (Côte d'Ivoire) 186, 200, 202, 208–9

Jager, Marjolijn de 207
James, Henry 90
Jansenism 7, 37
Japan 155
Jarry, Alfred 109–10, 112, 116, 152, 211, 213, 215
Jaurès, Jean 119, 171
Jesuits 7
Jeune Afrique 201
John (king of England) 6
jongleurs 14
Jospin, Lionel 159
Jouvet, Louis 152
Joyce, James 166
Judaism and Jews in France 2, 14, 33, 54, 87, 102–4, 117–18, 120, 121, 125, 130, 132, 136, 137, 141, 144, 161–2, 192, 217; *see also* Dreyfus Affair
Jung, Carl 195

Kafka, Franz 169
Kane, Cheikh Hamidou 187, 196
Kant, Immanuel 169
Kay, Sarah 17
kings of France: *see under individual kings; also* Bourbon dynasty; Capet; monarchy; Orléans dynasty

Koch, Kenneth 1
Kourouma, Ahmadou 202, 208–9
Kristeva, Julia 166

Labé, Louise 25
Labiche, Eugène 97, 109
La Bruyère, Jean de 29, 42–3, 110
Lacan, Jacques 140, 156, 166, 169
Laclos, Choderlos de 50–1, 66
Lafayette, Marie-Madeleine de 34, 37, 41, 46, 50, 59
La Fontaine, Jean de 30, 33, 34, 37, 38
laïcité 102–3
Lalonde, Michèle 202, 203, 215
Lamartine, Alphonse de 57–8, 60, 105, 184
Lang, Jack 172
Lanzmann, Claude 161
Laos 182
La Rochefoucauld, François de 34, 36–7, 44, 127
Larousse-Nathan (publishers) 162
Latin 2, 8, 17, 18, 19, 22, 68, 79, 221
Lê, Linda 202, 210–11, 215
Lebanon 182, 199
Leiris, Michel 167, 184
leisure 80–1, 131
Le Lionnais, François 154–5
Le Pen, Jean-Marie 159
Lévi-Strauss, Claude 1, 140, 150, 157–8, 177
libertinage: see atheism
libraries 77
Liking, Werewere (pseud. of Eddy Liking) 202, 206–7, 215
literacy 4, 75–6, 195; *see also* education
literary criticism 65, 156, 157, 169, 170, 176
littérature de colportage 48; *see also* Bibliothèque Bleue
Locke, John 44–5

Lombard, Jean 111
Lorris, Guillaume de 12
Lough, John 19, 26, 76, 127
Louis IX 7
Louis XIII 27, 78
Louis XIV 26, 30, 32–8, 43, 52, 53, 54, 78, 181
Louis XV 43
Louis XVI 43, 52, 53, 60
Louis XVIII 53, 58
Louisiana 181, 203
Louis-Philippe 54, 74–5, 82, 95, 122
Louverture, Toussaint 184, 190
Lubin, Georges 88
Lubin, Maurice 201
Lucey, Michael 123
Lugné-Poë, Aurélien 110, 152
Lumière, Louis 131
Lyotard, Jean-François 169, 170

Maalouf, Amin 199
Machaut, Guillaume de 16, 166
Madagascar 200
Maeterlinck, Maurice 110, 152, 178
Maghreb 202; *see* North Africa *and under individual countries*
Magna Carta 6
Magritte, René 178
Maillet, Antonine 202, 203–4, 206, 209–10, 211, 215
Maimbourg, Louis 68
Maintenon, Françoise d'Aubigné de 43
Maistre, Joseph de 69
'mal du siècle' 60–1, 104
Malesherbes, Chrétien-Guillaume de 55–6
Mallarmé, Stéphane 99, 113–17, 129, 134, 148, 154, 156, 205
Malraux, André 120, 133, 139, 142, 153, 171, 195
'Marianne' 101, 160
Marie de France 12, 14
Marivaux, Pierre de 43, 47

Marot, Clément 16, 18, 110
'Marseillaise, La' 57, 101, 171
Marseille 100
Martinique 181, 182, 185, 186, 187, 188–91, 195, 199, 202, 204
Marx, Karl, and Marxism 83, 88, 90, 140, 185, 187, 194
mathematics 10, 39–40, 43, 155, 176, 196, 220
'matière de Bretagne': *see* 'Bretagne, matière de'
Maupassant, Guy de 74, 105, 106, 116, 122
Maupertuis, Pierre-Louis Moreau de 43
Mauriac, François 120, 132
Mauritius 182
Maurras, Charles 118
May 1968, events of 140, 159–60, 163, 164, 169, 170, 199, 202
Mazarin, Jules (Giulio Mazarini) 30, 32, 33
McEwan, Ian 221
Meilhac, Henri 97
Méliès, Georges 131
melodrama 56–7, 78, 79
Mercure de France (publishers) 112
Mérimée, Prosper 213
Merleau-Ponty, Maurice 150, 184
Meun, Jean de 12
Michel, Louise 104, 108
Middle East 181; *see also under individual countries*; 'Orient'
Mills and Boon 163
Milton, John 191
Minuit, Editions de (publishers) 136, 145
Mirabeau, Honoré-Gabriel Riqueti de 56
Mirbeau, Octave 111
mise en abyme 147–8, 169
Mitscherlich, Alexander 149
Mitterrand, François-Maurice 159, 171, 172

Mnouchkine, Ariane 171
Modiano, Patrick 175
Molière (pseud. of Jean-Baptiste
    Poquelin) 15, 31–2, 34, 35–6, 37,
    38, 41, 51, 52, 78
monarchy 6, 26, 27, 31, 40, 44, 53, 54,
    87, 96, 126, 171; *see also* kings of
    France
Monarchy, July: *see* Louis-Philippe
Monde, Le 218–19
Monet, Claude 2, 108, 119, 126
Monnier, Henri 74
Montaigne, Michel de 1, 20, 22–4, 37,
    46, 62, 63, 117, 127, 166, 219, 220
Montesquieu, Charles de Secondat de
    45, 47, 48, 50, 68, 107, 179, 196
Moore, Will G. 35
'Moors': *see* Islam
'moralisateur': *see moraliste*
moraliste 34–5, 36, 42, 45, 73, 125
Moreau, Gustave 111, 113
Moriarty, Michael 65
Morocco 182, 186, 192–3, 200, 202,
    216, 219
Morrison, Toni 3
Moses, Claire Goldberg 88
Moulin, Jean 171
Mozart, Wolfgang Amadeus 1, 52
Musset, Alfred de 76, 96

Nabokov, Vladimir 206
Napoleon (Napoléon Bonaparte) 2, 6,
    20, 53–4, 55, 56, 58, 60, 66, 67, 68,
    69, 70, 71, 72, 73, 75, 80, 82, 83, 86,
    96, 99, 102, 159, 178
Napoleon III (Louis-Napoléon
    Bonaparte) 75, 76, 85, 91, 95, 99
Narcejac, Thomas (pseud. of Pierre
    Ayraud) 2
Nardal sisters 185, 187
Naturalism 107, 110, 111, 113; *see also*
    Zola
Navarre, Marguerite de 24–5, 31, 62

Nazism 52, 137, 142, 149, 168
'negritude' 185, 187, 195, 197
Némirovsky, Irène 120
Nerval, Gérard de (pseud. of Gérard
    Labrunie) 62, 86–7, 88, 90, 91, 134,
    136
New Caledonia 104, 182
New Novel 145–51, 152, 153, 157,
    161, 168, 169, 213, 221; *see also under*
    individual authors
New York School 1
Nietzsche, Friedrich 169
Nigeria 201
Nora, Pierre 101, 161
Norman Conquest 12, 177
'North', the, and Northern Europe 3,
    8, 159, 178
nouveau roman: see New Novel
nuclear deterrent strategy 139

OAS (Organisation Armée Secrète)
    183
O'Brien, Conor Cruise 141
Occitan 177
Occupation and Vichy regime 101,
    120, 132, 135–7, 138, 139, 141, 142,
    143, 145, 148, 149, 160, 161–2, 163,
    183, 188
Oceania 124, 182
Offenbach, Jacques 97
Ojo-Ade, Fermi 201
opera 1, 52, 57, 70, 97–8, 110, 171; *see*
    also under individual composers
Ophüls, Marcel 160–1
'Orient', the 2, 44, 94–5, 151, 179,
    180
Orléans (dynasty) 54
Ottoman Empire 182
OULIPO 154–5

paedophilia 134, 169, 180
Pagnol, Marcel 173
Pakistan 169

Pancrazi, Jean-Noël 168
Panopticon 32–3, 41
Papacy 6, 7, 58, 70, 153, 215; *see also*
    Catholicism
Paris 2, 4, 7, 19, 20, 31, 32, 35, 41, 53,
    55, 70, 72, 73, 77, 79, 83, 87, 88,
    91–4, 96, 97–8, 99–100, 110, 111,
    123, 129, 131, 134, 135, 138, 140,
    143, 146, 149, 152, 155, 171–2, 173,
    178, 185, 186, 188, 192, 196, 201,
    202, 218, 220
parody 14, 57, 97, 219
Pascal, Blaise 34, 37, 43
Pasteur, Louis 117
patronage 7, 20, 24, 26, 29–30, 31, 38,
    43, 80–1, 84, 131
Péguy, Charles 104, 132, 136
Pennac, Daniel (pseud. of Daniel
    Pennacchioni) 170
Perec, Georges 154–5, 219
Pernoud, Laurence 3
Perrault, Charles 2, 44
Perse, Saint-John: *see* Saint-John Perse
Persia 6
Pervear, Richard 78
Pétain, Philippe 120, 138, 149
Petrarch (Francesco Petrarca) 2, 15
phenomenology 150
philosophe 45, 48, 49, 50, 52, 93, 117,
    142, 156, 168, 196, 219, 220; *see also*
    Diderot, Montesquieu, Rousseau,
    Voltaire
photography 119, 132, 135, 166
Picasso, Pablo 2, 116, 189
pieds noirs 182, 183; *see also* Algeria
Pirandello, Luigi 152
Pitoëff, Georges 152
Pivot, Bernard 174
Pixérécourt, Guilbert de 56
Pizan, Christine de 12–13, 16, 17, 164,
    165
Plato 219
Pléiade poets 19

Poe, Edgar Allen 116
Pointillism 115
Polish-Lithuanian Commonwealth 45
political appointments, writers' 57–8,
    117, 187, 188–9, 198
Polity Press (publishers) 170
Pompadour, Antoinette Poisson de
    43, 50
Pompidou, Georges 159, 171
Popular Front 120, 131
Portugal 10, 197
positivism 107
postmodernism 169, 217
Pottier, Eugène-Edme 100
Poujadism (movement led by Pierre
    Poujade) 139
Poussin, Nicolas 126
précieuses 31, 32, 39, 164
Prendergast, Christopher 79
Présence Africaine 186, 201
Presidency of France 101, 139, 159,
    171–2; *see under individual presidents*
press and journalism (newspapers and
    periodicals) 55, 59, 75, 76–7, 79, 80,
    83, 89–90, 104, 112, 116, 117, 126,
    133, 139, 183–4, 188, 200, 212
Presses de la Cité (publishers) 162
Preston, Peter 221
Prévost, Antoine-François 46
printing: *see* book trade
prizes, named: Goncourt 131, 199,
    211, 217; Grand Prix Littéraire
    d'Afrique Noire 186, 211; Médicis
    155; Nobel 110, 120, 145
prose, perception and use of 18, 63,
    65, 79, 90–1, 127, 190; *see also* verse,
    free
prose poem: *see* Baudelaire; Césaire;
    Rimbaud
Prost, Antoine 161
Protestantism 7, 18, 20, 21, 24, 33, 58,
    67, 68, 78, 104, 181, 186; *see also*
    Edict of Nantes

Proust, Marcel 43, 59, 62, 75, 86, 89, 99, 104, 112, 113, 120–8, 131, 148, 156, 169, 172, 178, 191
'Prudhomme, Joseph' 74
Prussia: *see* Germany
psychoanalysis 49, 60, 62, 134, 157, 165, 166, 169–70; *see also* Freud; Irigaray; Kristeva; Lacan
Pushkin, Alexander 77

Queneau, Raymond 154

Rabelais, François 19–22, 39, 46, 63, 110, 136–7
Rachilde (pseud. of Marguerite Eymery) 112, 131
Racine, Jean 26, 29, 34, 37–41, 43, 59, 64, 70, 110, 154, 175, 179, 191
Radical Party 104
radio 174, 186
Rahimi, Atiq 199
raillery 36, 89; *see also* wit
Raoul de Cambrai 10
rap 218–19
'Realism' 85, 107; *see also* Balzac; Zola
Redon, Odilon 111, 113
Reggiani, Serge 173
regions and the regional 7, 10, 19, 20, 41, 55, 86, 87, 88, 89, 90, 91, 102, 172, 173, 204
Renaissance in France 17–25, 30
'Renaissance, twelfth-century' 7
Renoir, Jean 2, 131
Republicanism 101, 138; *see also* Republics
Republics: Second 75; Third 99–137, 138–9, 171, 180, 182; Fourth 137, 138; Fifth 138–9
Resistance, the 120, 136, 152, 163, 171
Restoration, the 76

Réunion, La 182, 189
Revolution (1789, 'French Revolution') 2, 52, 53, 54, 55–6, 57, 64, 66, 69, 70, 71, 79, 81, 93, 94, 101, 102, 109, 124, 171, 212, 220
Revolution (1830, 'July Revolution') 53–4, 74, 96, 104
Revolution (1848) 75, 91, 96, 104
Revolution, Russian (1917) 124
rhetoric 55, 56, 109, 113, 145, 156
Ricardou, Jean 147
Richardson, Samuel 46
Richelieu, Armand du Plessis de (Cardinal Richelieu) 30, 37, 78
Rilke, Rainer Maria 94
Rimbaud, Arthur 16, 99, 104, 105–6, 109, 117, 134, 173, 191, 219
Robbe-Grillet, Alain 146, 147–50, 173, 219
Robespierre, Maximilien 53, 56
romance 1, 163–4; *see also* Arthurian narrative; Chrétien de Troyes
Roman de la rose, Le 11–12, 13
roman-feuilleton (serialised novel) 77–8, 79–80, 91
Romanticism 3, 37, 46, 57–8, 60, 61, 63, 70, 78, 79, 84, 85, 86, 89, 97, 108, 117, 143, 153, 168, 178, 191
Ronsard, Pierre de 19, 26
Rops, Félicien 111
Roubaud, Jacques 154–5
Rouget de Lille, Claude-Joseph 57; *see also* 'Marseillaise, La'
Rousseau, Jean-Jacques 45, 46, 48, 49, 50, 54, 62, 63, 85, 89, 166, 178, 204, 212, 219
Roussy, Suzanne 188
Russia, culture and politics of 2, 45, 52, 53, 124, 152, 178; *see also* Catherine the Great; Soviet Union
Rutebeuf (pseud.; real name unknown) 14–15

Sade, Donatien-Alphonse-François de (marquis de Sade) 51
Sainte-Beuve, Charles-Augustin 89
Sainte-Chapelle, Paris 7
Saint-John Perse (pseud. of Alexis Saint-Léger Léger) 120
Saint-Just, Louis de 56
Saint-Ogan, Alain 132
Saint-Simonism 66, 164
salons 31, 50, 52, 57, 71, 88, 89, 112, 117, 185
San Quentin State Penitentiary 152
Sand, George (pseud. of Aurore Dupin, baronne Dudevant) 44, 76, 81, 84, 86, 87–8, 90, 112, 204, 219
Saracens: *see* Islam
Sarkozy, Nicolas 159
Sarraute, Nathalie 126, 146, 147–50, 167, 174, 175, 210
Sartre, Jean-Paul 29, 118, 120, 133, 135, 140, 141–3, 144, 145, 148, 149, 150, 153, 157, 167, 183–4, 188, 192, 195, 217, 220
satire 14, 35–6, 42, 56, 85, 104, 179, 211–15
Saussure, Ferdinand de 156, 178
Scarron, Paul 64
Schoelcher, Victor 180, 206
science 103, 107–8, 196; *see also* mathematics
Scott, Walter 69
Screech, M.A. 22
Scribe, Eugène 70, 97
Scudéry, Madeleine de 32
Second World War: *see* War, Second World
Sembène Ousmane 186–7, 193–5, 196, 208
Semprun, Jorge 161
Senegal 3, 181, 182, 186, 187, 196, 200, 201, 202, 211, 212–13, 218

Senghor, Léopold Sédar 186–9, 195, 196–7, 199, 211–12
sensibility 45–6
Serere people 187
Sévigné, Marie de 32
Shakespeare, William 1, 20, 22, 36, 38, 64, 133, 176, 178, 189, 205
Shapiro, Norman 92
slavery, slave-trade 33, 47, 59, 67, 77, 92–3, 102, 175, 179, 180, 182, 184, 190, 191, 204, 206, 211
Smaïl, Paul 175, 199
Smith, Adam 45
Smith, Annette 190
Socialism, Socialist Party 66, 86, 88, 104, 107, 111, 136, 159, 164, 171; *see also* Saint-Simonism
Solaar, MC (M'Barali, Claude) 218–19
song ('chanson') 55, 57, 100, 172, 173–4, 218–19
Sony Labou Tansi (pseud. of Marcel Sony) 202, 213–15
Sorbonne 18, 20–21, 186, 187, 196
Soviet Union 52, 100, 141, 142, 149, 171, 185; *see also* Russia
Sow Fall, Aminata 202, 211–12, 215–16
Spain, culture and politics 10, 46, 99, 131, 133, 172, 178, 181, 201, 221
spectacle and festivals 56–7, 75, 84, 87, 94, 116, 138, 140, 152, 171, 172, 219; *see also* fairground performance
Spinoza, Baruch 169
Sri Lanka 169
Staël, Germaine de 11, 58, 64, 67–8, 81, 89, 136, 149, 178
Stendhal (pseud. of Henri Beyle) 55, 57, 59, 63–5, 66, 68, 70–3, 74, 77–8, 82, 84, 90, 99, 107, 148, 151, 166–7, 178, 179, 211, 215, 219
Sterne, Laurence 3, 49, 148
Stevens, Wallace 94

Strasbourg oaths 17
Structuralism 157, 219
style indirect libre: see free indirect style
Sudan, French 193
Sue, Eugène 77, 79
suffrage 74, 75, 85, 101, 138
Surrealism 120, 134–5, 155, 170, 178, 188, 190
Swift, Jonathan 36, 132
Swinburne, Algernon 94
Switzerland, Swiss writers 58, 172, 178, 210; see also under individual authors
Symbolism 113, 116, 134, 214
Symons, Arthur 111
Syria 182

Tahiti 180, 182
Taine, Hippolyte-Adolphe 107
Tasso, Torquato 29
'taste' 65, 106, 110, 191
Taylor, Charles 82
technology: see industry and technology
Teilhard de Chardin, Pierre 188
television 160, 162, 174
Terror, the 51–2, 53, 54, 60, 71, 93, 99, 100, 104
theatre: see drama and theatre
Theatre of the Absurd 96, 148, 151–4, 156, 157, 202, 214
Thierry, Augustin 69
Thiers, Adolphe 100
Thomas, Evelyne 101
Thorez, Maurice 140
Thou, Jacques-Auguste de 68
Tintin: see Hergé
Tocqueville, Alexis de 151
Togo 186, 200
Tolstoy, Leo 2, 3, 66, 178, 195
Toubon Law 172
Tournier, Michel 168–9, 170, 199
Toussaint Louverture: see Louverture, Toussaint

tragedy 154; see also under individual playwrights; drama
travel writing 179, 180; see also Montaigne; ingénu, ingénue
Tremblay, Michel 202–3, 211, 215
Trenet, Charles 174
Triolet, Elsa 136
Tristan, Flora 88
trobairitz 12
troubadours 1, 10
Truffaut, François 221
Tunisia 3, 182
Turkey 192
Tynan, Kenneth 152

Ultramontanism 126
United Kingdom Independence Party (UKIP) 159
United Nations Security Council 139
United States, culture and world role of 1, 2, 61, 66, 88, 121, 140, 151, 155–6, 165, 170, 171, 172–3, 174, 175, 178, 184, 185, 190, 195, 202, 218, 221; see America; Americas
'universalism'/'difference' 164–6
universities 7, 20–1, 101, 117, 118, 140, 157, 160, 168, 171, 174, 176, 192, 196–7, 207, 217, 220, 221; see also Collège de France; Sorbonne
Urquhart, Thomas 21

Valéry, Paul 99, 104, 116, 120, 128, 129, 133, 148, 156
Vallès, Jules 104
Vallette, Alfred 112
Van Gogh, Vincent 4–5
Varda, Agnès 166
Vaux-le-Vicomte, château of 32–3
Veber, Francis 173
Vercors (pseud. of Jean Bruller) 136
Verdi, Giuseppe 1, 97
Verhaeren, Emile 178
Verlaine, Paul 105, 113

Verne, Jules 79–80
Versailles, Palace of 32–3
Versailles, Treaty of 100
verse, free 105, 187, 190; *see also*
    prose, perception and use of
Vian, Boris 151, 173
Vichy regime: *see* Occupation
Vico, Giambattista 81
Vietnam 3, 140, 172, 182, 185, 202,
    210, 215
Vigny, Alfred de 76, 80–1, 105, 174
Villon, François 16–17, 219
Virgin Mary 11
Voltaire (pseud. of François-Marie
    Arouet) 45, 46, 47, 48, 49, 68–9, 85,
    127, 179, 180, 211

Wagner, Richard 115, 126, 136
Walcott, Derek 181
Wales 8
Waller, Margaret 60
War, Cold 142, 144
War, Crimean 75
War, First World 103, 119, 120, 121,
    124–5, 126–7, 128, 129, 136, 137,
    182, 206
War, Franco-Prussian 9, 75, 99–100,
    104, 105, 115, 119
War, Second World 1, 101, 120, 130,
    132, 135–7, 138, 141, 143, 148, 151,
    153, 154, 155, 156, 161, 183, 188,
    194, 206; *see also* Occupation
War, Spanish Civil 133

War, Vietnam 140, 172
Wars of Religion 20, 24, 220
Waterloo, Battle of 53, 58, 67, 72, 99
Wiesel, Elie 161
Wilde, Oscar 4, 118
Williams, Raymond 155
wit 36, 37, 79, 89, 97, 115, 173
Wolof (language and people)
    187, 194
women, image and role of; writing by
    10–13, 28, 31–2, 50, 51, 60, 63, 65–8,
    75, 79, 84, 87–8, 89, 95, 97, 101–2,
    104, 108, 111, 112, 124, 130, 131,
    138, 144–5, 149, 157, 160, 163–6,
    169, 172, 175, 187, 188, 192, 193,
    194, 202–3, 207, 215–17; *see also*
    under individual authors
Woolf, Virginia 165
writer, income of 4–5, 7, 12, 26, 77,
    79–81, 83–4, 109, 122, 127–8, 131,
    138; *see also* patronage
writers, social origins of 26, 81, 118,
    148

Yeats, William Butler 176
'yellow novels' 4
Yourcenar, Marguerite (pseud. of
    Marguerite de Crayencour) 157,
    179

Zeldin, Theodore 65
Zola, Emile 99, 103, 106–9, 116, 117,
    124, 126, 132, 195, 208, 212, 219